CATER FROM YOUR KITCHEN

For those who want to get ahead, going back to the kitchen means success, not drudgery; independence, not slavery. CATER FROM YOUR KITCHEN is brimming with all the facts, step-by-step work plans, inventive ideas and expert know-how necessary to turn your home kitchen into a profit-making business.

If you earn raves for your cooking, you could be earning money doing what you love. If you're one of the many people who prefer to work for themselves, the autonomy and diversity of the catering business will suit you. You'll be a cook, salesperson, business manager, accountant, public relations expert, delivery service and creator of recipes. You'll have all the headaches, but the joys will be yours as well—and all the profits. You can test yourself, challenge yourself and feel the self-esteem that comes with being your own boss.

Food is fun, and eating, after all, is here to stay. CATER FROM YOUR KITCHEN tells you everything you need to know to make your kitchen work for you!

Other books by Marjorie P. Blanchard:

THE KITCHEN SCHOLAR

THE HOME GARDENER'S COOKBOOK

THE SPROUTER'S COOKBOOK

WHAT SHALL I COOK TODAY?
with Nika Hazelton

WHAT COOKS IN CONNECTICUT

TREASURED RECIPES FROM EARLY
NEW ENGLAND KITCHENS

THE OUTDOOR COOKBOOK

THE VEGETARIAN MENU COOKBOOK

BACKYARD HARVEST

SAUCE IT!

THE ORCHARD SAMPLER

THE MINIATURE GARDEN GUIDE

INCOME FROM YOUR OWN HOME BUSINESS:
❧CATER FROM❧ YOUR KITCHEN
MARJORIE P. BLANCHARD

PLAYBOY PAPERBACKS

CATER FROM YOUR KITCHEN

Copyright © 1981 by Marjorie Page Blanchard

Cover photo copyright © 1982 by PBJ Books, Inc., formerly PEI Books, Inc.

All rights reserved. No part of this book may be reproduced, stored in a retrieval system or transmitted in any form by an electronic, mechanical, photocopying, recording means or otherwise without prior written permission of the publisher.

Published simultaneously in the United States and Canada by PBJ Books, Inc., formerly PEI Books, Inc., 200 Madison Avenue, New York, New York 10016. Printed in the United States of America. Library of Congress Catalog Card Number: 82-81544. Reprinted by arrangement with Bobbs-Merrill.

ISBN: 0-867-21198-9

First PBJ Books, Inc., printing November 1982

To Donald

ACKNOWLEDGMENTS

I could not have written this book without the help of numerous old friends and new acquaintances, among them: Mildred Brand, Fort Wayne, Indiana; Nancy Carlton, Norwich, Vermont; Mary Carson, Coeur d'Alene, Idaho; Roberta Dowling, Cambridge, Massachusetts; Natalie Dupree, Atlanta, Georgia; Sally Duval, Greenwich, Connecticut; Edith Fillietazz, Southport, Connecticut; Kitty Gushee, Grosse Pointe, Michigan; Karen Hilliard, Odessa, Texas; Susan Layton, Fairfield, Connecticut; Gail Marcus, Encino, California; Ada Matchett, Warren, Indiana; Robert Salsman, Kansas City, Missouri; Donald Bruce White, New York, New York; Ken Williams, Griffin, Georgia; and Pug Youngblood, Augusta, Georgia. To them all, my most heartfelt thanks. Last, but far from least, I also want to thank my editors, Barbara Reiss and Stefanie Woodbridge, for their generous help.

CONTENTS

Introduction ix

SECTION I. FROM COOK TO CATERER 1
Chapter 1: Make Catering Your Business 3
Chapter 2: Starting Out 15

SECTION II. CATERER'S CRAFT 27
Chapter 3: Before a Client Calls 29
Chapter 4: Caterer and Client 44
Chapter 5: Doing the Job 51
Chapter 6: Success: The Story of a Young Caterer 68
Chapter 7: The New Wave: Fast Gourmet Food 73

SECTION III. THE BUSINESS OF THE CATERING BUSINESS 83
Chapter 8: The Law and Other Business Issues 85
Chapter 9: Equip Your Kitchen 92

Afterword 102

SECTION IV. A COOKBOOK FOR CATERERS 103
Introduction 104
Menu Suggestions 107
Appetizers 113
Soups 128

Entrées *132*
Side Dishes *156*
Vegetables *161*
Salads *168*
Sandwiches *174*
Crêpes and Breads *176*
Desserts *185*
Frozen Packaged Foods *214*
Index for A Cookbook for Caterers *234*

General Index *241*

INTRODUCTION

For the past twenty years I've done almost every job a food professional can do. I've taught cooking; written and lectured about food; tested and developed recipes; and even been up to my elbows, literally, in soufflé egg whites during a restaurant stint. I've also been a caterer, supplying everything from cakes to whole dinners.

Food experts are always being asked for information by the people they meet in daily life; doctors and lawyers aren't the only ones whose free advice is solicited at cocktail parties. Like my colleagues, I regularly answer all sorts of questions.

One day I realized that many people were asking me about catering. How should someone go about setting up a catering business? they wondered. Could it be a profitable career? When I thought about it, this development wasn't surprising. More people, both men and women, have taken up serious cooking in the last decade than ever before. Our newspapers regularly devote a significant portion of space to matters culinary. The sale of kitchen equipment has become big business. Magazines now feature articles with bright color photographs of psychiatrists or computer programmers who relax by baking Black Forest cake. Many of these people are excellent cooks. And some of them find they enjoy cooking more than their jobs. To them, catering looks like an ideal solution to the avocation-versus-job conflict. One professor, about to teach a class in sociology, remarked to a colleague, "I wish I were at home, making my pies." She has since left the academic world for the catering kitchen.

At first, I answered questions about catering simply by volunteering information from my own experience. For me, catering was a natural outgrowth of my food demonstrations and teaching. I have catered for wedding receptions, parties of all kinds, and for formal and informal dinners; my experience runs the gamut of situations in which caterers are used.

But I soon began to feel that people who were serious about going into catering as a business deserved to know more ways of doing things than just mine. Other caterers might have different advice. Catering is an informal business. There are few hard and fast rules to follow; instead, there are hints and tips and suggestions and procedures developed from experience. Since catering is also a very personal business, an expression of the caterer's personality in reaction to individual clients, I thought a would-be caterer might sometimes prefer Mr. Established Caterer's way of doing something to mine.

So I began to look for books and pamphlets on the subject. My search yielded only one book, a textbook for commercial caterers (*Successful Catering* by Bernard Splaver, Boston: CBI Publishing Company, 1975); that is why this volume has no bibliography or suggestions for further reading. No one had outlined a procedure for turning a good cook into a caterer. A book that met this need seemed to me a worthwhile undertaking. And a natural idea for me. Without planning to, I had informally taught my son Donald how to cater. From his development, I could see what the issues were for a neophyte. Moreover, having found that I could not cater and write at the same time, I eventually began to refer customers to Donald. I was free to write. So why not a book on catering?

I started by doing some research to see if catering has a future in an inflationary world, and I discovered that the 1980s are expected to be a period of increase—increased home entertainment, interest in good food, corporate and business entertaining, leisure time, and numbers of women in the work force (women, that is, with less time to cook). Although it will cost us all a bit more to entertain, apparently we will not give it up.

To widen the book's horizons I interviewed caterers all over the United States. Men and women in this business are friendly, personable, and voluble. They love their careers and are eager to volunteer helpful information. Far from resenting the revelation of professional "secrets" and "tricks of the trade," or wanting to discourage potential competitors, they all said there was room for newcomers to the business and willingly shared their experiences, hints, and tribulations.

In this book, you will make the acquaintance of these generous people from big cities and small towns all around the nation. I believe that in following the guidelines that they and I have established for caterers, you will find your way into a profession that is rewarding both literally and figuratively.

SECTION I

From Cook to Caterer

1

Make Catering Your Business

The Business of Culinary Pleasure

Do you love to cook? When people enjoy your cooking, does it please you down deep inside? Maybe dinner guests exclaim over your buttery chicken Kiev. Maybe your fresh baked breads or your full-bodied winter soups wow your family. Maybe your friends keep saying that no one, but no one, makes as rich and creamy a cheesecake as yours.

Whatever your specialty or your repertoire, if you earn raves for your cooking, you could be earning money, too. You may be male or female; young or older; bachelor, bride, or grandparent. If you love to cook, catering may be for you.

Today's verb, "to cater," meaning "to provide," began centuries ago as the Latin word meaning "to seize"; it became more civilized in Middle Latin, when *acceptare* meant "to buy" or "to acquire," and proceeded through Old French and Middle English meaning "to purchase." Down through history, a caterer has always been a supplier, a purveyor, the person who purchases and makes things available to others, as, for example, the purchasing department of a large business does, or a quartermaster in the Army. Both Chaucer and Milton mentioned catering as a profession. And Shakespeare used the word in its modern sense when he wrote, "And He that doth the ravens feed, / Yea, providently caters for the sparrow." (*As You Like It,* ii, 3.)

Today, catering is technically the business of providing food for any number of people, from one to one thousand. It can also encompass such auxiliary duties as hiring help to serve, and arranging for flowers, decoration, and rented equipment. This book deals with home or custom catering done by an independent cook, a freelancer—you. We're talking about a small business, just you and, ideally, your air-conditioned station wagon. Commercial catering is a much bigger business, complete with refrigerated trucks and uniformed drivers; it doesn't have quite the same personal touch a small caterer offers.

Your business can take any form. Some caterers make only wedding cakes; others supply everything for a wedding reception from petit fours and sandwiches to punch, coffee, and mints. Some caterers specialize in hors d'oeuvres, turning out trays of flaky cheese-filled puffs, prosciutto-wrapped melon balls, and shrimp-topped cucumber rings. Or they specialize in entrées, offering bubbling hot casseroles of beef in wine sauce or lamb Marrakesh. Dessert caterers make extravagant cakes, strudels, tarts, mousses, and airy soufflés. Yet another breed makes whole meals, from silken soups through veal with sour cream sauce, and salad, bread, and cheese, to a voluptuous dessert.

There are caterers of all kinds around the country today, men and women, teen-agers, too, who've gone into the business for reasons as different as the food they serve. Money, of course, is the obvious, universal motive. Otherwise, motives are varied. Ada Matchett, the wife of a farmer in Indiana, started catering because she didn't like to farm. She was just plain bored and wanted something to do. Gail Marcus of Encino, California, saw it as a good business for a woman tied down at home with a small child. Kitty Gushee of Grosse Pointe, Michigan, was tired of being a volunteer. She wanted the respect that comes with working for money. And Ken Williams of Griffin, Georgia, started quite by accident. He belonged to a club of gourmets who met once a month at different members' homes. One day he realized that more often than not, the group was gathering at his home to eat his cooking. When he finally decided to charge for his meals, he launched his business.

As these examples illustrate, the decision to try cooking for cash can be an informal commitment, not a make-or-break investment of time and money. And that's one of the advantages of home catering: It can be undertaken fairly easily.

A restaurant, by contrast, is an awesome enterprise. A popular restaurant can of course be very lucrative, and most good cooks—and not-so-good cooks—dream of opening their own place someday. There is something about the idea of starting a restaurant that seems to appeal to almost all of us. You know the vision. A charming atmosphere. The cheerful clink of silverware.

Deft waiters or waitresses coming and going. And at the center of things—whether red-checked tablecloths or white starched ones, country cooking or *nouvelle cuisine*—you, the artist, creating delectable dishes for beautiful, happy guests who glow with pleasure, while offstage, at the bank, your savings account grows by leaps and bounds.

Alas, the reality of a restaurant, even a small one, can be cruel. The physical labor alone is very taxing. Not only are you responsible for the food, but also for the surroundings in which it is served. Day in and day out. You oversee a staff that must be paid and fed, and that may present management problems. Again, day in and day out. Above all, offstage at the bank, everything may be written in red. A very large capital investment is the first basic reality of a restaurant.

Catering is a sound alternative. You can begin as modestly as you like. It doesn't require a large initial outlay. It can put a profit in your pocket. And it can satisfy the artist in you, fulfilling those dreams of happy customers.

Financial Realities

How much money can you make? That's hard to say, because your earnings depend on the sort of food and services you provide. Moreover, you can charge more in one community than you can in another for the same catered meal. Some caterers do an annual business in six figures and buy their own refrigerated trucks and uniforms for their help. Others simply earn money for family extras or for college tuitions. The field just doesn't lend itself to financial generalizations.

However, there is no question that you *can* make money. Here are some examples. Mary Carson of Coeur d'Alene, Idaho, caters whole dinners. Her business has a selective clientele, no commercial accounts, and no competition. It runs year 'round, with low spots in January and February and high spots in the summer, when there is a large summer colony in the area. Mary started her business eleven years ago in her own kitchen. Since then she has moved to a separate kitchen. The first year she grossed about $1,000. She did not make a profit for about four years. She has never paid herself a salary. In 1980 she could say that her business had grossed $50,000 that year.

Molly Brown started a catering business called "In a Basket" in New York City a couple of years ago, also supplying whole dinners, with a sideline of take-out food. She and her partner broke even the first year and were able to pay themselves a minimum wage the second year. (She said that they started the business in the month of January on a shoestring and had no money in February at all!) Sally Duval of Greenwich, Connecticut, started thirty-one years ago and made money immediately in the first year.

All the caterers I talked with agreed that the possibility of showing a profit sooner or later depends on the market for such a service. If your area is "ready" for the service you offer, you could make money over and above your expenses the first year. Don't count on this, however, because of our spiraling inflation. The characteristics of a good market are specified later in this chapter. The economic aspects of the business are discussed in both Section II and Section III.

A Closer Look

The Advantages

Interested? Let's consider more closely the advantages of having your own catering business.

The word "entrepreneur" is one you hear a lot these days. It's fashionable to be an entrepreneur, "someone who undertakes the risk and management of business," as Webster's Dictionary puts it. That is what you'll be: your own boss. No one will tell you what to do. If you're one of the many people who prefer to work for themselves, this aspect of the business will suit you. You'll be a cook, salesperson, business manager, accountant, public relations expert, delivery service, and creator of recipes. You'll have all the headaches, but the joys will be yours as well—and all the profits. You can test yourself, challenge yourself, and feel the self-esteem that comes with responsibility. You'll know for yourself what it means when a business must decide whether to expand or cut back. (Note that if time and experience teach you that having to make all the management decisions yourself is a burden, you can, like many entrepreneurs, take on a partner.)

A concomitant advantage is the feeling that your time is your own. It's more of a feeling than a fact, since your time really belongs to your customers. But to some degree you *can* schedule yourself as the mood takes you. If you feel like making quiches at midnight, you can. If you reserve Sundays as a family day, you needn't work that day.

Similarly, you can take on as much or as little business as you want to. If you want a full volume of business, you can arrange it. If you prefer to work part-time, that too is your choice. If you are planning to be away, then you can turn down a job or offer to provide frozen foods that can be prepared ahead of time, defrosted, and heated by the customer. Kitty Gushee's catering service in Michigan, for instance, doesn't work during July, August, or the Christmas holidays, and that doesn't seem to hurt business.

Furthermore, you may be able to work out of your own home. This is not entirely your choice, since some towns do not allow the sale of food that is cooked in a "family" kitchen. (Zoning and legal aspects are discussed in Chapter 8.) But even if you live in such a town, you can presumably start by working at home, which significantly reduces your financial risk.

In short, the home catering business offers a significant amount of flexibility and independence. Besides that, it offers side benefits. You'll be able to write off some fancy restaurant meals as research. You'll be prepared to entertain at the drop of a hat, because your freezer will usually be stocked with hors d'oeuvres, crêpes, cream puffs, croissants, or various entrées.

If you want to lose weight, you probably will—without trying. Most of the caterers I know are not overweight. Not only will you work off the calories you take in, you'll lose your taste for nibbling, because catering is a little like working in a chocolate factory. In fact, you become very discriminating about what you eat.

You won't get bored, either. I think that one of the most exciting aspects of catering is that every day brings something new. The world of food is always developing, and people's needs and desires change all the time. What Mrs. Jones wants today will not be what Mrs. Smith wants tomorrow.

Catering is also an opportunity to meet all kinds of people, to talk with them, and to help them. That's bound to interest you and make you more interesting. One husband told me he wouldn't have his wife give up her job for anything: She had become, as a caterer, a much more exciting person to converse with at the dinner table. If there's anything of the sociologist in you, or if you're a student of human nature, you'll learn a lot in a short time. People's likes, dislikes, and opinions about food are very revealing.

8 / CATER FROM YOUR KITCHEN

One more small but significant plus. If up to now your conscience hasn't allowed you to relax and read a newspaper or a book in the middle of the day, it will have to change. Part of your duty to your business is to keep up with the world, to know, for example, what the latest trends are, what's in, what's out.

The Drawbacks

If there are advantages, of course there are disadvantages. As a writer once said, every silver lining has a cloud. Let's be candid. There are two main disadvantages to the business. We can label them "Pressure and Hard Work" and "Family." Catering *can* be a high-pressure business. The orders can pile up, the fish market may run out of scallops the day before you're serving them at a luncheon. You may wish you had three heads and ten hands, even if you know how to juggle time and do two things at once. The phone will ring at all hours. Customers may be cross or short-tempered.

A young, attractive caterer, who prefers to remain anonymous, tells this story, calling it "A Day in the Life of a Caterer": "I awoke with a sense of foreboding. I *knew* there was something important I'd overlooked. . . . I ran through that night's party in my mind: Sure enough, I had completely forgotten to defrost some of the food! That was the beginning. While I was getting those things out of the freezer, I broke a couple of pie shells. Then the roulades I was making cracked. It seemed as if Murphy's Law ruled the day: If anything could go wrong, it did. The phone never stopped ringing, and I was late all around. I finally got the car packed and started off for the customer's house. Naturally, I got lost. My sense of direction isn't the best to begin with, and this place was way off the beaten path from anywhere. When I arrived, the hostess had all the children out on the road to flag me down. Because I was pressed for time at home, I had left some things to do on the site. Forget it! The house was full of kids, all of whom seemed to want to go into the food business, and they watched every move I made. On top of everything, I discovered that the customer's oven didn't work. Luckily my portable convection oven was still in the car from another job. Unluckily, the only place to plug it in was the laundry room, over the washing machine which was piled to the ceiling with Little League uniforms. The hostess must have volunteered to do the laundry for the whole team. I had to move those before I could even set up shop. To make it worse, she was nervous and couldn't handle the serving by herself. I usually do not make any appearances in front of the guests because I like to stay in the kitchen in control of the food. That night I had to do a little serving, and one of the men thought I was just his type and took to following me back into the kitchen. I put him to work serving, and with his hands full he couldn't create too much of a problem. But there were a few dicey moments. Was I glad to get home that night! Thank goodness that kind of day doesn't happen too often."

What About the Family?

If you have a family, they will definitely benefit in some ways from your work. If you've been a housewife up to now, your children may be happy to have a mother who is happy with a career. And there's no doubt they will enjoy some of the gastronomic fall-out. But they can't live on hors d'oeuvres and cream-puff swans, and sometimes they'll take it on the chin. On occasion you simply won't be available when your spouse or your children need you—because a cocktail party for 180 is under way, because a wedding cake must be delivered, or because there's a special rush order from one of your best customers. There are times when your family will feel neglected and you'll feel guilty—like the time, for instance, that Sue's husband broke two ribs. Sue couldn't take him to the hospital because she had to finish and deliver a wedding cake. Luckily a neighbor pinch-hit for her, but she wasn't happy about it and neither, of course, was her husband.

If you have young children, you may have to cope with their resentment over the loss of your time and attention. Here is how one mother turned that situation to her advantage. As she tells it, "One day my son asked me for a very expensive pair of sneakers. I said to him, 'Do you remember last week when I couldn't play tennis with you because I had to cater Mrs. Smith's party? Well, I made enough money on that party to pay for your new sneakers. That's what my working is all about.' Since then both my children have been much more cooperative. They are even proud of my job now."

Don't pretend to yourself or anyone you live with that he, she, or they won't be involved in your venture. When the pressure's on, bystanders are put to work. At the very least, a mate will be asked to make a delivery now and then to the kitchen door—something husbands, in particular, don't take kindly to. At the most, a bystander will be pressed into doing part of the cooking and marketing. (Keep in mind that it's risky to ask others to do your shopping for you: They tend to stray from the prescribed list, not understanding that only such-and-such a brand of pimientos will do, or that if substitution is necessary, the exercise of great judgment may be necessary. Emergencies aside, do your own shopping.)

One lucky woman got marvelous cooperation from her husband. During the first three months of a pregnancy, even the thought of handling food made her sick. But she didn't want to give up her new business, so she would stand at the kitchen door and direct her husband in the preparation of an order. Up to that time he had not been interested in her work. Today he can bone a duck as deftly as any French chef and more quickly than his wife. If your spouse can play any part in your business, include him or her. Then, if a night comes when chaos reigns and a deadline looms, you'll be assured of cooperation and understanding. Besides, cooking together can be fun.

Don't assume that because you're in the food business your family will eat better than any other family on the block. When you're preoccupied with a large order, they may eat worse. I do know of one caterer who deliberately saves out a portion of an order and freezes it for future home meals. If you can do that, fine. But keep in mind that a steady diet of boeuf bourguignon and chicken Kiev becomes tiresome. Have some fail-safe suppers in mind just in case. And discuss your interest in catering with those who may have to sacrifice on your account. It can help if things are understood at the outset.

If you're single, don't think that you're safe from complications. One caterer who lives alone opened the refrigerator one day to find that visiting friends had eaten two of the éclairs, four of the stuffed eggs, and all of the shrimp. (The moral of that story is: Label "business" food, "Hands off!")

One more thing. Any business has its share of the pitfalls that come with human nature. Inevitably, people will sometimes try to take advantage of you. Catering is a personal service business, and personalities are at its center. Be friendly, but be businesslike in your dealings. Business *is* business.

Basic Requirements

What traits and skills are needed to be a successful home caterer?

First, you must be a Cook.

There are two kinds of people in the kitchen: Cooks and People-Who-Have-To-Get-Something-Ready-For-Dinner. If you're one of the latter, you may like food. You may well turn out tasty meals. You just don't like to prepare them. It's no disgrace, and circumstances allowing, it's no misfortune. But if you're just doing time when you're in the kitchen, if you're just getting the job done, catering is probably not for you.

If you're a Cook, you prepare food better than the average person. (Modesty has no place here: You need to know you're good, better, best.) And you would rather make things to eat than do anything else—read or watch television or jog or play paddle tennis. A Cook's idea of a good time is to be busy in the kitchen, lost to the world, unaware of the passing hours. In sum, a Cook loves to cook. And what we love to do—the old adage goes—we do well. (After all, you wouldn't want to offer for sale a product you weren't proud of.)

So I repeat the opening lines of this book: Do you love to cook? When people enjoy your cooking, does it please you down deep inside? If your answers to those questions are "Yes!" you may be very happy as a home caterer.

Now, some Cooks are fascinated by the chemistry of food, by the interaction of butter and eggs in a hollandaise sauce, for example. And there are Cooks who can start with nothing, or so it seems, opening cupboard doors to see what's on hand. They hum to themselves, chop and mix, put in a little of this and a little of that, and voilà, something delicious arrives on the table.

Imagination and creativity, in other words, are two critical qualities to have, as is some understanding of how basic materials behave. If you're a Cook, you probably have these talents in some measure. They are part of your stock in trade, and you would be wise to cultivate them. Indeed, Cooks are always interested in new ideas. Observe, and keep your eyes and ears open. And read, read, read. If you've always enjoyed cookbooks, catering is your chance to revel in them.

A good sense of organization is vital. Catering requires efficiency. You need to be able to organize both time and materials. The successful caterers I know seem to accomplish more in a day than most people. They are all early risers, partly because they can get more done before the phone starts ringing. By 9 A.M. they've scheduled the day's activities, started dough rising, made a couple of batches of pastry, boned fifty chicken breasts, and planned a party or two.

Clearly, you must have a lot of energy. Basic good health is important. Catering involves physical work and sometimes long hours, and you will need stamina. Besides, good health always improves your appearance, and your appearance counts when you're selling your culinary services.

So does your personality. Do you like people? Can you deal with them, relate to their needs, and, in some cases, their problems? All catered occasions are not necessarily happy ones: Someone has to provide food for the sick and the bereaved. Men sometimes have the advantage in this area. Ken Williams has found that he can handle little old ladies better than his own daughter can. Sensitivity to such matters pays off. Catering is not just working with food, it's working with people.

It's also working under pressure at times, as I've suggested. Are you flexible? Can you keep your head? Can you ride with the punches if they come? You'll need to learn to bounce back and, on some days, to leap like a mountain goat from one peak crisis to another. If you're fairly easygoing, you'll have an easier time of it.

One More Requirement

What is the market in your area for a catering business? Even if you're the world's best cook, there's no point in setting up shop if there's no one to buy what you make. Take a fresh look at your community. If nobody is attempting a catering business, you had better find out why not. If there are already several caterers, large and small, there are customers. Where there's competition, there's something to compete for.

Ideally, you need a fairly affluent and sociable population. You want people who like to entertain and do so fairly frequently, who have some awareness of good food, and a certain degree of sophistication—enough to think that hiring a caterer is money well spent. The more clubs and organizations the better; they are an excellent source of revenue. A diversity in age groups also helps. Older people may like to entertain, but they just can't handle it themselves. The presence of a sizeable number of young couples in the community is also a good sign. These days many younger couples both work, so their time is limited; but they have a large combined income, one that covers such extras as catered parties. In places where there are pockets of professionals, you will find young adults who are very well off financially. Their incomes have six figures and they like to live well.

Local businessmen are another profitable market. If you live in an area where there is an influx of corporations, you're in luck. Big business has been moving to the suburbs; many corporations make their headquarters in rural areas today. But they miss certain aspects of city life, however, such as restaurants and the availability of good food. Their new facilities do include executive dining rooms and cafeterias, but for special entertaining they may yearn for what they had in the city. That makes a market for you. Corporate accounts are good ones to have because they are both dependable and profitable. They do not quibble about costs, they are flexible and open to suggestions, and they pay on time. On the other hand, a corporate account demands a sizeable capital outlay, because you need more than standard home equipment—for instance, various portable ovens and large coolers—to serve it.

Another market is on-location meals for film or television companies. This is a natural for the Los Angeles area, of course, but such meals are needed in the suburbs of big cities as well. Sue Layton, a caterer in Connecticut, has her dog to thank for bringing her in contact with this category of business. Like many people who have a very rare kind of dog, Sue knows other owners of the same breed. One was a woman who had provided her house and kennel—complete with the dog—for a dog-food commercial. She was also requested to provide a midday meal for the crew, producer, director, and others. The woman called Sue, who came through with a smashing French restaurant lunch—no hero sandwiches for her. She has gotten the business for their on-location filmings ever since. That's very nice business to have.

Crystal Ball Time

If the advantages appeal to you, if the disadvantages don't discourage you, and if you're confident that you can fill the basic requirements, you're on the brink of an exciting career.

The catering business offers a good chance for success.

Longevity is a reliable indicator of prosperity, since no one stays in business if he's losing money. Ken Williams has been a caterer for twenty years. Ada Matchett has been in business for twenty-one years. When she started, some people in her area didn't even know what the word "catering" meant. Today, brides-to-be call Ada before they set their wedding dates. Sally Duval was in business for twenty-one years and then sold out. She has been a consultant for ten years.

There's more. Roberta Dowling worked out of her own kitchen for three and one-half years, then moved to a store. She now has seven people on her permanent staff. Karen Hilliard has been catering for seven years. Pug Youngblood set up his shop six years ago. He started with $4,000 on a ninety-day note and now has a business valued in six figures. When Gail Marcus decided to go back to school, her hors d'oeuvre business was so lucrative that she was able to sell it. And Kitty Gushee reports that in Detroit, which she considers "a depressed area," business is booming.

Market surveys for the coming decade show a trend back to at-home entertaining, with more gatherings of family and friends around the fireplace or the home video screen. That bodes well for the catering business. And pundits explain that in the last two decades the United States has awakened to a significant interest in good food, an interest they expect to continue and grow. You and your business could grow with it.

2

Starting Out

How to Proceed

If catering appeals to you, read this book all the way through, recipes and all. You will see that it divides the field of catering into two main types. First is the "traditional" type, in which the caterer prepares a meal or a specific food (e.g., dessert or the main course) and either delivers it to the customer's house or serves it there. The caterer may also perform duties beyond serving, such as decorating the table and renting necessary equipment. The second form, which I have named "new wave catering" because it is a very recent development, is the preparation of food for customers to pick up and take home. The same foods may be involved, but there is less menu-planning and no delivery or service. New wave catering is a species of fast-food operation.

Reading about both types will enable you to make the decisions that mean a good start for you. You will then be able to use this book as a reference work. If you're interested in traditional catering, you will be concerned mainly, but not exclusively, with Chapters 3 to 5. If you are going to ride the new wave, Chapter 7 is especially for you.

When you've gotten your bearings, you'll be ready to make the transition from cooking for family and friends to the business of cooking for strangers. You'll be ready to go public.

At this stage, you need to be sure of yourself and your product. Established caterers, who have trod this path before you, advise that you take some time to get practical professional experience. The amount of time is best decided by you. One woman, who has been running a successful business for over five years, first spent nine months working in a small restaurant.

There she learned two important basics: organization and the knack of making every moment count. Time *is* money. You must know how to do more than one thing at a time. While the soup is simmering and the cakes are baking and the bread is rising, the soufflé base can be made and the ratatouille started. In part, pressure makes a restaurant a valuable training ground. If you can get a job in one, the investment of time will be worthwhile. You will learn many tricks of the trade that will stand you in good stead.

You don't want to be an amateur when you make your professional debut. If you have sagging spots in your repertoire, or if some of your creations look too much as if they were fashioned at home by loving hands, take some lessons. A show-and-tell lesson can perfect your techniques much faster than hours of experimentation by yourself in the kitchen. Some of the best caterers go to cooking school periodically for inspiration or a brush-up. (Just make sure that the instructor is expert enough to teach you something you don't know or have always wanted to learn. Some of our cooking schools are just one jump ahead of Fannie Farmer and are mainly geared toward the host or hostess who wants new dinner party suggestions. If you are a professional, you should learn from professionals.)

This is also the time to investigate zoning in your area. As I mentioned in Chapter 1, the zoning regulations in some towns prohibit the sale of food cooked in a family kitchen. The laws in your city or town and surrounding towns will influence your decisions about the nature of your catering business—for instance, where you will cook, where you will sell. (These matters are discussed in Chapter 8.) While you are making the transition from cook to caterer, you may decide to be temporarily on the fringe of legality, if your town's rules would require you to invest more money in a kitchen than your initial catering activities justify. But you will need legal status sooner or later if you want the publicity and advertising that make business grow.

Decisions, Decisions

What are you going to offer to customers?

You must get used to asking yourself a lot of questions. You'll need to answer dozens to make up a sensible business plan: How much time can you work, full-time or part-time? What are your objectives? Long-term? Short-term? Et cetera, et cetera! But the answers all depend on the most important question: What are you going to offer?

Well, what can you cook best? What do you like to cook? Is pastry your strong point? Do you have a flair for cake decorating? Would you consider extending a gift for cakes and pies to all kinds of desserts?

Or are you clever at whipping up hundreds of intriguing little hors d'oeuvres? Would you rather make casseroles? Then again, do you want to do full meals, soup to nuts?

In Indiana, Ada Matchett started with what she calls "cake and punch parties"; the cakes were wedding cakes. Kitty Gushee's catering service is called "The Main Course" because she started by providing just the entrée. (She found that people really wanted her to serve the whole meal, and preferably "warm from the oven.") Karen Hilliard in Odessa, Texas, started with cocktail buffets, luncheons, and dinners.

Pug Youngblood of Atlanta, Georgia, is becoming a new wave caterer. He believes, as do others, that the food service business is changing: The influence of a generation that has grown up with fast foods is moving the business away from elaborate private parties with help to serve to the convenience of "pick-up, take-home, and warm-up." The efficiency of fast foods is in demand, though people are tired of hamburgers and want better foods and a more interesting variety. In response, Pug provides take-out quail and take-out prime ribs.

This trend poses a fundamental choice: to serve or not to serve? Is yours going to be a take-out business? Or are you going to provide your customers with staff to serve your food? Established caterers agree that you must be able to provide service unless you're running a business like Youngblood's. Thus, if you spurn the ins and outs of serving, which is discussed in Chapter 5, you might consider a specialized food service that doesn't deliver, doesn't go into the home—but does offer marvelous food, extremely well packaged, with complete no-fault instructions.

In choosing your offerings, you must consider the tastes of your particular area of the country. Is it basically conservative like Boston and the Midwest? A Boston caterer says that in The Hub, chicken and beef are *de rigueur*. She has to vent her creative urges on desserts. Midwestern caterers tell me that preferences there, except in the large cities, are still for fairly plain and simple food—meat, potato, vegetable, salad, and dessert. But they must all be of high quality. A Detroit caterer says that she serves so many chicken dishes that one day she'll probably cackle. In Kansas City, green noodle salad with dill sauce is a winner. The large cities offer more room for variety. Can you introduce some unusual and ethnic dishes as they do in Texas, California, and some of the larger cities?

Regional specialties, particularly authentic ones, such as beef and kidney pie, jambalaya, cioppino, real chile con carne, plum duff, bourbon pecan pie, and whiskey pudding, are always popular. Quiches and crêpes tend to be done too much in metropolitan areas, but they can be good basic business, especially if you create some varieties that are yours alone. In general, the experts predict a return to the simpler foods of yesteryear; freshness, good quality, and excellent preparation will be the hallmarks of success.

When you have chosen the dish or dishes you're going to start with, practice, practice, practice. Cook them for friends and family until you've gotten the dishes to work every time. This is particularly necessary when you are adapting a recipe designed to serve eight to serve forty. You need to be able to depend on your recipes and yourself.

Whatever your product, caterers all agree that you should make lists of what you offer, and you should have them ready to show or give to prospective clients. Even if you are going to specialize in entrées only, be sure to have suggestions for a whole menu. Most customers like to have an idea of what is appropriate with moussaka or boeuf en gelée.

Going Public: Your First Step

When you're ready to offer your wares to strangers, start small. You can grow big in time. One of the commonest mistakes entrepreneurs in all fields make is to start out too big. At the first sign of success, they expand or take on more business than they can handle; interpreting those first signals of positive forward movement requires sensitive judgment. Experienced caterers advocate a modest beginning.

Starting small lets you feel out your market. One woman made sure of hers by offering free cooking for every charitable organization in her town. She did this for two months during which time people also asked her to do parties on the side. Thus, she got positive evidence that there was an opportunity to do more.

STARTING OUT

Selling through a Women's Exchange is a good way to start. Is there one in your town or nearby? A Women's Exchange is just what it implies—a place for women (and men) to buy and sell. Presumably in the old days it was a place of barter—my onions for your butter. No money changed hands and no income tax had to be paid. Today it is a nationwide organization with rules and regulations, but it is still a shop where the work of local men and women is taken on a consignment basis and sold to the public. Exchanges continue to spring up in unused railroad stations and gas stations and are usually completely manned by volunteers except for one paid bookkeeper or accountant. If there is an exchange nearby, you have an excellent opportunity to see just how you can handle catering. You will also learn something about packaging and freezing. (These topics are discussed thoroughly in Chapter 7.)

Since things are taken on a consignment basis, the first step is to take in a sample of your product. The product's general saleability is evaluated. Someone in authority checks how it looks in its frozen packaged state, whether the directions given are explicit enough, how it looks after it is heated, and, of course, how it tastes.

If the product is accepted, you negotiate its price with the Exchange. You explain your costs and the amount you'd like to charge. Let's say a fancy casserole cost you $5 to make and you'd like to charge $11. The Exchange representative may say, "Eleven dollars is too steep. No one will pay it. Nine fifty." The Exchange is in effect a distributor, responsible for knowing current prices. Note that in return for selling your product, to cover its own costs, the Exchange will take 20 percent of the gross price: for instance, $1.90 of your $9.50, leaving you $7.60, or a profit of $2.60.

As initial exposure, this is good for you because exchanges generally have high standards; their clientele is middle to upper-middle class. If you become a dependable and regular supplier, you'll probably be asked to handle catering orders for them. This is another way of becoming famous for your food without too much hassle. (But you *are* paying a percentage of the take.) Especially if you are interested in a take-out catering business, selling through a Women's Exchange would give you good preliminary experience.

You can also start out by offering to do the food for the church fair, the school fund-raiser, the newcomers' tea, or other such occasions. If you are interested in the more traditional forms of catering, this kind of experience can be the making of you. Check your local newspaper for names of organizations that would be likely candidates to contact. If you belong to any clubs, so much the better—you know just how they work.

Give unusual, imaginative suggestions for menus. That will distinguish you from the other cooks in town, lending you the aura of expertise that you need. Present different options: an Indian party featuring a complete curry dinner; a French picnic with pâtés, breads, and quiches; a brunch of ham loaves, codfish cakes, and corn fritters; an omelet party where the guests can choose from ten different fillings; an English tea with treacle tarts and seed cakes; or a wine and cheese tasting. In addition to the food, you will also have to handle details of decorations, table arrangements, and serving. You'll learn a lot that will be valuable when, later on, you are challenged by bigger and more financially productive jobs.

A very successful caterer in my area got her start when she took over the lunch concession at the annual art and antiques show of her daughter's school. In previous years, lunch had been merely a hot dog, hamburger, and Coke affair. She produced sandwiches made on homebaked breads with fillings of curried egg and avocado, meat loaf and watercress, chicken and bean sprouts. She gave away recipes for homemade zucchini and bean soups and furnished lemon squares and baby cheesecakes for dessert. In addition to coffee, she gave the hardworking concessionaires coffee cakes and a restorative wine and chicken broth soup. She then moved on to handling the school patrons' party which had always been a fairly mundane cocktail party with hors d'oeuvres. She gave it a theme, served a buffet with such unusual dishes as cold fish mousse in aspic, pastry-wrapped spinach rolls, beautiful baskets of crudités, cold rice salad, and tiny cream-filled éclairs and pastries. From this simple beginning, and a lot of hard work and hustling, she has become one of the foremost suburban caterers, commanding and getting New York prices.

Stimulating Business

Find ways to create a market for your services. Remember the woman who donated her cooking to charitable organizations? To build on that, she got their mailing lists and sent out 1,800 cards announcing her business intentions. She got a 2 percent return. In the mail order business, that is considered excellent. She knew she was really needed. And people were alerted, waiting for her business to open.

Being able to generate interest in the minds of people who would use a caterer if they thought of it is important. In the world of finance, people speak of "making a market"; caterers need to do the same thing.

Money Matters

How do you charge at this stage? One answer is, get paid in publicity.

Chapter 3 gives the general rule for calculating your fee: Three times the cost of the ingredients includes overhead and some compensation for your time. When you are just starting out, however, you need business and publicity more than you need the going rate. You're trying to establish yourself with a clientele.

So charge your first customers a reasonable amount, one that is less than the current rate. In exchange for giving them a break, ask for publicity. At this point, that is worth more to you. Again, one woman worked for free for two months. In return, she got mailing lists of 1,800 names. If it hurts to charge very little, remember that you are a beginner. Experience and reputation entitle seasoned professionals to charge more than you do. Moreover, if your work is for a charitable organization, your "food" is tax deductible.

Make Yourself Known

Any fund-raising affair must have lots of publicity to be a success and if you're the caterer, you want a share of it. If posters are put up around town, make sure your name is on them: "Special Omelet Luncheon Catered by ———." After all, food is a best seller. If the committee wants action photos, don't be bashful. Include yourself in.

One good reason to get a license to cater from your kitchen is that you can invite publicity—and the business it brings—with an open mind. Obviously, if your business is not legal, you will not consider advertising or even looking for publicity, unless you're also willing to consider a fine and/or a jail sentence. Our health inspector once showed me a feature article in the local paper about a woman who had just gone into the catering business from her own kitchen. "She won't answer her phone," he said, "but I'll track her down!"

Free advertising is available if you search it out. Think up a story with a good angle to give the local newspaper. Invite the social or food editor to lunch (or breakfast or tea) to sample your wares, or at least take him or her some of your better products. If you are not clever with words, ask a friend who is to write a press release on you and send it in to the paper. If you have a friend who does public relations professionally, so much the better. An official letterhead works wonders. Have some good photographs taken of yourself working at your trade and send them along with the release.

What do the established caterers say about paid advertising? They all agree that one free mention is worth a thousand paid words. "Our parties are our best advertisement," says Roberta Dowling of Cambridge, Massachusetts. A Texan caterer did put her name in the Yellow Pages and got two big commercial jobs out of it. If you are living in a big city, you might try a small ad in a major newspaper or regional magazine. But most professionals say that paid ads tend to bring in the wrong kind of business. The Junior League or Garden Club bulletin is a different matter.

Word of mouth is really unstoppable, anyway. If you're good, word travels. It travels if you're not, too. People are on the lookout for the new and the exciting. So when you're starting out, approach each assignment as a chance to get another one. Do something special that will make people talk.

Underway

If all goes well, sooner or later you will find that you are underway. By selling through an outlet like a Women's Exchange or by volunteering to cater for local groups, you've begun to feel comfortable in your new role. People are beginning to hear of you. Maybe they're even beginning to call you.

This is another transition point in your development, as important as the moment when a plane lifts off the runway, climbs, and settles at its best cruising height in the sky. To negotiate this stage smoothly, you need to think of two things at once.

First, craft. This is the time to refine your mastery of the elements of the caterer's craft: menu-planning, pricing, rapport with clients, organization of time; also, service, if you are going to provide that; packaging, if you are not. They are discussed in the next section. Your craft is all-important. It is the basis for your enterprise.

But business is also important. This is also the time to start thinking seriously as an entrepreneur. There is no prescribed timetable for specific business decisions in catering. But you will need to be aware of the following matters, and above all of their theme: Be businesslike.

Are You There?

Publicity is meant to bring business—that is, phone calls. Having made yourself known, you must be available when people seek you out. Many customers will not call more than twice. If you cannot arrange to cover the telephone yourself, hire an answering service or buy a recording device to take messages. Otherwise, word-of-mouth will spread the news that you're unreachable, and business will go elsewhere.

Appearances

As your activities gain momentum, consider the appearance of your business. What, for instance, will you list in the phone book? Today's world is one of splashy logos and catch phrases; it's important to have a distinctive name. Like your food, your business stationery, bills, and packaging labels should look professional, not amateur.

How do you want to name your business? This question merits real thought. Your own name will lend a personal touch. Is your name long or short? Do you like it? Is it neat, easy to say, easy to remember? Or would it attract attention because it's unusual? How would it look printed on cards, labels, stationery?

Do you prefer to "make a name" for yourself, to create a clever phrase? "Crème de la Crème," "Glorious Food," "Catered Affair," "Feast Without Famine," "Party Box," "Country Host," "Cuisine sans Peur," are just some that have earned renown.

Will you have a logo?

Whichever you choose, name or phrase, make sure it can catch attention and be remembered.

(When you are ready to invest in printed stationery, etc., read about it in Chapter 7.)

In Business

When you're first starting out, it probably doesn't matter too much if you're informal about the business aspects of your activities. But as you make the transition to professional status, you should set your business up properly. It's time, then, to open a set of books for record-keeping and for taxes. Refer to Chapter 8 in Section III, "The Business of the Catering Business."

You will find in Chapter 9 a discussion of the kitchen equipment needed to go into business. Again, if you've been getting by with just a few additional utensils, you will find at some point that you have to equip yourself to handle more tasks and varied ones. As gleaming pots and fish poachers dance before your eyes, remember, it's good business practice to make capital investments as the current and projected volume of business justifies them.

More Publicity

It is *always* time to stimulate business. In fact, let's put it this way: When you've had to turn away business for six consecutive months, you can stop thinking of ways to stimulate it. As your confidence and your business build, new forms of publicity will open up.

Write to the manager of the radio or television station in your area and offer your services as a food consultant on a talk-interview show. Follow up with a phone call if you don't hear from him or her. Letters get lost on busy desks. You'll find that most local stations need free guest artists; if you sell yourself convincingly they will give you a chance. Don't forget that there is a kind of magic in the printed word and even more in visual appearances. They become a part of your credentials. You can also offer a story on your coming TV stint to the local paper.

If public appearances do not faze you, you might give a cooking class. It will add glamour to your image and eventual profits to your business. If the local high school has an adult education program, offer to teach some cooking classes. You might feature a session on vegetarian food, one on low-calorie dishes, one on economy meals. If there is a cooking school already established in town, offer to give a demonstration of the kind of thing you do best. My friend Sue started by demonstrating desserts at a church fund-raising kitchen tour. She went on to give a class in garnishing at a new kitchen store. Her fame is spreading far and wide and she can't keep up with the orders.

There is more to teaching or demonstrating than meets the eye, however. Observe first before plunging in. We are not all born teachers. Painful experience has shown me that more goes into the making of a teacher than just opportunity and an audience. My own first teaching session came close to disaster because I had not realized the importance of the preliminaries. I should have gone through the whole lesson by myself beforehand, step-by-step, taking notes on timing, techniques, and distinguishing between what should be prepared in front of the class and what should have been done earlier. I did not know, for instance, that you should never chop onions as part of the lesson. By the time I got my face mopped up, two men had walked out. I once watched a woman who was a superb cook in her own kitchen fail miserably when doing a demonstration because she hadn't done her homework, literally. By the time she had sifted the flour, measured the baking powder, greased the pans, and melted the chocolate, her audience had left.

Don't let these two stories stop you from attempting a public appearance or two. Just organize in advance, and have confidence. As a well-known lecturer once said to me, "Before you go on, just say to yourself, 'If all these people have paid to hear me speak, then I *must* know more than they do about the subject.'"

If you happen to have a particularly interesting or unusual kitchen, you might try to promote an interview with a magazine or Sunday supplement. Write or call the media and tell them what you've got and why it should be of interest to their readers. They may turn you down, but you will have made a contact. The next time they hear your name they may recognize it. One caterer made the most of her restored house and old-fashioned kitchen, which has a Garland range; she placed articles and pictures of it in every magazine and newpaper she could. Today she combines her catering business with a contributing editorship on a national magazine and uses her kitchen for photographs of party setups.

Cook to Caterer: A Guide

- Take time to become professional.
- Investigate the zoning laws in your environs.
- Specialize in food that you do well and that you like to do—ideally, something that is always in demand.
- Start small. Grow gradually.
- As you're getting started, charge less. Trade for publicity.
- Make yourself known to the public.
- When people call, be reachable.
- Give your business a professional appearance.
- Set up your business records properly.
- Equip your kitchen as need and business volume allow.
- Stimulate business imaginatively. And constantly.

SECTION II

Caterer's Craft

Introduction

If you go into traditional catering, whether you provide whole meals or just a specific food, such as the hors d'oeuvres for a cocktail party, you will find that there is a basic order of events to a catering job:

1. a client calls you, asking you to provide food;
2. you and the client discuss various foods and their cost;
3. if you get the job, you and the client reach an agreement;
4. you shop for ingredients;
5. you prepare the food;
6. you deliver it; or serve it and clean up afterward.

There is more to catering than these six steps, however. Before you can talk to a client, you must have selected the foods you will offer, set their prices, and decided on your general business policies. Otherwise you would not be able to negotiate steps 2 and 3.

Logically, then, a catering job can be divided into three main parts:

1. the tasks you perform before a client telephones;
2. the caterer-client arrangements;
3. the tasks you perform after reaching an agreement with a client.

In the following chapters you will find guidelines for the procedures that comprise a catering job. These generally apply whether you are providing a complete meal or one element, such as hors d'oeuvres, an entrée or a wedding cake.

3

Before a Client Calls

Let's begin with what you need to do before a client even telephones you—the skills of menu-planning, pricing, and policy-making.

All About Menus

In Chapter 2, you were urged to choose your specialty. If you chose wedding cakes, you should learn a repertoire of different cakes to offer clients. Brides today tend to want untraditional cakes, like carrot cake, for their weddings. As one young woman remarked, "To me, an old-fashioned, traditional wedding cake tastes like sawdust with sugar on it." Remember that if the wedding is a small one, with the reception at home, only one cake will be needed. But if it is a large wedding, with the reception taking place at a club, you may need two cakes: a large one that the bride cuts and a second one in the kitchen, which is the one actually cut there and served to guests. The reason is simple: Large, tiered wedding cakes are mainly for show—they are held together with dowels; the understructure is not meant to be seen.

Note that busy customers, burdened with all the details of a wedding, may not be content to let you provide only the wedding cake: You may find that they really want you to do the whole reception—sandwiches, coffee, punch, etc. This means more menu-planning: What kinds of sandwiches? What kinds of little cookies or petit fours?

If you choose to specialize in hors d'oeuvres, you will need an extensive, flexible repertoire of different kinds that complement each other. Some caterers prefer to limit the selection at a given party to four or five, offering those in quantity. Often caterers like to do ten or twelve different hors d'oeuvres, both hot and cold; perhaps three may be different raw vegetables, three different deep-fried foods; three canapés; or three kinds of filled pastry. The greater the variety, the fewer of each kind you offer. The rule of thumb for hors d'oeuvres is to allow ten per person. Remember that things like shrimp will be very popular. Guests will eat more shrimp and less of something else, so plan accordingly.

In choosing your selection, consider a variety that offers different textures and tastes and colors. You should plan hors d'oeuvres as you would a dinner menu, with sensitivity to the relationship of the component parts. With hors d'oeuvres, aesthetics are particularly important. Your preparations should look irresistible. (Plan carefully to avoid presentations that will leave the buffet table looking like a scene of carnage after the food has been eaten.) Note that while some clients may be content to have you deliver the hors d'oeuvres to their door, others will want you to arrange the platters for them or supervise serving.

If you are going to cater whole dinners, the first thing to do is equip yourself with menus for three budgets: high, medium, and low. Customers can then choose a price range without embarrassment; you will have something for everyone. Ideally, you should have several menus for each price range. If you are just starting out, have at least one set of three. Keep these menus, with approximate prices, by the phone for quick reference when a client calls.

Once the menus are made up, be prepared with alternatives to replace a course if the customer requests a change, of if you discover at the last moment that the necessary ingredients are not available. Whenever you propose a menu to a client, always give yourself some leeway for change. A client may say, "I'm happy to pay top dollar, and I like your most expensive menu—except for the beef. For the entrée, could you substitute something else?" Without missing a beat, you should be able to say "Of course. You could have lamb or veal." To do this, you must know what foods are in the same price range, what's expensive, what's reasonable, what's cheap. It's a good idea to cultivate your consciousness of cost.

Seasonal Thinking

Menu-planning and shopping go hand in hand. All serious chefs practice "seasonal" cooking: They plan menus around foods that are in season; in fact, they plan their menus while marketing. The ability to do this well comes with experience, with such an extensive knowledge of recipes, for instance, that the sight of a seasonal food—say, winter squash—brings to mind two or three ways to prepare it. Work toward this ability. The larger your knowledge of recipes and menus, the larger your stock in trade.

Here, for inspiration, is a chart of seasonal fruits and vegetables and some unusual suggestions for their use.

SPRING

Artichokes: stuffed (hot or cold); as hors d'oeuvres with curried mayonnaise
Asparagus: mimosa; with prosciutto; raw for hors d'oeuvres
Rhubarb: sauce for game hens, ring filled with strawberries
Strawberries: cold soufflé with raspberry sauce
Peas: puréed as filling for pastry barquettes; spring soup
Watercress: sauce for chicken loaf
Spinach: roll en croûte; puréed base for poached chicken breasts

SUMMER

Cucumbers: baked; stuffed
Mangoes: mousse
Cherries: clafouti; jellied with rum custard sauce
Peaches: poached with raspberry sauce; tarts
Beans: vinaigrette; bundles tied with scallion tops
Corn: timbales on fried tomato slices
Zucchini: grated and stir-fried; crust for pizzas

FALL

Melons: sliced with figs, prosciutto, or smoked salmon; in ice cream
Grapes: cheese-stuffed for hors d'oeuvres; garnish for veal scallops

Pears: stuffed with nuts and dried fruit and baked
Apples: custard pie; stuffing for pork scallops; soup
Eggplant: moussaka; cannelloni; oven-fried
Pumpkins: purée baked in a ring; diced in beef stew
Cranberries: sugared and baked for a garnish
Sweet potatoes: pudding with Grand Marnier; stuffing for pork roast
Jerusalem artichokes: soup; provençal

WINTER

Citrus fruits: baked with brandy and caramel; glazed slices as garnish for meat and poultry
Carrots: filling for veal roulade; puréed with cheese and ginger
Avocado: guacamole; garnish for soup, chicken, and fish dishes
Onions: amber baked; glazed rings with apple rings
Leeks: vinaigrette
Cabbage: lasagne; stuffed
Mushrooms: herbed vinaigrette; raw with brandied cheese filling

When you plan a menu for profit, you must consider two basic elements: interest and cost. Seasonal menus obviously save money; they can also make your meals more interesting by giving them a theme. Thinking seasonally, you will always be ready to suggest something interesting to a client. It is like knowing what will be in the supermarkets ahead of time.

A "seasonal sense" is also helpful when you must change a menu because a food is unavailable or suddenly too expensive. The ability to adapt in an emergency is part of being a caterer. As we have learned recently, crop failure can raise the price of a staple to unreasonable heights. You need to be alert for substitutes. Winter salads do not have to be greens: They can be fruits or vegetables, coleslaw with a Caesar dressing or a julienne of root vegetables in a rémoulade sauce; and don't forget white turnips and celery root.

As illustration, here are two seasonal menus, a winter dinner for eight, which suits a medium-sized budget; and a summer buffet for thirty,* which is more expensive. The winter dinner be-

---

*The recipes for both these menus can be found in Section IV, "A Cookbook for Caterers."

gins with seviche, a delicious cold scallop dish; next is tarragon chicken with artichokes; puréed broccoli; julienne of endive with watercress; refrigerated rolls; and cold mocha soufflé. The seasonal elements here are the scallops, the artichokes, the broccoli, and salad greens, all of them winter foods. Note that the inexpensive foods balance the cost of the more expensive ones. The art of menu planning is the blending of cheaper and costlier ingredients. The trick is to make low-budget items more elaborate in appearance and preparation; high budget items can be much simpler. This will be discussed further in the section on pricing. For the moment, observe that the dessert and vegetable are low-budget items; the first course is elegant and expensive, and the entrée is medium in price.

The summer buffet for thirty calls for salmon or striped bass in aspic; chicken breast in green sauce; vegetables à la grecque; cucumber rings; brioche-and-pâté sandwiches; and mango mousse. There are many seasonal elements here: the vegetables à la grecque, the cucumbers, the parsley and watercress for the green sauce, and the mangoes; although the fish is available all year round, salmon is particularly good in the summer.

An Artist's Eye

Good menu-planning involves two other elements as well. These are the ones that show your expertise, the ones which confound most party-givers. Foods must be complementary to each other in terms of *texture* and *color*. As one caterer put it, "I consider myself an artist; my trays are like paintings."

Picture a group of foods as they will appear on the plate. The classic example which we have all encountered is the all-white plate — fish, mashed potatoes, and cauliflower. Our winter dinner counterpoints chicken in a golden sauce against green broccoli, highlighted with pale artichoke hearts and ivory mushrooms. The summer buffet is a bright medley of colors and textures. In another dinner for eight, you can have a buttery entrée in a chicken Kiev and, for balance, two plain but colorful vegetables — a green purée of broccoli and amber squash. A salad will always add texture and bite. As you plan menus, review them for texture and color. And keep these qualities in mind whenever you look at or taste other people's cooking.

Do Your Recipe Homework

Revise your menus periodically, and always try to include new recipes. One catering establishment in our town has some of the same things on its list that it had ten years ago. The result? Predictability and boredom. Wouldn't you prefer to have people say, "Betsy catered last night's dinner and I've never had such a good and unusual chicken dish"; rather than "Betsy catered last night's dinner and she's still doing that same chicken dish"? Donald Bruce White, one of Manhattan's major caterers, says he is constantly researching new recipes. Otherwise, with his competition, he'd be out of business.

Creating new recipes is part of the fun of catering. Styles in food are constantly changing. Where do you get new recipe ideas? From magazines and trade journals, for starters. Food magazines publish many down-to-earth, well-tested recipes; if some are a bit too esoteric, at least they give you ideas to work on. Some restaurant reviews are so detailed they can start your creative juices flowing. Cookbooks on entertaining are helpful; but don't get carried away and attempt dishes that are too elaborate; they take time, and your time is a precious commodity. Instead, adapt classics. Improvise. A clafouti is really a cherry pudding in batter. For a summer buffet, Martha Stewart, a very creative caterer, took the idea of a clafouti and made it with eggplant. It was sensational. Try serving some classically hot dishes cold and classically cold dishes hot. In this way you achieve the element of surprise that distinguishes your food from that of other caterers.

Collect cookbooks of all kinds. Some of the best are the regional ones put out by women's organizations; the food is good and the selections give you an idea of what people like to eat. (Test the recipes, however; they are not as dependable as recipes in commercial cookbooks.) Two particularly good regional cookbooks are *Recipe Jubilee*, put out by the Junior League of Atlanta, Georgia, and now sold in bookstores and the Women's Exchange; and *Forum Feast*, published by The Forum School in Waldwick, New Jersey.

Most of the caterers I interviewed say they constantly test recipes and try to create their own dishes whenever possible. The best have specialties that become their trademarks. People invariably ask for these distinctive dishes. Karen Hilliard describes an art gallery supper she had prepared of sliced beef tenderloin; homemade breads; raw vegetables with her specialty, spinach dip; a giant guacamole; and great big bowls of fresh strawberries. When people see the spinach dip they recognize Karen Hilliard's signature on the meal.

You should especially test recipes that you are going to adapt to serve a larger number of people than originally intended. If you want forty servings from a recipe which yields eight portions, think in terms of a half-pound portion per person. Whenever you increase a recipe, remember that it will take longer to prepare. Here are some tips for increasing recipes:

1. Casseroles of meat and vegetables: You can increase the number of portions by doubling the meat and vegetables, but don't double the sauce; use one and one-half times the amount, or the sauce will drown the food.
2. Soufflé recipes cannot be doubled. You will have to make a separate soufflé for each set of servings.
3. Soup recipes can be doubled.
4. Baking recipes (anything that must rise) cannot be doubled successfully; a cake will not rise properly if the recipe is doubled.

Otherwise, recipes can be doubled successfully.

How Much to Serve?

Be generous with the portions you serve. Clients would prefer to have generous amounts and pay for them rather than skimpy ones and risk the danger of running out of food. Your clients will not want to look chintzy to their guests. For accuracy, it's best to work with a scale. In general, allow one-half pound of meat per person; and one-half cup of vegetables. Portions of desserts like mousse should be about one-half to three-fourths cup; use the lesser amount if it's very rich. Salad is measured by the handful, one handful per serving.

One footnote: People are becoming increasingly knowledgeable about food. Tastes are more sophisticated than they were ten years ago. On one hand, that means there is a receptive audience to inspire you. On the other, it means that the audience sets a high standard for you, especially perhaps on the two coasts. It is a little risky to be just one jump ahead of your customers. Some of them are excellent cooks themselves; they know too much. For instance, recently I was playing around with an idea I'd had for a new recipe. It involved wrapping large sea scallops in lettuce, poaching, and masking them with a light wine sauce. I went off to the fish market, where I explained that I just wanted five or six of the biggest scallops to wrap in lettuce. "Oh," came a bright female voice over my shoulder, "and you're going to steam them and serve them for a first course. Hot or cold?"

Pricing

How do you price the food you provide?

When you set up a personal service business, one of the most difficult things to do is to put a price on your product, an amount that will both appeal to your customers and give you a fair return on your investment. When your own labor is involved, pricing is particularly hard. Sometimes prices become simply "what the traffic will bear." When I asked caterers all over the country how they handled pricing, many of them sighed. One way or another they all said the question was just too hard to answer concretely.

The basic rule of thumb for catering is this: Charge three times the cost of the ingredients. The resulting amount is meant to allow for overhead, labor, and profit.

You then divide the total by the number of guests, getting a cost per person. This is the figure you will quote to the client; then the client can easily decide whether to invite those extra four people or not. Actually, the "three times" rule currently applies outside New York and other big cities. In places like Los Angeles and New York, inflation has forced caterers to multiply the cost of ingredients by four or even five. For example, at this writing, in 1980, the price per person in New York City for a cocktail party with hot and cold hors d'oeuvres is $8 to $10. A sit-down dinner is about $18 to $25 per person, a figure which does *not* include wine, rented equipment, and service.

In the suburbs prices are scaled lower. You will have to evaluate the difference between a wealthy suburb and a middle-income small town. Price your wares to fit the clientele and the competition. Sometimes a decision on price may be based on what the customer can afford. This is not a businesslike approach to making money, but many caterers adopt it because the business is so personal. One caterer says she is unfortunately very soft-hearted; if a customer looks a bit worn, she lowers her price and hates herself for doing it. As a result, she advises setting prices and sticking to them, no matter what!

"Three times the cost of the ingredients?" you may think to yourself, "I can *never* offer seafood!" Yes, you can—with clever menu-planning. The cost of the ingredients for some dishes far outweighs the labor involved. Seafood Newburg is a simple dish to put together, but the seafood is expensive. To control the price of a menu on which it appears, plan a lavishly decorated dessert which may take time to make but contains nothing but eggs, cream, and ladyfingers—inexpensive ingredients.

In short, plan your menus to balance the cost of an expensive, easily prepared dish with menu items whose ingredients are inexpensive—the bread, for instance, or the dessert. Again, you will need to learn the price ranges of various foods—those which are high (e.g., beef, lamb, veal), medium (chicken), and low (pasta).

Our winter dinner for eight was planned this way. Let's see what it costs to make.

*WINTER DINNER FOR EIGHT**

Coquilles Seviche: 1 pound of scallops @ $7, and 1 pound firm white fish @ $4 plus herbs, etc.	$14.00
Tarragon Chicken with Artichokes: 4 whole chicken breasts @ approximately $1.60 per pound, artichokes, staples	20.00
Puréed Broccoli	2.00
Julienne of Endive and Watercress	2.00
Refrigerator Rolls	1.00
Cold Mocha Soufflé	1.75
Total cost of ingredients	$40.75
	× 3
Total cost to customer	$122.25
Cost per person ($122.25 ÷ 8) =	$15.28
	or $15.00

*The recipes for this menu and the two that follow can be found in Section IV "A Cookbook for Caterers."

In our inflationary world, it's impossible to give hard and fast prices. In the winter of 1980–81, this dinner at $15 per person would be in the range of medium-priced meals, which run from $11 to $17 per person. The range for expensive meals is $18 to $25 per person (and beyond, too). Low-cost menus are $5 to $10 per person. I emphasize that these rates are approximations which vary in different parts of the country. As a rule, city prices are the highest.

Our summer buffet is an expensive meal:

SUMMER BUFFET FOR THIRTY

Salmon or Striped Bass in Aspic 15 pounds of fish @ $6 per pound, plus other ingredients	$92.00
Poulet Vert (Chicken in Green Sauce) 23 pounds of chicken breast @ $1.60 per pound plus parsley, watercress, etc.	42.00
Vegetables à la Grecque	20.00
Cucumber Mousse	10.00
Brioche Stuffed with Chicken Liver Pâté	8.00
Mango Mousses with Rum Sauce	20.00
Total cost of ingredients	$192.00 ×3
Total cost to customer	$576.00
Cost per person ($576.00 ÷ 30)=	$19.20

Rounding off, you could charge $19.50 or $20 per person for this meal.

A meal that features pasta is inexpensive:

LASAGNE SUNDAY SUPPER FOR SIXTEEN

Lasagne (pasta, meat, cheese, sauce, onions, herbs)	$12.50
Salad bar	6.00
Bread	2.10
Walnut rolls	2.50
Cost of ingredients	$23.10
	×3
Cost to customer	$69.30

Cost per person ($69.30 ÷ 16) = $4.33

With time and practice you will find that you become adept at gauging the approximate cost of basic dinner menus. If you keep up with changing costs of ingredients, you can usually know what those menus cost for four or six people. Working with multiples of four and six, you can easily give a customer an approximate estimate of a meal for almost any number of people.

Similarly, it's wise to develop a sense of the cost of a couple of cocktail party menus in units of ten people. You can easily deduce the cost per head for fifty-five people. Compute the cost of the ingredients, multiply by three, and divide the total by ten to get a price per head.

You must also be prepared to price platters of hors d'oeuvres, casseroles, or desserts separately for customers who simply want a given quantity of food delivered to their homes. Again, charge three times the cost of the ingredients. A price-per-portion may be optional.

Wedding cakes are a separate case. The price for a wedding cake is calculated by the portion: A portion cost $1.00 to $1.25 in 1980. Caterers whom I talked with expected the 1981 rates to be $1.25 to $1.50 per portion. A wedding cake for 100 guests will cost $150.

Finally, here are two important tips based on the experience of caterers I interviewed. First, do not quote flat prices for your food. If you do, it will be difficult to change them if supermarket prices rise. Just as you should give yourself leeway in creating a menu for a customer, give yourself flexibility by quoting approximate prices.

Second, don't underprice. Charge the full amount. Women, in particular, sometimes lack the confidence to charge what their services are worth, because they are afraid that they may overcharge and cheat a client. Experienced caterers agree that if you err, it is better to err on the high side, rather than the low. You are not in as much danger of cheating as you may suppose.

Basic Policies

Will you charge to deliver food? Will you ask a client for a contract and a deposit? If so, how large a deposit? What arrangement will you make in case of a cancellation?

Before you discuss a catering job with a customer, you must set your business policies. Experience may modify your thinking, so don't cast your first ideas in concrete. But do anticipate the issues.

You should charge for all services you perform—for delivery, for serving food, for arranging rentals. Particularly if you are working in an area where people are conservative in their spending, or a feeling of recession has taken hold but food prices are changing every day, you can hold your own and not lose money by charging small fees for anything extra that you do.

Delivery

Given the price of gas, most caterers are adding delivery charges for small items. When they do a large party some of them will absorb the delivery in the overall charge, but for a couple of casseroles or desserts they add one or two dollars to the price and mark it specifically as a delivery charge. Gail Marcus, whose extremely successful catering business offered only frozen hors d'oeuvres, charged for delivery of orders under 500 (quantity, not price). One small caterer located in a large city now charges taxi fare for single orders. She would just as soon discourage them, and calculates that a $2.00 surcharge on an $8.00 order will do the trick.

Overhead

Another consideration in your prices is overhead—electricity, heat, insurance, equipment, etc. Some of these are fixed costs; some are floating. Since it is difficult to figure overhead exactly, most home caterers do not. Instead, they take whatever tax experts allow them as a figure. Probably the stickiest question is how to assign a dollar value to your own time and effort. (If you are a woman who has been out of the labor force for a while, you may have trouble giving your own time appropriate value. Remember, you earn the money by honest work; it is not an unexpected blessing.) You can pay yourself a wage, although many caterers do not. Your tax man or the local IRS representative can give you the best advice on how much to charge the business for your labor.

Agreements

Contracts and deposits are also a matter of judgment. Those caterers who insist upon both—all New York City caterers do—generally ask for a nonrefundable deposit of 15 to 50 percent of the total price and payment of the balance on delivery. The contract is really a letter of agreement detailing the menu, equipment (rental), number of people in help, who pays for what (such as liquor and flowers), and the total price. Here is a sample form for a letter of agreement, listing the categories to be filled in.

> Date of agreement
>
> Date of party
>
> Services to be provided by _____ (caterer) for
> _____ (patron)
>
> Menu:
>
> Bar service:
>
> Home visit to inspect space and equipment:
>
> Staff:
>
> Tent, dance floor, and lighting:
>
> Referral to other services (music, flowers):
>
> Total price of menu, staff, and services (to be confirmed):
>
> Rentals (We will arrange for rentals to be delivered and picked up. You will be billed directly by the rental company):
>
> Deposit of _____ % to confirm date and arrangements.
>
> _____   _____
> Patron   Caterer

Some caterers I've talked with insist upon contracts. Others, including one man who runs a very large service, never use them. Perhaps because he himself is a Southern gentleman, he believes that a man's word is his bond. On the other hand, a (Northern) caterer whose fees for parties run into the thousands, not only uses contracts, she sues if she doesn't get paid.

With business accounts, charity benefits, and organizations, I believe it is more efficient to arrange for both a written agreement and a deposit; they are used to doing things that way. If it is a person-to-person arrangement in which a deposit and/or contract seems inappropriate, tell your customer that you will present your bill when you deliver the food, and that it is payable then. You can also give her the option of being billed, if you are able to wait for your money.

Cancellations

How you handle cancellations is also a matter of judgment. Most of the caterers I talked with assured me that cancellations are rare; usually, they occur when there is a death in the client's family or something equally momentous. If you have obtained a nonrefundable deposit, you are protected. Otherwise, you simply charge for the food that has been prepared and cannot be used. Caterers told me that they didn't charge for their labor in this situation, preferring to cover just the cost of the ingredients. The charge probably will be small because most foods can be put to another use.

I also asked established caterers what happens if the caterer must cancel for some reason. Most of them had no ready answer; apparently it just doesn't happen. There was only one story: of a caterer who broke his leg before a job. A friend carried on for him while he gave orders from his bed. All the caterers said they would muddle through somehow. It might be wise, however, to give some thought to a contingency plan in case "the worst" happens, and you cannot carry out your side of the catering agreement.

4

Caterer and Client

First Contact

Your menus, with prices, are finally set, and so are your basic business policies. The phone rings, and when you answer, Mrs. Boniface, a prospective customer, introduces herself, explaining that she's heard of you from her friend Mrs. Baker, for whom you had catered a committee luncheon. Mrs. Baker was delighted with your food and recommends you highly. Mrs. Boniface would like to discuss with you a summer buffet dinner that she plans to give for her husband's birthday next month.

What happens next?

First, see if you are available. Ask for the date and check your calendar. If you're free to take the job, you can go on from there. (If you are not, explain so with regret. You want Mrs. Boniface to call you again.)

Next, find out if you are the only caterer Mrs. Boniface is calling. If she's looking for bids, are you willing to compete? (Usually, people ask for bids when the affair is a big one, but you should be prepared for competitive situations.) This is another policy decision you'll have to make.

Ada Matchett of Warren, Indiana, says she never puts in bids. But she admits that she has gotten very independent and that she can afford not to compete because she has been in business for a long time. Another caterer, who claims, "My food is so good you don't need to know the cost," says her "snobbish" air pays off because people automatically think she's the best. These women are in the minority, however. They are definitely quality caterers, and they may be the only caterers in their towns. Most people have to compete. While you are establishing yourself, you will probably have to submit bids.

Competing for a job means presenting your plan for the occasion in question, describing the food you would provide, other related services, and the price. This is a job of salesmanship in part, and you should make your "pitch" as irresistible as possible.

Sometimes you can win a job by pricing—by a lower bid. Sometimes you get the job because you offer the type of food that is wanted. Style, offering something special, can win for you in a competitive situation. As Elsie de Wolfe, a famous interior decorator, once said, "Style is what counts."

Remember that competitors are not necessarily enemies. When I described this book to Sally Duval, a highly respected caterer in Greenwich, Connecticut, she welcomed the idea of bringing new people into the business, saying she'd like some reliable referrals to whom she could pass along her overflow business.

Chat with Mrs. Boniface for a moment to get information and confirm her good impression of you. Has she decided how many guests she will invite? Since the occasion is a birthday, does she want a fairly special dinner? Does her husband like lamb? What doesn't he like? Is there any particular food she'd like or does she want you to suggest something exciting? From the range of menus you've planned and keep handy by the phone, you can mention possibilities to entice her.

The aim of this conversation is, first, to get some sense of Mrs. Boniface and her occasion, and then to make an appointment to see her in person. In the time between the call and the appointment, you can use the information gleaned from your talk to tailor some suggestions that will please Mrs. Boniface and win you the job.

Visit the Client

Whether or not a situation is competitive, you should always see a client at her house. The catering business is one of personal expression, both the client's and yours. Rapport—or its absence—can make all the difference to both of you. Donald Bruce White, a leading New York City caterer, advises, "Always, if possible, meet and talk to your client on her home grounds. Number one reason: If you take the time and trouble to go to her home, it shows you care about the job. That is the all-important personal touch. Also it gives you a chance to size up her tastes, surroundings, and the type of food she would like." Gail Marcus adds that when she was in business she not only went to the client's home, she took samples of her product, hors d'oeuvres, with her. "The product sold itself," she reports. Roberta Dowling of Cambridge, Massachusetts, takes along a book with photographs of her food. Bob Salsman of Kansas City also visits the client's home and checks the layout; in addition, on the job he tries to use as many of the hostess's things as possible. He also likes to cook in the customer's home, doing charcoal broiling and clambakes in a pit. He prides himself on creating menus to fit the individual. Again, the personal touch.

Thus, your visit with Mrs. Boniface has a sales purpose and what we might call a "logistics" purpose.

An additional reason for conducting the interview in the home of your customer is that your own kitchen may not look like the perfect *House and Garden* caterer's kitchen. Although the food you produce is beautiful and hygienically sound, sticky fingerprints, spilled milk, and general clutter can do a lot to ruin your image. One ant crawling across the floor can multiply into an army on the counter with a little loose talk.

A cautionary note: A visit of this sort is informal, and the discussion of the client's personal tastes can easily lead to gossip. Like the family doctor or lawyer, you as a caterer will be privy to a lot of personal information about your customers. If you've ever had a penchant for gossip, give it up or resist it. You should be as circumspect about privacy as other professionals are. Your reputation, like theirs, would suffer if you breached confidences. In the course of your career you may learn a few things about human nature that you'll wish you hadn't. And on occasion you may have to practice the fine art of disappearing into the furniture. That's part of the job.

You Are the Authority

A client hires and pays for something he or she either cannot or does not wish to do. Mrs. Boniface has confidence that you can handle the job better than she could. Your knowledge of food is as important to you as a law degree is to a lawyer.

Encourage the customer's confidence as much as possible. Never discourage it. If Mrs. Boniface should ask for a dish you do not know how to prepare—"Can you do veal Prince

Orloff?"—do not reveal your ignorance. Say yes; you can look up the recipe and test it later.

Although customers will sometimes request certain foods, they will be most interested in your menu suggestions. You are the authority on planning the meal—what goes with what, what is in season, what is reasonably easy to eat at a buffet, what is elegant enough for royalty. Introduce your thoughtfully planned menus flexibly. Be authoritative, but be careful to elicit your customer's tastes. Does Mr. Boniface like fish? Has he given up beef? Even people who sit on the fence on domestic, political, and international issues have definite likes and dislikes about food. Like an interior decorator, you must create a showcase for your client's personality.

Tact is a necessary asset. What is absolutely basic knowledge to you may be astounding, surprising, and completely unknown to other people. Don't talk down to clients. Explain carefully what each dish consists of, how it tastes and looks. If you must use a French or Italian phrase for a certain dish, be sure you translate as you go. Translated from the Italian, "vitello tonnato" is veal with tuna sauce, a delicious cold buffet dish that can also be made with chicken or turkey instead of veal. Nothing overwhelming, but it *sounds* formidable. One person may come right out and ask what you mean; but if Mrs. Boniface is too embarrassed to ask, she may assume it is just too fancy for her tastes.

Negotiation

With menus at various price ranges, you are well prepared. Since price often governs the choice of food, raise the question of budget early in the meeting.

If Mrs. Boniface has not used a caterer before, explain that caterers work on a cost-plus basis, and that she will be charged so much per person for food. If you provide staff to serve, or if you arrange the rental of any equipment for her, the charges are separate. Don't prejudge your customer's pocketbook. People will surprise you. Those who may not seem affluent are sometimes the least concerned about cost, while the Rolls Royce owners have been known to haggle over the extra charge for bread. And just because we are all talking about inflation and the high cost of eating these days, don't make the mistake of offering only chicken tetrazzini and moussaka. There will always be takers for the veal Orloff and the sole and crabmeat turban. One caterer I know can't shake a frugal streak. She literally chokes as she mentions veal or asparagus or some of the other foods that have skyrocketed in price lately. She hates to recommend them, but she knows it is not good to get a reputation as a "budget caterer." It isn't.

And when it comes to cost, be firm. Don't let customers pressure you. State your prices and stick to them. Don't be talked down. When you are starting out, especially, some people will call you thinking that they can get a bargain. It is true that at the outset you should charge less than more experienced caterers; but that simply means that your profit margin should be smaller than theirs. You should still make a fair profit.

You will find that conveying firmness, a "Business is business" attitude, is easier when your menus, with prices, are typed up on paper. Caterers all agree that you should have lists of what you offer ready to show or give to prospective clients. And you will find that people bargain less with paper and ink; printing gives prices the status of objective, unchangeable *fact*.

Let's say that there will be thirty people at the Boniface birthday. It's summertime, and the Bonifaces have a covered terrace outside their living room. Looking it over, you and Mrs. Boniface agree that a buffet on the terrace would be lovely; there is enough space. Mrs. Boniface is willing to spend top dollar, and you and she work out the menu for the summer buffet mentioned in Chapter 3 at $19.50 per person. Make sure that she understands that this is a *tentative* menu and a tentative price. The occasion is a month away, and prices may rise in the interim. Explain that you will call to confirm all the tentative arrangements you make at this meeting.

Other Business

Feel free to take note notes during this client consultation. The best of memories falters at times. If you are going to serve the meal rather than just deliver it, you might even do a quick sketch of the room or rooms that will be used and take special note of the kitchen facilities, counter space, ovens, refrigerator, and freezer. *Don't* count on the availability of kitchen equipment. The most expensive kitchens sometimes lack the basics. I once gave cooking lessons in a brand new, terribly elegant kitchen that didn't even have a strainer. What is important to one cook is not to another. Ken Williams of Griffin, Georgia, feels so strongly about this subject that he tries to plan the menu around the available facilities in the home. He then says firmly, "Take everything else you will need with you."

Ask Mrs. Boniface if she wants to use any of her own serving dishes. She may have some spectacular pieces hidden away on the top shelf, or a wonderful collection of pottery or baskets. If she does not have anything that will do your food justice, tactfully suggest your own serving ware. You want to do yourself as proud as you can before her guests. They are all your potential customers.

As you can see, a meeting with a client is work. You have an agenda, so to speak, that you must cover point by point. When you come away from this meeting, you and the client should both have a clear idea (and the same one!) of what you plan to do and how much she will pay. You should have arranged such issues as who gets any extra food. If you are going to prepare some food at the client's home—as you would do with the summer buffet—you will also have a definite idea of her facilities and what you need to bring.

Ideally, you will have given the client an impression of yourself as appropriately personable, competent, and businesslike. She should feel that her trust in you is well placed; she should not feel that she can exploit you. (When you are just starting out in business, you may feel very anxious to please. Resist that feeling. It invites trouble.)

You will also have sized up your client, feeling out both her tastes and what you can expect from her as a client. Is Mrs. Boniface direct? Is she going to change her mind a lot? Will she be easy or hard to satisfy? Again, people will surprise you. A good set of antennae never hurt a caterer. It is best to be ready for whatever human nature brings. That is another advantage of a businesslike attitude.

Human Nature

Let's be candid. Unfortunately, some customers may try to cheat you. How? By feeding more people than they have contracted or arranged for. Mrs. Boniface has ordered a dinner for thirty people at $19.50 per head. Suppose that as the guests are being served on the night of the party, you suddenly realize that there isn't enough food because, without telling you, she has asked eight extra people; she expects the food planned for thirty to feed thirty-eight. She has no intention of paying for food for thirty-eight.

Insufficient food definitely hurts your reputation. (It hurts the hostess's, too, but she may forget that.) A friend tells of a nightmare job when she had to cut chicken breasts in half to feed the extra guests her client had invited. There were no snacks for the help that night. My friend admitted that she had been a little short on backbone up to that point, but sheer anger made her stiffen up. The nightmare has not recurred.

When you encounter such a situation you may have to accept it, because there is nothing you can do. You cannot have it out in front of the guests. But once burned, twice shy. If you work for Mrs. Boniface again, take extra food. Explain to her that to run short of food damages your reputation. If there are more guests than she contracted for, you have enough food for them and you will charge accordingly.

There are only a few of these bad eggs. Most of the people you meet will be honest; if you're good at catering, they will be enthusiastic about you and your food.

Crisis in the Kitchen

Things can go wrong just before or during a party. Kitty Gushee's gazpacho salad mold once ran out onto the platters in liquid form. She thought fast and suggested that it be served in silver pitchers and cups. That saved the day. But what if there's no saving solution? Those are the moments when you need your client's good will and trust.

Pug Youngblood believes you must build your customer's faith by maintaining absolute honesty in all your dealings. He does not pretend to be superhuman. If a dish that's been ordered turns out wrong and there is no time to do it again, Pug calls his customer, explains, and suggests an appropriate substitute. Usually, he says, the customer is perfectly agreeable to his suggestions. In making your arrangements with a client, don't promise more than you know you can deliver. You are human, and an accident can put you at your customer's mercy. At a moment like that, you'll value a customer's good will and confidence.

5

Doing the Job

After the Meeting

Your next step is to confirm the arrangements and prices. Adjust your recipes for the proposed menu to fit the number of the client's guests, and make out a detailed shopping list. Off to your favorite markets you go, menu and list in hand. Will the foods you need for the Boniface buffet be available? What will their prices be? In short, will you be able to produce the meal you've described for the price you've quoted?

In a discussion with your friendly fishmonger, you learn that he expects salmon to go up in price in the next two weeks. And a consumer authority concurs, predicting a rise in food prices across the board. After some thought and time with your calculator, you conclude that you really cannot hold the tentative $19.50 price. It will have to be $21.00.

When you are sure of all your food and prices, call the client and make firm arrangements. If Mrs. Boniface accepts the $21.00 fee, and if you have opted to use a letter of agreement, fill it out and obtain her signature; if it is your policy, get her deposit. The job is now confirmed. When you're off to market this time, you're ready to buy.

Marketing

Intelligent shopping is one way to control your food costs and therefore your profit margin.

First, except in emergencies, do your own shopping. No one else will do it as assiduously as you, and if you do it, you'll know you have what you need (or not). That knowledge is a comfort, particularly if you're working under pressure.

Can You Get It Wholesale?

Wholesale sources are everyone's first thought when it comes to shopping economically. Try the wholesalers in your area. You may find, as many have before you, that there is no substantial saving. Caterers' opinions differ. Roberta Dowling thinks that "wholesale" as applied to food has lost its meaning these days because of inflated prices. But Ada Matchett does most of her buying from a wholesaler. Their different experiences may be explained by geography. Your orders may be so small that the few dollars you save is not worth the effort.

One way you *can* save is to buy in quantity. A well-stocked freezer is a good hedge against inflation. It also saves energy. Sit down with your local newspaper twice a week, usually Wednesdays and Sundays, and check the market ads not only for sales but, again, to see what's in season.

Friends in the Right Places

It helps to make friends in the local markets, especially with the butcher and the greengrocer. I don't necessarily recommend using a small butcher shop rather than a supermarket. It depends solely on what you are buying. When one of our local supermarkets has a sale on plume de veau, it is the best buy around and worth going the extra mile for. Find a meat man who will cater to you on your special orders. At one time I used to make a lot of ham loaves en croûte. My special butcher would bone out and grind up a shank for me. In addition he taught me how to bone a veal breast, chicken breasts, and a leg of lamb. It is equally good to be known in the fish market for those times when you need special items like shad roe or tiny soft-shell crabs. Knowing where to buy fresh phyllo pastry, fresh pasta, and assorted ethnic foods is important. These are the things that help to make your food stand out.

Plan Ahead

When you have your menu set, pull out the recipes and check over all of the ingredients. Don't assume you have everything on hand without looking for it on the shelf. And do your marketing for staples early in the week. Order ahead—order the salmon for Mrs. Boniface's dinner in advance, for instance. Try to buy in bulk on staples such as nuts, flours, sugars, cheeses, canned fruits. If you have been running to the market often, cut it down to once or twice a week.

It is useful to know that supermarkets plan their specials a week in advance; you can order specials ahead too. Always check specials. If you have been asked to plan a menu way in advance of a party, as for Mrs. Boniface, give yourself some leeway by asking the client if there can be a substitution of one dish for another at the last moment depending on what's in the market. There are occasions when you can get caught short even with the best of planning. For instance, towns in the East have California strawberries starting in February, but they are not in the market every week. Sometimes a supply of perfectly ordinary items unexpectedly dwindles to nothing or, as a friend discovered, a holiday will clean out the local markets. She was planning lamb as a main dish and just didn't think about Easter. There wasn't a leg of lamb to be had. (She finally drove a great distance to buy one because she had absolutely promised it.) The key to smart marketing is planning ahead and a minimum of impulsive, or compulsive, buying.

Time and Organization

In the catering business, there is never enough time.

Therefore, you must learn to organize the time you have. There will always be unexpected demands on it; things will suddenly come up that you hadn't counted on. As I've warned, catering is sometimes a pressure business. Remember "A Day in the Life of a Caterer"?

When a dinner like the summer buffet is approaching, make a list of all the tasks to be performed, and spread them out, in order, over the right number of days so that you can do the work comfortably.

Here are three sample work schedules: one for Mrs. Boniface's summer buffet; the other two for the winter dinner for eight and the lasagne Sunday supper planned in Chapter 3.

WORK SCHEDULE
FOR SUMMER BUFFET FOR THIRTY

As soon as date is set, order rental equipment to be delivered on the day before party. Arrange for serving help.

At least one week before party: Order fish, arrange to borrow extra poacher, buy mangoes, ask hostess for final number of guests.

Monday: Market for staples and chicken breasts. Bone breasts, wrap and freeze. Make brioche and freeze.

Tuesday: Make liver pâté.

Wednesday: Check on fish order to be picked up on Friday.

Thursday: Make mango mousse and rum sauce. Make cucumber rings. Thaw and poach chicken breasts. Make green sauce. Cook vegetables à la grecque.

Friday: Thaw brioche and make pâté sandwiches. Poach salmon. Cool. Cover with aspic. Decorate. Chill on platters. Check to make sure rentals have arrived.

Saturday: Pack up food:
   Leave mango mousse in molds.
   Leave cucumber rings in molds.
   Pack sauces in plastic containers.
   Pack vegetables in plastic containers.
   Pack garnishes in plastic bags.
   Put fish in last.

If table setting and decoration are up to you, be at client's home at 3:00 P.M., with one in help to serve. Otherwise arrive at 5:00. At client's home: Chill fish. Explain the plan of the evening to helper.

Look over table and rentals to be sure everything is there. Unmold mousse onto serving platters and chill. (Pray that it is not a hot day.)

Put vegetables à la grecque into serving bowls and leave at room temperature.

Cover chicken breasts with green sauce and leave at room temperature.

Make sure ice and bar setups are ready.

Make coffee.

At 7:00 P.M. put all food for main course out except fish.

At 7:45 P.M. put out fish. Light candles.

When party is over clean up.

NOTE: This timetable presumes that the guests will eat on time and not linger too long over drinks. The fish can wait only twenty minutes on a hot night, or the aspic will run.

WORK SCHEDULE FOR WINTER DINNER FOR EIGHT

These instructions are for a meal to be delivered to the client's home rather than served.

Monday: Shop for staples. Order scallops, endive, watercress, broccoli for Thursday. Order chicken breasts for Wednesday. Make roll dough and refrigerate.

Tuesday: Make rolls and freeze.

Wednesday: Bone chicken breasts. Wrap in plastic and chill. Make mocha soufflé and chill.

Thursday: Pick up scallops, broccoli, and salad greens. Marinate scallops in lime juice. Put together chicken dish. Make vinaigrette.

Friday: Prepare endive and cress. Arrange in salad bowl and cover with damp paper towels. Put vinaigrette in glass jar. Cook broccoli and purée, adding remaining ingredients. Turn into baking dish and cover with plastic wrap.

Arrange finished chicken dish in casserole and cover with foil.

Finish seviche and put into bowl or plastic container.

Thaw rolls, split and butter. Place in brown paper bag.

Whip cream and pipe rosettes on top of soufflé. Garnish with marrons. Keep chilled.

Write out cooking or serving instructions on separate sheets of paper and tape onto each dish:

"Seviche: Divide among 8 shells or cups. Serve with small forks as a first course or with drinks."

"Chicken: Reheat in 325°F. oven for 35–40 minutes until sauce is hot."

"Broccoli: Heat in 325°F. oven for 35–40 minutes."

"Rolls: Sprinkle paper bag with water and heat in 425°F. oven for 10 minutes."

"Salad: Toss with dressing at table."

"Cold soufflé: Remove from refrigerator 15 minutes before serving."

Pack car and deliver dinner by 5:00 P.M.

WORK SCHEDULE
FOR LASAGNE SUNDAY SUPPER FOR SIXTEEN

This meal is to be delivered rather than served.

Monday or *Tuesday:* Buy staples, such as pasta, flour, nuts.
Wednesday: Bake bread and freeze.
Thursday: Buy perishables, such as meat, cheese, salad ingredients.
Friday: Make lasagne.
Saturday: Make walnut rolls; prepare labels for food packages explaining how to serve.
Sunday Afternoon: Defrost bread; prepare greens and accompaniments; pack food with labels; deliver.

Pace yourself. Do not leave things to the last minute. Do not leave them to chance. Get used to using extra minutes or hours for cooking ahead on "back-up" foods such as chopped onions, grated cheese, chopped parsley, and bread crumbs. Be sure to put into the calendar reminders about when to thaw frozen dishes and when to heat them. When you're going off to serve a meal, allow enough time to pack the car properly and drive at a reasonable speed to your destination. Also allow enough time to get lost if it's your first trip to that house. (If, like me, you are one of those born without a sense of direction, you know too well the panicky feeling of driving through strange country in the gathering dusk, knowing it's later than you think.)

Also allow enough time when you get to the house for emergencies. I don't know of a caterer who hasn't gotten off track at some point because of a situation not of his or her own making. One woman was doing a wedding reception at a temple. While the couple was being married in the next room, she was setting up in the main hall. Suddenly she discovered that she was short two tablecloths and that the chafing dishes were missing. Luckily she had arrived early; there was time (provided by a long ceremony) to call the rental service and get delivery of the missing items.

Be fair to yourself. In the beginning, especially, allow yourself more time for a project than you think you can possibly need.

Beautiful Food

Garnishing and Decorating

When you prepare food for a job, remember that half of catering is showmanship—flair, style, pizzazz. Food must appeal to the eye. If a dish looks good, people are attracted to it. If it tastes good as well, it is a winner.

You don't have to be an artist and create lovely still lifes with every dish you put together. But it does help to be able to produce an attractive display of food. One caterer told me that two things make his food distinctive, his garnishing and his hot hors d'oeuvres. Another said, "I do each party as if I were doing it for myself." Another: "A *lot* of my budget is spent on garnishing." You can train yourself, as they have, in the basics of garnishing. Once you have them down pat, all you need to do is keep an alert eye for new ideas and file them for future use.

In the food business two terms are used interchangeably: "garnishing" and "decorating." "Garnish" applies to savory foods, "decorate" to sweet foods. The main purpose is to complement and contrast the basic food.

There are only a few rules to follow. First, practice restraint. When you have a pastry tube in your hand, you're tempted to decorate everything in sight. Go ahead, but leave most of it off the food. Do a few swirls and a couple of rosettes on the foods, then squirt where it doesn't count. Second, all garnishes should be edible. No plastic flowers, please. Third, a garnish should never hide the flavor of a food. Fourth, a garnish will not make a silk purse out a sow's ear. A lot of parsley can hide the cracks in a soufflé roll, but it will not hide a fallen soufflé. Finally, edible garnishes should enhance the prevailing flavor of the food. They should be tasty in their own right and should make a basically good dish even more inviting.

For example, kedgeree is a plain dish of flaked fish and boiled rice in a little curry powder and cream. It's very good for a brunch, but unassuming in appearance. By covering the center of the top with sieved egg yolks and sprinkling chopped parsley all around the outside edge, you can make it an eye-catcher. The color is hard to resist, and once the guests have tasted it, they will like the flavor. Similarly, vitello tonnato does not have much eye appeal. But when you have garnished it with shiny black olives, bright yellow lemon slices, green parsley, and capers, it looks like an Italian painting. People can't wait to try it.

Some garnishes and decorations are part of the tasting as well as the beauty. This is true of appetizers and small finger desserts. The tiny shrimp on the canapé, the rolled anchovy, the slice of green olive with pimiento, the slivered almond, the candied peel—all are part of the recipe, not just afterthoughts.

When a dish is finished and ready to be served, give it a critical eye. What does it need? Color? Texture? Shape? Many delicious foods are, unfortunately, lacking in one or all of those things, even though they are high in flavor. Eggplant is a good example. If only that beautiful, shiny purple skin could be kept after cooking. I am sure that one reason children object to eggplant is that it is gray and soft. It cries for red tomatoes, green zucchini, and golden onions, as in ratatouille. A chicken breast is just a chicken breast until it is perked up with parsley or paprika or lemon slices. A pork fillet wouldn't take any beauty prize dressed as it is, but the addition of plump black prunes and golden apricots makes it a winner.

Here are more suggestions for garnishing and decorating.

Hors d'Oeuvres and Individual Appetizers: Capers, parsley flowerets or chopped parsley, olives (sliced green with pimiento or crescents of black), radish roses, paprika, pimiento (chopped or in crisscross strips), sieved egg yolks and chopped whites, pickled onions, red or black caviar, nuts (chopped, sliced, or slivered), fruit rinds (candied, grated, or in curls).

Soups: Popcorn (buttered or lightly salted with garlic or cheese), croutons, salted whipped cream, bacon bits, thin apple slices, chopped cucumber, chopped herbs, tiny cream puffs.

Entrées: The above suggestions plus mandarin orange slices, preserved kumquats, dried fruits plumped in brandy, asparagus tips, watercress (dip leaves lightly in oil), canned whole baby carrots with parsley tops, fluted mushroom caps, tiny pickled beets, celery leaves, stuffed cherry tomatoes (peeled), vegetable cups, toasted bread crumbs, chopped aspic, ribbons of sour cream, anchovies, canned french-fried onions, crushed pretzels, stuffed orange or lemon halves, fried parsley.

Vegetables and Salads: Fried bread shapes, green and red pepper rings (blanched), pickled beets, branches of herbs (tarragon, basil, thyme, lemon balm), miniature vegetables, sliced water chestnuts, Chinese pea pods, mint leaves, thin mushroom slices, grated carrots, scallion fans, melon spears.

Desserts: Nuts (halves or chopped), crushed candy (lemon drops or peppermints), coconuts, praline, chocolate (curls, cutouts, cups, leaves, grated), caramelized nuts, chopped ginger, candied citrus peels, frosted fruit, glazes, marzipan fruits, tiny meringues, raisins, chocolate bits, glacéed strawberries, glacéed nuts, pastry shapes and cutouts, powdered sugar sprinkled through a paper doily placed on cake layers, icing drawn with fork tines to make geometric patterns, whipped cream and icings piped through a pastry bag.

A final word: When you test recipes, also practice your garnishes and decorations.

Serving Dishes

The size, shapes, and colors of serving dishes play an important part in the composition of a picture that is pleasing to the eye and the palate. A ham loaf looks better on a rectangular or oval platter than a round one. It looks better on heavy white china than on stainless steel or brown pottery. Chicken hash does not do well on clear glass, but brightens up immeasurably on china with a patterned border. A peasant dish such as paella or cassoulet does not belong on Limoges. A dacquoise deserves a silver platter, bread and cheese a handsome board. Look through some of the food magazines for ideas. These days food is photographed with finesse. The people who put food pictures together spend hours picking out linen, crystal, china, flowers, and fruit. Great care and imagination is used to make the food look its best. Also, today, thanks to the "truth in advertising" rules, the food is real.

Table Decoration

If you can suggest some decorations for the table, you will be helping your customer. Moreover, an attractive table will certainly show off your food to better advantage. Step carefully, however; don't tread on your hostess's toes. Offer suggestions tactfully, and if she responds affirmatively, press on. If she doesn't, back off and save your inspirations for someone else.

An edible centerpiece could be part of your menu. Usually a

client will welcome the idea because it lets her off the flower-arranging hook. Here are a variety of table suggestions:

Brunch: Fill a wire hen two-thirds full with white and brown eggs. Set it on a round shallow basket "nest." Make a loaf of whole wheat bread in a round cake tin. Cut off the top and hollow out the bottom, making a nest. Fill it with deviled egg halves and cover with plastic wrap. Set this next to the hen. About an hour before serving put a lot of parsley under the hen and among the deviled eggs (remove wrap). If you are using a tablecloth, make it bright and flowered. If you don't have matching napkins, use contrasting paper napkins of a good quality.

Informal Luncheon or Supper: Get a very large squash and decorate the outside by carving a design in the skin. Cut the squash in half lengthwise and scoop out the flesh. Cut a piece off the bottom so the squash will stand without tipping. Make a casserole using the flesh of the squash, meat, and additional vegetables. Bake it, and just before serving, fill the squash, using it as a serving dish. You can surround the squash with other smaller squash, gourds, and a few fall flowers.

Christmas Eve Supper: Use a large bûche de Noël, a rolled cake also called a Yule Log, as your centerpiece. Place it on a board or platter and surround with greens or holly. When it's time for dessert, just carve up the centerpiece.

Small Dinner with a French Theme: We are frequently criticized by Europeans for serving our dinner backward. By that they mean that we have large pieces of cheese for hors d'oeuvres when, for balance, the cheese should end the meal. A large Brie cheese can do double service as a centerpiece and a last course. Leave it at room temperature all day so it will be properly runny when it is served. Make a wreath of bread or brioche dough to go around the Brie. Place the cheese inside the wreath on a large tray, basket, or board. Arrange apples, pears, and grapes around the cheese. You can use some grape leaves, if available, to fill in. If the hostess thinks there should be something sweet in addition, suggest madeleines.

Other Ideas: Fancy breads in baskets are decorative by themselves, depending upon the type of dinner served.

DOING THE JOB / 61

A very large brioche, scooped out, is an elegant container for small hors d'oeuvre sandwiches.

Crudités can be arranged in ice-packed glass flower pots and set in the center of a table. This would do only for a cocktail party because they will be picked at and the table will be a shambles when the party is over. Be careful not to arrange the crudités too artistically, as a friend of mine did, because nobody will touch them.

Make an arrangement of citrus fruits with lemon leaves and create napkin rings from circles of lemon rind.

Bamboo steamers are wonderful serving dishes for cold foods.

Small pumpkins hollowed out make excellent individual soup bowls.

Graceful leafy cabbages or heads of lettuce in baskets are effective in the centers of round tables.

Group together a lot of herb plants in pots.

Fill small baskets with fresh garden vegetables, contrasting colors and shapes. Small red potatoes, white onions, plump mushrooms, pink runner beans, long green beans, baby carrots.

Place shaped breads on beds of greens.

If you are serving bread and butter, put the butter on the table in tubs with a small design marked in the top.

Tie colorful bandannas around the necks of wine bottles.

Use glass soufflé dishes for salads and for crudités arranged in layers.

For a Christmas dessert party centerpiece make a lot of meringue mushrooms in assorted sizes. Coat the undersides (gills) with chocolate buttercream. Pile them up in mushroom baskets.

Fill market baskets full of young vegetable plants in small individual pots. If your client wants to buy the seedlings for her own garden, fine. Or she might want to give them to her guests. Otherwise, they should go home with you.

For an informal buffet, suggest using trays cafeteria-style. Obviously the trays must be attractive, but it is much easier to balance a tray instead of one or two plates, silver, napkin, and glass.

Always be on the lookout for unusual ideas. Tag sales, auctions, and flea markets may have things you can use. When you see a bargain in baskets, trays, or decorative serving pieces, buy it.

Before a party, make sure the table decorations can be assembled easily without fuss. When you arrive at the customer's home with the food, there will be no time to practice.

The Complete Party Planner

If you specialize in wedding cakes, or hors d'oeuvres, you'll find yourself asked to handle everything for the reception or the cocktail party.

The more services you can offer in addition to providing the food, the better your reputation will be. More business will come your way. This is the other half of the advice: Start small—grow big.

How much you undertake is up to you. You can become a jack-of-all-trades by handling the rental of equipment as well as hiring waitresses, bartenders, designing table decorations, and arranging flowers. If you want to do all this, it will pay off. Once people have made up their minds to "buy" a meal, they would just as soon hand over all the responsibility for the party. Bob Salsman calls himself a "party planner plus." He does everything except the invitations; that includes suggesting a theme for the party and coordinating all of the details.

Rentals

Caterers all say that a good, reliable rental service is indispensable. Your summer buffet for the Bonifaces is outdoors, for instance, and you may need lights as well as an extra table. Rent them, and a portable bar, if necessary. How do you keep Mrs. Boniface's salmon in aspic cold if refrigerator space is at a preminum? Rent an ice chest or a wash tub, which is also good for wine bottles and soft drinks. It is not necessary to make a large capital investment for serving equipment. But don't hamper your imagination for lack of accoutrements: Rent them. With diligent searching, almost everything is within the realm of possibility. Start in the Yellow Pages.

Caterers generally agree that overseeing the rental of needed items is a major aspect of the service you perform for a client. If you want it done right, you should handle the rentals yourself. One caterer left the rentals to the host. The night of the party, she set up a very elaborate dessert table, then discovered there were no dessert plates. In the guests' eagerness to sample her desserts, they were reduced to scooping up samples with their saucers.

Rented equipment is delivered separately to the customer's home; it is also billed directly to the customer.

When you are planning a party, keep a list of available rental items in front of you. Then you can easily suggest certain dishes or come up with creative ideas for service. For example, look down the list: food warmers, glassware, stemware . . . aha! What can you do with stemware besides drink out of it? Answer: It's wonderful for serving mousse or cold soups, or raw vegetables with dips, or the condiments for a curry, or possibly the seviche for our winter dinner party.

Flowers

Where does flower-arranging fit in? It is really an art in itself. Unless you're particularly good with flowers, you would probably be wise to leave them to a professional. However, if you can honestly recommend a good florist with whom you work well, so much the better. A connection can be established that may bring you customers.

Service

As I have said, caterers agree that unless you are running just a take-out, take-home, and re-heat business, you must be able to provide service. (Even if you have a take-out business, people will ask you to recommend staff to serve at their parties.) It behooves you to cultivate a bevy of efficient, dependable waiters and waitresses of all ages. They may be friends of friends, associates of an acquaintance—anyone you hear of who is willing to do the work and interested in the pay. Experienced waitresses and waiters who really know the ropes are in great demand; you have to sign them up a long time in advance of a party. A popular alternative are the less experienced teen-agers, college students and, if you live in a city, young men and women whose goal is a career in the arts.

Caterers have been criticized for having sloppy help. If waitresses are serving in a variety of messy costumes, or their long hair falls into the soup, it detracts from the pleasure of the food and the general elegance of a party. Insist upon a uniform appearance: white blouse or shirt, dark skirt or trousers; you must supply aprons. Make sure they wear comfortable shoes. You do not want to spot bare feet halfway through the evening.

When you call to hire a young person, be definite about the

time he or she should arrive, ready to work; estimate also, to the best of your knowledge, how long the job will take.

You may have to teach young people how to serve. Before the evening begins, hold a brief training session so they will understand their responsibilities. Explain where you will be and what you will be doing. Tell them exactly what is being served and how to serve it. Explain how food should be presented. And give them a timetable of the evening. Do not expect them to second-guess you.

If things go wrong—if something is missing or out of place, if time is running short—keep your head. Don't take it out on the help. By losing your temper, you will lose their cooperation. And the next time they may not want to work for you. It is ideal, of course, to develop a good relationship with a couple of young people who will work for you whenever you ask (their schedules permitting), because they will know how you like things done.

A young woman I know worked for two very different caterers. Her first experience was discouraging. The boss was an artistic, talented person, and the food merited, and got, raves. A serene, cooperative appearance was presented to the hostess, but the help saw a different side. From the beginning, the atmosphere "backstage" was charged with tension; as the evening wore on, it got worse until the help were all snapping at each other. The young woman said it was very clearly a matter of not enough time to do things perfectly and too much left till the last moment. Happily, her next experience was different. She actually had time to sit down for ten minutes and read a book before serving. Everything ran like clockwork, and the whole party went according to schedule.

Which caterer would you rather work for?

In a restaurant, for formal arrangement, the help is given a meal before serving. In catering, the arrangement is informal: The help just make do with snacks of whatever is available. It is unreasonable to ask people to work with food and not feed them something.

You should pay your help when the job is finished; they are working just for the money. In the suburbs of New York City, 1980s rates call for help to be paid $7.00 to $9.50 per hour. Predictably, city rates go higher. It is customary to pay the help for travel time, door to door. Additionally, some caterers tip their help if their work has been good. You may consider doing this because having "repeat" staff is as desirable as having "repeat" customers. If you can develop your "own" staff, so to speak, you will not have to train new helpers for each occasion.

Delivery

Caterers really need large cars or station wagons, preferably air-conditioned. Given the price of gasoline and the need to conserve energy, that is unfortunate. But there are times when anything short of a panel truck will seem too cramped for all you have to handle. A van is probably ideal.

At best, delivery is a problem and a challenge. Rental equipment can be delivered directly to the customer's house, so you don't have to worry about that. All you have to worry about is the food in its various sizes and shapes. That will be enough. Packing the car must be done carefully, with thought given to how things will ride. (Everything I own has been christened with some type of sauce; happily, some sauces do not live on, as stains, into eternity.)

Crumpled newspapers, small rugs, and towels are good padding. Set everything on flat, non-slippery surfaces. Use a lot of plastic wrap, foil, and rubber bands. Plastic baskets and tubs are handy. Coolers with trays will be necessary. Get containers that are as lightweight as possible. Large old-fashioned laundry baskets are great. So are big foil pans and Tupperware types of containers with foolproof lids. Sometimes it is easier to carry produce in the baskets it came from the market in. If you have help, and time allows, take along the ingredients for the hors d'oeuvres and make them at the party. For a dessert such as fruit tarts, the pastry shells can be stacked, the pastry cream taken in plastic cartons in freezer bags, and the prepared fruit in baskets.

Handle your foods carefully—beware of butterfingers (not the kind you eat). On one occasion, as a car was being unloaded, the doorman of a New York apartment house dropped the cold lemon soufflé. Salvage was out of the question. The day was saved only because there was another soufflé at home in the caterer's apartment.

In short, you need good organization, strong arms, and a lot of stamina when you leave your home to serve a meal at the home of a client.

Charging for Auxiliary Services

If you are responsible for such services as hiring help, ordering rental equipment, and providing bar setups (ice and soft drinks), you should charge for them. Your final bill should list these items separately. For instance, if there are 100 guests at a party, you may provide one waitress for every ten people. At $9.50 per hour for seven hours, the labor cost will be $665.00. There is also a charge of $1.25 per person for bar setups. (Again, rental equipment is billed directly to the client.)

Here is what your final bill to Mrs. Boniface might look like:

SUMMER BUFFET FOR BONIFACE FAMILY

30 dinners at $21.00 per person	$630.00
Serving help: 1 waitress at $9.50 per hour for 7 hours	66.50
Bar setups for 30	37.50
	$734.00

Clean Up

Your very last service is to clean up when the party is over. Pack up all your belongings so that the client will not have the nuisance of calling you to tell you to come and get your electric beater, and so that you won't be wondering where it is. Leave the kitchen and dining rooms in order. A client who wants to be a guest at her own party doesn't want to clean house at midnight.

Caterer's Craft:
Guidelines and Procedures

Before a Client Calls:

- Plan menus carefully, considering seasonal foods, texture and color. Balance costly and economical ingredients. Have expensive, inexpensive, and medium-priced menus, and be ready with substitutes for a particular course.

- Constantly add new recipes to your repertoire, testing and adapting them; be creative. When you test, also practice garnishes and decorations.
- To set prices, charge three times the cost of ingredients. Divide the total by the number of guests, getting a cost per person.
- Develop the habit of pricing your recipes mentally for four or six people so that you can estimate the price of a meal for any number of guests. (For cocktail parties, think in units of ten.)
- Do not quote flat prices. And do not underprice.
- Set basic policies for delivery, cancellations, etc.

Caterer and Client:
- When a client calls, check your schedule; ask if the job is competitive; chat with the client to obtain useful information.
- Always visit the client at home.
- Encourage the customer's confidence. Never reveal ignorance of a requested dish.
- Be diplomatic, and be firm. Project a businesslike attitude.
- Set a tentative menu at a tentative price and confirm it after research.

Doing the Job:
- Sign the contract and obtain your deposit when arrangements are confirmed.
- Organize your time carefully. Make a list of all the tasks to be done for a specific job and spread them out over enough time to do them comfortably. Allot more time than you will need. Do not leave things to the last minute or to chance.
- Do your own shopping. Your costs control your profit margin.
- Shop intelligently, making friends with your butcher, greengrocer, etc. Buy in quantity, following specials.
- When you prepare food, strive for eye-appeal as well as taste. Follow the rules of garnishing and decorating.
- Use serving dishes that show your food to good advantage.
- You can extend your services by handling equipment rental as well as hiring help to serve, designing table decorations, and arranging flowers.
- Charge for all extra services.
- If you provide help to serve, supervise them and pay them well. Cultivate "repeat" staff to avoid retraining.
- When the party is over, clean up.
- When you deliver food, pack it in your car very carefully. Unpack carefully, too.

6

Success: The Story of a Young Caterer

Introduction

To illustrate the development of a caterer, as well as the informality of the custom-catering business, I'm going to tell you the true story of one caterer who happens to be a teen-ager. I chose this example in part to reiterate that catering is for everyone: male, female, young, or old. Age does not matter; what counts is ability. For the young, catering can be a good answer to the problem of employment, a welcome improvement over mowing lawns, weeding, or baby-sitting for those who like to cook.

The hero of the story is my son, Donald. "Oh," you may say, "here's another mother overwhelmed by pride. Her son the caterer and all that." To which I must reply that I am indeed proud of my son. But that is not my reason for telling his story. Rather, I tell it because he was my first catering pupil, the forerunner (or guinea pig) for all readers of this book. It is true that in getting started he had an advantage: I helped him plan menus; I showed him how to shop and taught him how to make certain dishes. At that time, I had not yet written this book. If he were starting today, I'd just give him this book. (Well, maybe I'd throw in a cooking lesson.)

The Story

At twelve, Donald had spent some time in the kitchen and had learned, for instance, to make crêpes. This is actually easier for children than for adults because their motor coordination is better. He had eaten in some fine restaurants and was sensitive to the presentation and garnishing of food.

SUCCESS: THE STORY OF A YOUNG CATERER / 69

Donald got his first job by chance. A simple dinner had to be prepared for the faculty at his school. If a caterer took the responsibility for the main course, the school kitchen would furnish the rest of the meal. When the headmaster's wife asked Donald to sound me out about the catering, Donald suddenly saw dollar signs. Or visions. Whatever he saw, he replied that *he* would be glad to do the meal, and suggested crêpes cannelloni. Happily for him, the headmaster's wife, who is good with young people, thought that dish—the only one he could have offered her—sounded fine, and hired Donald to make it for forty people. It consists of crêpes filled with chicken and spinach and served with a béchamel sauce.

I taught Donald how to make the filling and the sauce, and then he was on his own. That first time, he spent hours and hours in the kitchen. But he produced a good meal. Not only was the headmaster's wife pleased, Donald found he was hero for a day at school, treated just as if he were the star of the football team. He also discovered that cooking is no longer considered a sissy occupation. One of his friends, a big jock, quietly confided that he loved to cook—would Donald need some help next time?

The next time was the chance to do the meal for a fund-raising dinner-theater evening for his sister's school. Donald wanted a stereo set at the time. He bid for the job and got it. Nepotism may have helped, but he had to hold up his end; his sister is a tough taskmaster and she did not intend to be disgraced at her own school. Again, Donald presented his cannelloni. The evening was a success, with a plus he hadn't counted on. His kitchen helpers were all girls from the school. Donald found himself surrounded by attractive young women all following his orders. "Put that in the oven. Take those out. Heat the bread. Serve this. Slice that." Caterer's bliss!

The irony of Donald's success with his cannelloni dish is that it involves spinach. Vegetables are not on his preferred list of taste sensations. Like many boys in their mid-teens, he is somewhat fussy about what he eats. Having a professional cook for a mother definitely does not dictate his likes and dislikes. Despite my hopes that his catering career would widen his dietary horizons, they have remained the same—heavy on the pasta, light on the vegetables. At home we have all learned what to expect when Donald decides to add a vegetable dish to his catering list. If you don't like eggplant and zucchini, how do you make a decent ratatouille? By getting your family to taste it as you go along!

Donald was invited to do the dinner-theater job again the next year; this time it was to be held for two successive evenings. New dishes were needed. With some help from me, he presented two menus, which were accepted:

Menu I* Chicken Florentine
Tossed Salad with Vinaigrette Dressing
French Bread
Frozen Coffee Mousse

Menu II* Veal Ragout
Buttered Noodles
Spinach Salad
Mocha Five-Layer Torte

This assignment taught Donald something about coordination. He was also learning about quantity cooking, pricing, freezing ahead, shopping, and service.

The next summer he went into business seriously. At age fifteen, he catered dinners, picnics, cocktail parties, even a wedding. He earned a lot of money, and he learned a lot, too. Here is his advice, in his own words, to other young people who would like to start a catering business:

"I started out small. I didn't cook very many different things. Mostly I took jobs that were too small for bigger caterers. I learned to do quiches and crêpes very well. You should pick one or two things you can make easily, like a simple chicken dish and a good stew. Then you can specialize in them. Plan meals with dishes that you can prepare ahead and freeze. That's important. When I catered the large dinner-theater parties, I cooked and froze everything beforehand except for the bread and salad.

"If your customer wants hors d'oeuvres, offer a limited selection, maybe four or five kinds at the most. Doing more than that is too complicated. I usually include a cucumber or shrimp sandwich. I've also found that one can of crabmeat mixed in with cream cheese goes a long way. For dessert, cakes are best since they can be frozen in advance. No matter what I cook, I go by one rule my mother taught me: 'Keep it simple, and concentrate on appearances.' I can make even a crumbling ham loaf look great if it's garnished well. Garnishes can be anything—parsley, olives, capers—as long as they're edible. Use your imagination.

---

*Recipes are in Section IV, "A Cookbook for Caterers."

"Occasionally a customer doesn't use my menus. She knows exactly what food she wants to serve. If I get a customer like this, I *never* admit that I don't know how to make the soubise or cream puffs or whatever it is that she wants. You don't have to know—you can always follow a recipe. Just look it up.

"When I started out, I didn't have a driver's license, so my mother and my older sister drove me everywhere I needed to go—to the market or to deliver the food. Also, my mother helped me with the pricing. She recommended that I charge my customers three times the cost of the food. Sometimes I charge less than that for more expensive items. I usually make up for it by charging more on desserts. They're cheap to make. If a customer also wants me to serve at her party, I charge her an hourly wage and include this service charge in the total bill.

"I would say that the hardest thing about catering isn't really the cooking, but managing my time well. I usually have to cook two or more things simultaneously. Whatever you do, leave yourself lots of time to prepare food; it always takes longer than you figured."

Donald also learned not to let people take advantage of him. Initially he was charging five dollars per person for his dinners. Then he was asked to do one that included fresh fruit tarts and homemade bread in addition to soup, entrée, pasta, and salad. With fear and trembling, he raised his price to seven dollars—and got it, because the dinner was of professional caliber. His age was irrelevant to the quality of the food—though it was a good novelty for public relations. The hostess was overwhelmed with compliments and felt she had made a hit with her young caterer.

How does a young person get business at the start? A school is a fertile source of contacts. Teachers entertain on weekends, and they don't have much time for cooking. Many of them would probably like to hire a caterer but they are leery of the expense. Put up a sign in the faculty lounge or on the bulletin board. Then put signs around town in busy places like the Y or any community clubs. List some menu suggestions for dinner, casseroles, and desserts. Since food prices change rapidly these days, write "Prices on Request." Give your name and phone number. Don't be discouraged if business is slow at first. After you've done a few parties you can give references. Once you've gotten started, word of mouth will bring you most of your business.

Donald did one other thing that helped his reputation. He took a course in professional cake-decorating and captured a lot of work doing birthday and wedding cakes around town. This is a specialized field, one that many caterers and most mothers will not get into. He became so good at decoration that someone dubbed him the "Michelangelo of the pastry tube." That didn't hurt his business at all.

Today, at seventeen, Donald is an established caterer in our area. In fact, he has taken over my business. Whenever anyone calls me, I refer them to him. He has even been photographed in our kitchen for *House Beautiful*. That was another unusual experience that came his way through catering.

If you, too, are a teen-ager who likes to cook, you may find that catering is the start of an exciting career.

7

The New Wave: Fast Gourmet Food

The Traditional and the New

The traditional caterer's role as producer of a social event may not appeal to you. Perhaps you're happy to prepare the food, but not to deliver it or hire and oversee help to serve it. Perhaps you don't like the pressure of managing a social occasion. If so, you may prefer to ride the new wave in catering, the take-out business I described in Section I.

Whatever the reasons—a changing economy, more relaxed lifestyles, the two-career couple—the elaborate party with lots of service at so much per head is giving way to a pick-up, take-home trade. Pug Youngblood, who sells take-home quail and prime ribs, calls it fast food with a difference. The difference is the gourmet menu.

The take-home business is still too new for anyone to judge whether it is more or less profitable than traditional forms of catering. But this kind of food service has definite advantages that may suit your schedule or your personality. Your time is even more your own. You decide how much money and food you want to make each week and then produce it. If you will be away, you can make the food ahead of time and freeze it. Many of your dishes will be frozen in any case. No need to worry about flowers, tables, rentals, liquor, service, or dealing with clients.

Two Essentials

Is it as easy as it sounds? Let's see what's involved. To sell the food, you must have an outlet. To present it, you must have good packaging. Both of these are essential and sometimes they are not easy to come by.

For an outlet, you can rent a store, which will give you a basic overhead cost. If zoning allows, you can sell from your own kitchen. Since customers will come at their convenience, the premises must constantly be manned during business hours. You can also tie in with local stores, farmers' markets, or Women's Exchanges. One group of women took over the abandoned railroad station in their small New England town, decorated it, and now use it to sell their cottage industry wares.

To offer and sell your homemade foods through any outlet, you must package them well. Packaging must solve the problems of appearance, practicality, and cost. A visit to a commercial paper products company should be one of the first things on your agenda. (Look in the Yellow Pages under "Paper Products.")

But before you can consider different containers, you need to know what kind of foods you plan to sell and the size of the servings.

How Much in Each Package?

First, let's discuss portions. You should allow one-half pound of meat per person. If you're serving chicken, each person gets six ounces, boned, which is about one and one-half cutlets. Measure salads by the handful—a handful per person. Vegetables are measured in four-ounce portions (a half cup). It is best to work with a scale for complete accuracy. And you should note the amount of servings on the product's label.

I believe that one good market for take-home food is the two-career couple. They need and can afford good, convenient food. But few commercial food companies make single or double servings, especially of main courses. Various dishes lend themselves to double portions. Chicken breasts which can be prepared in countless ways, are a natural for two. So is veal. Beef stew is welcome because ordinarily it is too much trouble to prepare for two. Crêpes as entrées or desserts are good possibilities as are stuffed peppers, stuffed cabbage, curries packaged with their condiments, and roulades of sole filled with mushrooms or shrimp. Small tart shells are natural individual containers for quiches, fruit desserts, or shepherd's pies. Even mousses can be packaged singly; cakes and breads can be divided into tins for two.

Be Creative

When you visit the paper products company, you will get ideas just from looking at the various containers. For instance, what would you do with a foil pizza pan? You could make an oversized fruit tart. How? Line the pan with a thin layer of short pastry. (You could even use a type of cookie dough that gets pushed in place rather than rolled.) Bake the shell. Spread it with a thin layer of flavored cream cheese. Then arrange fresh berries or grapes in a decorative pattern on the cheese and glaze with melted currant jelly. If these are to be sold fresh, they must be refrigerated; or they may be frozen. In either case, chill the tarts until set. Then wrap well in plastic wrap or in oversized plastic bags. The wrapping must be clear, not opaque, because the appearance of a fruit tart is part of its appeal.

Thin bamboo skewers are wonderful for hors d'oeuvres. Stack miniature cream cheese balls combined with marinated cucumber cubes on them; or glazed sausage bits and figs; scallops seviche with avocado cubes vinaigrette; a variety of crudités; melon balls wrapped in thin prosciutto or pear cubes wrapped in smoked salmon. These can be laid flat in shallow plastic trays, probably four to a tray. Bag them and tie with a twist.

Cakes are best made, frozen, frosted, frozen again, and then placed on cardboard rounds. Then they can be bagged and sealed. The visual aspect is important because a cake is just another cake unless it looks particularly decorative and attractive. Cold (frozen) mousses can be made in pretty molds, frozen, and then turned out onto cardboard rounds and wrapped or bagged in clear plastic.

Cake logs, such as the bûche de Noël, and other long shapes, such as spinach rolls, can be a packaging problem. There are two ways to handle these. One is to freeze the roll and, when it is really stiff, slide it into a long plastic envelope. If you do this, your label must include instructions for removing the roll to a platter while the roll is still frozen. Otherwise it will bend or break at the moment of serving. The other method is to freeze it on long sheets of cardboard salvaged from boxes or the cleaner. Again, the roll should be removed to the serving platter before it starts to thaw.

Cold soufflés can be frozen in round foil containers; the soufflé should rise above the top rim at least one and one-half inches for appearance's sake because it will have to be served from the container. A curry packaged with its condiments is an interesting entrée, one not difficult to handle. The curried meat, fish, chicken, or whatever can go into a foil container and be frozen. Then you can put the chopped peppers, nuts, bacon, marinated avocado cubes, crystallized ginger, and chutney in smaller cups. These can be all gathered together in a large plastic bag or arranged on a foil tray and frozen. Instructions on how to serve and present the dish must be clear.

Currently, the Dixie Company is test marketing a line of disposable ovenware that should be a boon to the take-out business. It can be used in a regular oven up to 400°F. and in microwave ovens. The containers are coated so they don't get soggy, and they will go from oven to freezer, or vice versa. They come in various sizes and shapes, all with lids, and, best of all, they are neutral in color so that they don't detract from the food served in them. They will not do for the formal dinner party, but they are more attractive than aluminum foil.

Baskets are marvelous containers for almost everything and you should start a collection of them. They are a natural for picnics, something that you should offer. Another container that is good for picnic food and very inexpensive and disposable, is the heavy paper "dish" that holds meat products in the supermarket. Sometimes they even have pretty red-and-white checks on the side. These are heavy enough not to leak or collapse, and will hold a really decent amount of food: two sandwiches, a plastic cup of salad or fruit, and cake or cookies. The Dixieware I mentioned also comes in a good size for individual picnics.

The Picnic Trade

Picnics, or portable feasts, have become very popular recently. I have heard of catered picnics on boats, planes, beaches, benches, and even one on the Metroliner from New York to Washington. Picnics may be simple or elaborate. Whichever they are, they require careful planning. To prepare food to travel well can be a challenge.

Containers are, again, the first thing you must consider. The berry baskets that fruit growers use for strawberries and raspberries are inexpensive and attractive. Another useful container is the brown bag, which now comes in all colors. Be sure to get the type that is coated and has handles. You will need small plastic containers for soup, salad, or fruit.

Thermoses of all sizes up to the large box type are necessary. You can invest in the metal type or use the styrofoam kind. Thermal bags and commercial ice packs are also helpful. Don't try to use dry ice because it is virtually nonexistent and very expensive. Also it tends to freeze things too hard.

When you are ready to order containers, be sure you know the quantities you will be using. Have a proper place to store containers. And be sure to order see-through tops. Again, foods sell by their appearance. Containers are a business expense that will increase along with everything else. At the present time, a round foil container which holds six servings costs 15¢. A rectangular foil container for four costs 12¢. Individual foil containers are 10¢ apiece. See-through rigid plastic lids are 3¢ and plastic bags are 1¢ apiece. (These are wholesale prices.)

Pricing

How to price take-out foods? Again, the basic rule is three times the cost of the ingredients. Inflation may force you to multiply by four or five, as your judgment dictates. It's probably a good idea to check the competition's prices to see what the going rates are, and to test what the traffic will bear. You will probably find it very helpful to have sold through a Women's Exchange or an equivalent outlet to develop a sense of the marketplace.

Here are two samples of pricing. The first comes from Nancy Carlton of Norwich, Vermont, who says she is known locally as the "box lunch queen" because she does a big business in box lunches, hors d'oeuvres, and desserts. Her business is mostly pick-up. She charges for ingredients plus $10.00 an hour for her labor plus 10 percent overall for the nebulous overhead. She gave me a sample menu for a family picnic: mushroom pâté en croûte, spinach and onion quiche, salad, egg and chicken finger sandwiches, and Grand Marnier cake. Here are the figures using that menu for six people at mid-1980 prices:

Pâté	$ 4.10
Quiche	2.50
Salad	1.00
Chicken sandwiches	1.50
Egg sandwiches	1.00
Grand Marnier cake	1.50
	$11.60
2½ hours labor	25.00
10% overhead	3.66
	$40.26

This averages out to approximately $6.70 per serving, which is not bad for a fancy picnic, with each serving packed individually. And Nancy adds that she stresses presentation and appearance.

Next is a sample breakdown of a typical main course you might offer for the two-career couple. The dish is chicken breasts in white wine sauce, for two. Again, prices of ingredients and materials are given for 1980.

Chicken breasts (buy it with bones in and bone it yourself)	$1.79
Sauce (wine, cream, broth, herbs)	1.00
Container, an aluminum dish with plastic top	.15
Label	.01
Total cost of materials	$2.95

If you follow the rule of multiplying the cost of materials by three, you would charge about $9.00 ($8.85, strictly speaking) for this dish; that price would include labor and basic overhead. The dish then costs about $4.50 a head which, in urban areas in today's economic circumstances, is reasonable for a meal that needs only a salad and bread to be rounded out, plus dessert, if it is wanted.

Compare the fact that one New York City take-home establishment charges $10 to $12 per pound for its entrées. Since a portion is considered to be a half-pound, one serving costs $5 to $6. At another popular Manhattan store, entrées begin at $5 and go to $8 per serving.

Freezing

Most of your stock will have to be frozen. The subject of freezing is one about which there are many misconceptions. To do any kind of catering, particularly for outlet sale, you need to master the techniques of freezing food. Ideally, all foods should be flash-frozen. And your freezer should have a below-zero temperature. To quick-freeze in a home freezer, place the wrapped food—cooled or at room temperature—as close as possible to the cooling unit or on top of it. Don't just dump packages of food into the baskets and expect them to freeze. If you do, they will sometimes be slightly soft days later. Your customers will object to being served somewhat mushy, flavorless foods and will not come back for seconds. Commercial ice cream makers advise you always to wrap an ice cream carton in a plastic bag before storing it in your home freezer, since the cartons are not moisture proof. The ice cream will keep longer without crystallizing.

I cannot emphasize the next point enough: *Always* test the freezing capability of a dish you intend to freeze for sale to a customer. Otherwise the customer may have an unpleasant surprise. One home caterer produces packages of stuffed zucchini and eggplant by the dozen, freezing them at home for resale. At best, zucchini is soggy when thawed. Home-stuffed, it is a disaster. Charts are available that give the recommended times of freezer storage for home-prepared foods, and one should be tacked up next to every freezer.

Many people insist upon cutting the meat off the carcass of the Thanksgiving turkey, wrapping it up and freezing it. They should not wonder why, when they pull it out two or three months later, it is tough and dry. If you want to freeze leftover poultry, it should always be covered with broth or sauce to retain its moisture and then quick-frozen as best you can. Cooked whole roasts, fried chicken, and meat loaves should only be frozen in case of emergency and then just for a short time.

On the other hand, baked goods, including tiny cream puffs and pastry shells to be filled for appetizers, freeze beautifully. You really should not freeze filled puffs and shells except for a short period of time. Cake layers freeze best unfrosted, but a short spell of freezing won't hurt a frosted cake. The best way to freeze a number of small items is to spread them out on a cookie sheet. It is safe to freeze them uncovered, then put them into plastic bags. But don't leave them uncovered longer than overnight; they will taste slightly "off."

There are three or four good books available on the subject of freezing food. Buy one—such as, *Complete Book of Home Freezing* by Hazel Meyer, New York: J. B. Lippincott Company, 1970—and study it carefully.

Non-Frozen Items

Before you develop many products that do not freeze, are perishable, and must be refrigerated, check on the facilities of your outlet. Is there enough refrigerator space? Can you make a delivery every second or third day? Will your food be well displayed in open cases or on shelves? And, most important, how much turnover is there? In some cases it might be better to take orders. At the outset, you will want to know how well certain items sell, so you should check with the store fairly often. Eventually a sales pattern will emerge. All food stores have their regular customers, and you will soon know how many quiches, crêpe dishes, entrées, or cakes you have to make in a week. At first you may have a storage problem in your own kitchen, but as your estimate of the turnover rate becomes more accurate, it will be alleviated. Remember that there will be distinct upward trends in the graph at holiday times and downward trends during January and February. Use these slumps to test new recipes and regroup.

Labeling

Labeling is another important element in the sale of take-home food. When you are shopping, monitor your own reactions to different packages. Companies like General Foods spend enormous sums on design and graphics because they are important in the overall sell. Eye appeal again. A professionally designed and printed label is a good investment if you want your products to be noticed. You might be able to trade a free meal for your graphics.

Printers vary in their prices, so get estimates. The more you order, the less the cost. And examine samples of their work. Ask to proofread the copy before they go to press. A careless printing job will not help your image.

There are two reasons to opt for "one-color" printing. The

first, naturally, is cost. One-color does not have to be black and white. It can be blue on green, or red on yellow, any color combination that is clean, clear, and appealing. Freshness and clarity are your second reason. For food advertisements, "busy" combinations of colors do not appeal. Nor do you want people to associate your products with muddy grays and browns. One of the most appealing print jobs I have seen comes from a two-woman operation called "Crème de la Crème," which makes and sells delicious desserts and main courses. Their label is white and shows their logo attractively printed in red. They also use off-white paper, size 9 × 12: On one side is the logo; the other side of the sheet has the address, phone number, and their menu specialties. The paper can be folded in three for mailing. The owners use sheets of matching paper in a smaller size for bills.

The label that goes on the package of food should be large enough to catch the eye; it must be readable. There should be room enough, below the logo, for the name of the dish, its contents, instructions for serving, and the number of servings. Use a good, descriptive, persuasive adjective along with the name of the dish. By law you should also include a list of ingredients. If the product is particularly healthy or nutritional, low in fat or salt-free, be sure to mention it. Following are some examples of succinct, saleable labeling:

AU BON GOÛT

Spicy Madras Curry

Lamb, meat stock, apples, onions, spices, chutney, seasonings, 1½ qts. 6 servings. Thaw and heat. Serve with rice, sliced bananas, and attached condiments. (Nuts, peppers, bacon, raisins, chutney.)

AU BON GOÛT

Summer Blueberry Bread

Flour, sugar, spices, orange juice, eggs, butter, blueberries. 12-oz. Thaw and serve thinly sliced with butter or cream cheese.

AU BON GOÛT

Frosty Lemon Mousse

Eggs, cream, lemon juice and rind, sugar. Six 6-oz. servings. Remove from freezer 30 minutes before serving.

AU BON GOÛT

Fragrant Herb Cheese
Cream cheese, herbs, spices. 6-oz. Use as filling for raw vegetables or mushrooms, stuffing for chicken breasts, quiche filling, salad dressing.

The New Wave: Guidelines for the Fast Gourmet Food Business

- When you start, test your wares, the marketplace, and the rate of turnover and production by selling through a low-overhead temporary or "test" outlet.
- When you're sure of your products and the pace of the business, choose your utlimate outlet carefully, balancing problems of overhead, refrigeration, space, sales staff, etc.
- Choose packaging to meet three criteria: eye appeal, practicality, and low cost.
- Order containers and tops in quantity and store them carefully.
- Design labels to be distinctive and informative.
- Labels should list ingredients, number of portions, weight of contents, and instructions for serving.
- Practice to master the intricacies of packaging difficult foods. If you offer picnics, develop ways to prepare food for travel.
- Master techniques of freezing.
- Test the freezing capability of any dish you plan to sell frozen.
- Price your foods judiciously, checking the going rates.

SECTION III

The Business of the Catering Business

Introduction

Becoming a caterer is not simply a matter of cooking professionally. It also means running a business. The long arm of the law reaches right into your kitchen. When you go into business, city hall becomes interested in you and so does the Internal Revenue Service. Your insurance man perks up, too.

In this section you will learn about the business aspects of catering: its legal issues; the need for insurance; the necessity for record-keeping and some of the intricacies of good records.

You will also encounter the issue of equipping yourself for business. If you like to cook, you probably have a lot of kitchen tools already. Going into business will bring the need for new or better ones, even duplicates of what you already have. Buying equipment for a business is different from buying it for yourself: Before your business can show a profit you will have to earn back the money you advance for equipment. That sobering thought may temper urges to spend.

Remember, the purpose of business is to make a profit. "Success" is spelled with black—not red—dollar signs and numbers.

8

The Law and Other Business Issues

Zoning

Zoning is an issue that applies to any home business; it applies to you if you opt for traditional or new wave catering. Whether you choose to obey the law or evade it, as some caterers do, you had better know what it says.

One of the first things you must do when you're considering an independent catering business is check the local zoning regulations: Are you legally allowed to prepare food in your own home kitchen and then sell it outside? In Connecticut, my state, more than 50 percent of the towns do not allow the sale of food cooked in a family kitchen. If you live in such a town, by law you have to have separate kitchen facilities for any business cooking you do.

Some towns require that any food sold in their town be cooked in a business kitchen. It doesn't matter whether you live there or not. For example: Let's say you live in Town A, and Town A requires a business kitchen. Town B does not. You can cook at home in Town A and sell it in Town B. But to sell food in Town A, you must cook it in a business kitchen. If you live in Town B, you can sell your home-cooked food there, but you can't sell it in Town A.

You can, and should, find out all about this from your local health officer, who gives out the licenses and inspects your kitchen. Most communities do have an established health code for food purveyors. In my town, anyone who violates this code is liable for a fine of "not less than $100.00 and not more than $500.00 and/or thirty days in jail for each offense."

The reasons for health officers, licenses, and zoning laws are fairly obvious. Nothing could put you out of business faster than illness caused by something from your kitchen. Whatever dismay you may feel as a prospective caterer ("Isn't there enough challenge without zoning problems?") should be offset by the recognition that these safeguards also protect you as a consumer from germs or unhealthful conditions that could endanger you. Before you feel too frustrated, find out what kind of town you live in.

Coping

Many caterers operate outside the law, especially in big cities where zoning is an issue. They count on nice neighbors who don't object to the smells of cassoulets, chocolate cakes, and brioches floating through the halls of the apartment building. (It is advisable to give nice neighbors an occasional gift from your kitchen.) One big city caterer handles this technicality by finishing her cooking at the site of the party, thereby qualifying as an itinerant cook. Defensive maneuvers or not, so far she has had no brush with the law.

One country caterer installed a business kitchen in her basement, a cool idea in more ways than one because she did not have to invest in air conditioning to protect her buttercream icings, puff pastry shells, and aspic dishes. Roberta Dowling used her own kitchen for three and a half years, then moved to a store. She felt that limited storage and freezer facilities made it too difficult to work in her home.

Kitty Gushee rented an industrial kitchen in a church, equipped with professional ovens and refrigerators. Churches and other nonprofit organizations are usually willing to listen to a proposition designed to supplement their incomes. Today most of them have well-equipped cooking facilities. Ken Williams's family believes that catering is best done outside the home. He uses a kitchen in a farmhouse that is not used for anything else. In my interviewing I discovered that it was the men who were most interested in doing their cooking away from home. They simply could not get used to the constant interruptions that crop up at home. They wanted to be sure that when the telephone rang it was a business call for them, not a date for one of the children. They also felt that although it was appropriate for a woman to conduct a business from her home, it was unseemly and unbusinesslike for a man to do so.

THE LAW AND OTHER BUSINESS ISSUES / 87

Inspection

A food service inspection is really a long list of requirements to be met. Your food sources must be approved. Especially in the case of dairy or fish products, you can see why this would be essential. The design, construction, and installation of equipment is checked. Your water supply, sewage disposal and plumbing, as well as washing facilities, garbage disposal, lighting, and ventilation must be approved.

Most important is cleanliness of personnel and equipment. The main concern is disease-prevention. You should be concerned because, again, nothing could ruin your business faster than sickness traced to food you prepared. A young man I know spent a summer vacation working for the local franchise of a national fast-food hamburger chain. When I asked about his job, he said "I know you don't like our product, but you would certainly approve of our environment. We have to scrub the tables and counters down every fifteen minutes, and if a hamburger is ordered and for some reason rejected, it must be thrown away. Not even the cook can eat it. And the hamburgers cannot sit around longer than five minutes." I did approve of his "environment."

The inspectors who come around to view your working premises are generally pleasant people who can help you with tips and information you might not get otherwise.

Useful Information

A health inspector can tell you that temperature requirements are very important. Even if you don't need a license to sell home-cooked food, you should know all about this for your own protection.

All potentially hazardous foods, while being stored, prepared, displayed, served, or transported, should be maintained at 45 degrees or below, or 140 degrees or above, except during necessary periods of preparation and service. When placed on display for service, food to be served hot should be kept at 140 degrees or above. Food to be served cold should be prechilled to 45 degrees or below and the temperature should not exceed 55 degrees. Certainly custard and cream fillings, hollandaise sauce, poultry stuffings, and pork products are "potentially hazardous." The most important point to remember is that you should cool food rapidly. Do this by putting the food into shallow containers and immersing the containers in cold water. For a really rapid chill you can set them in ice.

Protecting Yourself

After the local health department, your next port of call should be your insurance agent. It stands to reason that if you are in a business where there is any possibility of being sued, you should be insured to the hilt. One insurance man told me that a home caterer should carry a minimum of $3 million additional insurance coverage. He added that all personal liability policies are business exclusive. In other words, any insurance policies on your home do not cover a business, even if it is conducted out of the home. If an employee is burned—even if it is your next-door neighbor just helping out—the doctors and damages are on you. Keep in mind that the most unexpected people will decide to sue. Naturally, a rampant run of salmonella could not only put you out of business but might take away everything you possess. Don't put your head in the sand about insurance or you might find yourself in the soup.

Record-Keeping, Part I

Undoubtedly you have been told about the wonderful deductions you can take when running a home business. Yes, you can take deductions. But to do so, you have to file with the IRS, just as any wage earner does. You will be responsible for federal, state, and local taxes. The only way to back up your tax information is to keep complete records of income and expenses. They should include the cost of every strainer you buy, expenses for recipe testing as well as utility costs, maintenance, and such. I find the checkbook a handy recorder for my expenditures. Pay by check and write in a description of what the check is for. For example, "Pottery Barn, 2-qt. casserole, business expense." Get a courtesy card from the local supermarkets that you use and pay for your food by check with a notation that the food is for recipe testing. These checks, however, must be for the exact amount on the register, not blanket $40 or $50 amounts. If you are trying out a group of new dishes on friends, write the menu in your calendar with the amount spent. Keep track of your traveling expenses to and from jobs. Gasoline adds up these days. Get a copy of the government publication entitled "Tax Guide for Small Business" from your local IRS office. You might also meet with your local tax man to learn what you can and cannot deduct.

Numbers Talk

Keep a separate record for every job with costs carefully noted. This can help you judge just how well you are doing from month to month or year to year. It will give you a good idea of when you should raise your prices or drop certain items because they cease to make money. Add up your hours and pay yourself a salary, figuratively if not actually. That is the only way you will know if you are really making money. You can put the profits back into the business if you wish. But first you must find out if there *are* profits. Don't neglect your pride either; it is a very nice feeling to be able to pay a tuition or buy a vacation with your earnings.

If you are hopeless at bookkeeping, if you know you'll make a mess of it, pay for a friendly part-time accountant. It is an investment that will pay for itself. You can check over the records daily if you wish. The important thing is to get it all in writing.

Record-Keeping, Part II

Not only do income and expenses have to be recorded. It is very helpful to have a written record of what you have cooked for your customers in the past. They do not want repeats, no matter how good a meal was, and they will count on you to remember. Also, they do not want to serve the same meal the woman down the street served last week. You can keep the necessary records in a ledger type of notebook. Here is an example of the information you need to keep:

Mrs. Ernest Jones	Dinner for 8	Melon with prosciutto
48 Brookside Dr.	5/10/80	Chicken Marengo
Westford, Va.	$66.00 pd.	Stuffed mushrooms/Spinach
234-5678	Cost $22.00	Salad/Fr. bread/Cheese
		Cold walnut soufflé

NOTES: likes large portions, wants someone to serve, welcomes suggestions on table decor., pays on deliv.

You should also keep track of your time: how much time you spend on this project, how much on that. Consult your accountant about the need to do this, and start ways to record the hours you allot to different jobs. Such questions can be complicated.

To help organize your time, you might consider installing a large blackboard in the kitchen. Use different colored chalks to indicate what has to be done immediately, partially done or finished tomorrow, delivered today, etc. Or you can glue a piece of corkboard to the front of the refrigerator and put up reminder signs in bold bright lettering. A large card file is very useful, and so is a legal-sized pad entitled "Check List for Today" made up the night before. These records can all help you establish your use of your working hours.

Get into the habit of writing down everything you discuss on the phone—not on the backs of old bill envelopes, but in a special notebook. It is unbusinesslike and embarrassing to have to call a customer back to repeat the arrangements for a party.

Again, if all of this record-keeping appalls you, hand it over to someone else. Records must be kept.

An Oracle

One of your main sources for advice when starting out is the Small Business Administration. They have field offices in every state, in all of the big cities, including Honolulu, Anchorage, and Hato Rey, Puerto Rico. Their advice is free and the offices are manned by retired businessmen who know whereof they speak. Their publication list covers everything from "Is Your Cash Supply Adequate" to "Preventing Employee Pilferage." There is a booklet devoted to a bibliography for home businesses. Their "Restaurants and Catering" booklet has an excellent list of publications that would be helpful to anyone considering either venture.

If you are a woman with little business experience or confidence, you should take advantage of a free telephone counseling service available to any woman who is either already in business or planning a new enterprise, such as her own catering business. A nonprofit organization, the American Women's Economic Development Corporation (AWED), 1270 Avenue of the Americas, New York, N.Y. 10020, telephone: (212) 397–6880, makes this counseling available for women anywhere in the continental United States. It has already assisted over 6,000 women. (In New York City, AWED has also run a seminar on catering, featuring established caterers as speakers.) If you are interested, call or write for an application to the service. After it is approved, you are entitled to two telephone counseling sessions with relevant experts at AWED's expense.

Do You Need a Lawyer?

I have managed the fairly neat trick of giving you a chapter on the law without once mentioning a lawyer. If you are going to start small as a one-person operation without any hired help, if you are not renting space, signing leases, borrowing money, incorporating, or taking on a partner, I see no reason why you should incur legal fees. If you're nervous about doing anything without a lawyer, choose someone you can communicate with who understands your business. Hire him on an hourly basis and prepare all your questions before you consult him. Don't forget that lawyers charge even for phone calls. And don't ask for advice at cocktail parties.

9

Equip Your Kitchen

Start Small

This chapter is about the equipment caterers need. At the end of the chapter I have listed in detail all of the possible items you should require. Use my list to take inventory of what you have. You will probably be surprised at how much you already own. When you are ready to buy, go to a reliable kitchen supply store which sells professional equipment, not a gourmet gift shop whose cookie sheet will warp when the oven heats up. (It's very disturbing to hear the Twang! and know that the filling of your quiche just went over the edge.)

With equipment, established caterers again advise that you start slowly and grow. Pug Youngblood has gained an excellent reputation over the years; among other things, he now caters some twelve to fifteen parties a day for the annual Masters golf tournament at Augusta, Georgia. He started his firm, "RSVP," as a hobby. Seven years ago he set up a shop away from his home and started buying secondhand equipment for it. He says, "I have a walk-in cooler with McDonald's written all over it. That's fine with me!" He adds that that's the kind of equipment you have to be on the lookout for, unless you have a lot more capital than he did. Another caterer rents space in a commercial freezer because the bulk of her business is in frozen hors d'oeuvres. Still another says she had a "humble beginning" and reinvested all of her profits in equipment.

Two Basic Investments

You do not necessarily need the largest food processor now. You do, however, need a food processor. It will make your work go much faster and, in most cases, more efficiently. Chopping alone can take up too much valuable time. Besides, a whole new world of mousses and quenelles is open to you with this amazing machine, to say nothing of puréed vegetables that can be passed through pastry bags into decorative mounds and will survive standing on a buffet table much better than vegetables cooked any other way. Which brand to buy? Check with other caterers, knowledgeable friends, and consumer journals. New machines with new capabilities come on the market all the time. GE has just introduced a processor with a new feature that makes the machine much easier to use. Called a "continuous feed tube," this device enables the processor to work the way a meat grinder does. Instead of having to empty the processor's bowl when you're chopping vegetables, for example, you can open a shutter in the machine, allowing the chopped vegetables to flow directly into a bowl placed on the counter. This feature can really save you time. Make sure you get a solid machine that doesn't "walk" the counter under stress, one that will handle the constant use it is sure to get.

Another investment you should consider, a large one, is a heavy-duty mixer such as the Hobart Kitchen Aid; it is valuable especially if you are going to bake a lot of breads, brioches, cakes, and pastries. I recommend the Hobart specifically because it is the only machine of its kind available to the noncommercial cook; it is worth its weight in bread dough alone. The Model k-45 is the smallest size; it will probably last a lifetime. It comes with a whisk, paddle, and dough hook that will save you literally hundreds of hours of kneading. During the holiday season I use this machine exclusively and constantly. Invest in an extra bowl at the same time.

If the Kitchen Aid is out of reach for the moment, get a mixer with a stand. Don't try to work with a portable. A portable not only wastes time, that most valuable commodity, but also it will not get the volume out of egg whites or cream that most recipes require. Is a portable mixer necessary at all? Yes, for your portable feasts. There are times when you may be preparing a banquet in a garage and only an electric plug is at hand. Caterers are unanimous in their opinion that you should take whatever you will need when you go out on a job; don't count on anything being available. This advice holds for lectures and television performances as well. Get a small, efficient hand mixer with no more than three speeds.

Major Appliances

Now for the large things. Two ovens? They are a help on big jobs. So are six burners, but you only get this on a professional Garland-type range. One thing to be said for the professional stove is that the ovens are big enough to handle oversized pots and pans. Big baking pans for sheet cakes simply will not fit into a standard oven, and improvising wastes both time and materials. If you have to buy a stove, but don't want a six-burner professional range, which is expensive, look for one with the largest possible oven. There is a difference in depth and width according to the manufacturer. For your second oven, consider a portable, and look into the convection type. It works on a circulating hot-air principle which ensures even baking on all levels, even if one pan is directly on top of the other. You can even cook bread on one shelf and meat on another. If you are doing "on location" cooking, this oven will extend the range of your menu; behind the scenes preparation will also go much more smoothly.

Microwave ovens are strictly a luxury unless you really know how to use one, and do so. A microwave does not bake the way a standard oven does; to make it worth the investment of money and space in your kitchen, you must concentrate on learning what it will and will not do. A microwave is wonderful for thawing and heating up foods quickly; thus it is very helpful to a caterer. One catering friend says she can't live without hers because of its speed. Make sure your ovens are correctly calibrated. Have them checked, then keep accurate thermometers inside them so that you'll always know the temperature. An appliance man told me that no oven is absolutely right on temperature all the time because of power drains, grayouts, and such, and if you have two going at once, one is bound to pull on the other. Also, always take an oven thermometer with you when going out on a job. You wouldn't believe how inaccurate some people's ovens can be.

You have probably seen those wonderful stainless steel refrigerators with glass doors: Everything is in plain sight and so easy to organize. Most of us simply cannot afford them. Make do with an ordinary one in the kitchen and another in the basement or garage. Buy a secondhand model to store bags of greens, extra cold lemon soufflés, and the salmon-in-aspic on the oversized platter. If you do invest in a new model, make sure it has only the gadgets you will really use. An automatic icemaker might be

EQUIP YOUR KITCHEN / 95

useful. Adjustable shelves would certainly be handy, as would dual-temperature controls for setting your own temperatures in various sections of the box. The ideal refrigerator for home use would be designed like the commercial refrigerators with separate controls for meat, greens, dairy products, etc. Whatever your refrigerator, organize its contents. Energy escapes whenever you open the door to hunt for some lost item.

Next, you need a decent freezer. The one that is part of the refrigerator is merely a storage area for already frozen foods, and it will not do for freezing from scratch. Unfortunately, most home freezers do not have flash freezing units. Ideally, all foods should be flash frozen to preserve flavor, texture, and quality. If foods, especially prepared dishes, are frozen too slowly, they tend to deteriorate faster than they would otherwise, losing vitamins, color, and flavor. So you will have to buy an independent freezer. Whether you get a chest type or an upright depends upon its location. Chest freezers usually give more storage space, but they are not as easy to organize, although the wire baskets do help. The upright takes up less floor space and you can see at a glance what is in it, and where. You lose more cold air in the upright because it "spills" every time the door is opened. Don't buy a freezer that is too small; it is an investment that you won't repeat again soon. However, remember that to run a freezer economically, it must be at least three-quarters full. Approximately one foot of space will store twenty to twenty-four pounds of food. Once again, I repeat, it's important to be organized. You can't afford to waste time rummaging around in the bottom of the freezer looking for that small package of lobster butter or duxelles. If your freezer does not have baskets or compartments, invest in some and put all your birds in the same basket. That goes for baked goods, hors d'oeuvre components, pie shells, fillings, icings, etc. Label and date everything. Spend a day chopping nuts, grating citrus rinds, assembling garnishes, making melba toast, tarts, cream puffs, bags of crumbled bacon, seasoned bread crumbs and croutons—anything you use frequently that takes time to prepare, even with the food processor.

On a Smaller Scale

Now for a look at the smaller, equally essential items. Large kettles for lobsters, corn, mussels, and quantities of stew and soup are basic and important. They can be either stainless steel or aluminum; stainless steel is preferable because aluminum reacts unfavorably when it comes in contact with high-acid foods. Stainless steel cleans easily, does not become pitted, and, with an aluminum inset in the bottom, is an excellent heat conductor. These large pots are expensive; to buy them, you should go to restaurant supply houses and any auctions of restaurant equipment that you might hear about.

A boon to the man or woman who is going into cooking as a business is the recent appearance in the market of what was previously sold only as commercial cooking equipment. Now we can buy the heavy pots and pans that are actually made for restaurant use. This is strictly no frills, utilitarian equipment. A fish poacher is essential and expensive, but it will be useful for more than just the two salmon you will cook during the summer. Sauté pans are necessary, as are nonstick pans.

The newest nonstick material is another boon for the caterer, because it is superior to the old type of coating. The new surface is smoother, will not peel off, and coats pans that are of a good weight. There is a range of equipment for the top of the stove and the oven.

You should have roasting pans, baking sheets (heavy ones that don't buckle with heat), all sizes of bread pans and muffin tins, brioche tins, tart pans, cake pans in different shapes and sizes, and all the molds you might happen to see around. Molds are fun to pick up and tag sales will yield some of the more unusual shapes. What for? Not only jellied salads but wonderful flan, mousses, ices, sorbets, and old-fashioned desserts like coffee and wine jellies. Try a rum praline Bavarian cream decorated with tiny meringue mushrooms for an elegant dinner party.

For serving dishes, copper is not only dramatic in appearance, it keeps things hot for a long time. But it is also becoming prohibitively expensive. The new copper pans presumably do not need retinning as often as the old ones did; that in itself is an investment. If you don't have any copper chafing dishes, you can and should rent them if necessary.

You will need an assortment of casserole and baking dishes, with some freezer-to-oven-to-table ware. They should be attractive in appearance, easy to serve from, and able to withstand wear and tear. Plain white or off-white or sparsely decorated ovenware is best, although the Royal Worcester ovenware seems to go well with almost anything. You want to show the food off to best advantage and also blend in with the hostess's tableware.

EQUIP YOUR KITCHEN / 97

A couple of sets of glass soufflé dishes are excellent because you can do lovely layered hot or cold dishes in them. There are some very attractive heavy glass bowls in all sizes from France that are inexpensive and worth having. They are ovenproof, and the smallest size would be fine for individual soufflés.

A Smaller Scale Still

The smaller, varied assortment of cooking utensils should include all those things you've always wanted but never could bring yourself to buy in quantity: lots of measuring cups—all sizes, some glass, some plastic, and metal for dry measure. Make sure the cups have metric measurements on them. Lots of measuring spoons. Take them off their rings and put them into a convenient container on the countertop to pull out as needed. Buy good Taylor thermometers for your stove. A meat thermometer is essential unless, like James Beard, you can work by touch. Interestingly enough, some children's cooking classes are now being taught the "touch method" to make them independent of thermometers, broom straws, etc. This was the way our ancestors cooked, even judging the temperatures in bake ovens with their hands. If you are interested in the touch method, learn to use your fingertips, which are extremely sensitive. When a layer cake has been in the oven for thirty minutes, lightly touch the center. If it springs back, it is done. Chicken will feel firm, not slippery. So will beef. After a soufflé has been cooking for twenty-five to thirty minutes, give the dish a little shake. If the center wiggles, it is not quite done.

Have two peppermills, one filled with white and one with black peppercorns. It helps if the mills are of different colors or shades. Buy your peppercorns in quantity; they are much less expensive than in little bags or boxes. Whisks come in various sizes and shapes and you may prefer the flat to the round, or the elongated to the round. Rolling pins are also a matter of personal choice; it is too bad you cannot practice with them in the store because weight as well as shape is important. I have owned various rolling pins, including one four feet long that I carried home on the plane from Italy. (I was convinced that it would perfect my pasta, but I soon found out that I lacked the sheer physical strength to use it, so I bought a pasta machine instead.)

There are dozens of fascinating gadgets from all over the

world. One I find quite useful is a zucchini-corer which reams out the center of the zucchini, leaving an outside shell to be stuffed in the Turkish manner. Another is a plastic disc with measured holes in it that produces a lattice pastry crust. The number of gadgets you buy is up to you. As you progress in your business, you will find out what you really need.

Kitchen Arrangements

How is your kitchen set up for convenience and workability? The baking supplies should be near the mixer, with flour and sugar in large wide-mouthed containers. The more tools that are out within easy reach, the better. Buy some crocks and put small implements in them. If your counter space is limited, consider a table on casters for mixers or blenders. Store potatoes, onions, and other vegetables that do not need refrigeration in hanging baskets so they get air circulation. Anything up in the air is out of the way.

You will need a desk of some kind. It may be just a small counter, possibly a pull-down, but it should have your datebook, schedules, and all essential information on it, not to be touched by others. You probably have a lot of cookbooks already and will have more. Keep the most important ones in the kitchen and the others not far away. In them note changes you make in recipes, ingredients, and methods. Many printed recipes do not come out exactly as stated, as you have probably discovered. You might also keep a separate notebook in which you note which cookbook contains which much-used recipe.

The final piece of kitchen equipment that will save your disposition, your energies, and your time is a long cord for the telephone. Make it a present to yourself or put it on your birthday list. You will be amazed at how much you can get done while listening to a client or friend ramble on.

Rentals

By now you may have taken an inventory of your pantry shelves and decided that not only do you not have the equipment to go into the catering business, you'll be starting out with a capital loss if you try to buy everything you need. Don't despair. In the United States today you can rent almost anything. Sometimes it makes more sense to work that way. As I mentioned earlier,

EQUIP YOUR KITCHEN

the local rental center can work with you on parties and may even get business for you on occasion. Knowing where to get dance floors, tents, flowers, canopies, tables, chairs, linens, outdoor grills, torches, and bars is part of your professional responsibility. Pick a place that has the type of equipment you want, a wide selection in good taste. No matter how much equipment you invest in yourself, you will probably never have things like 174-cup coffeemakers, silver services, sixteen-quart punch bowls and three-branch candelabras. One caterer always uses all clear glass serving platters, plates, and bowls, rented, for her parties. It has become her trademark and she knows that the food, which is extremely decorative, shows off best this way.

Chafing dishes and hot trays? They are wonderful to use, especially for brunches where the food has to stay hot for three to four hours. Tablecloths and napkins? Even if you are handy with a needle, they are one more thing to do. Realizing that many beautifully catered parties use disappointing linen, one woman recently began to rent out cloths and napkins to caterers. By renting from her, I have access to many more decorative fabrics than I could hope to own myself. If you don't want to buy something, or if you can't, rent it.

Renting is also a hedge against the pitfall of overequipping yourself. At the outset, give yourself an equipment allowance for the things you absolutely need, and stick to it. Don't buy "too much too soon," and burden your business with an unnecessary capital investment. That will simply postpone the day your records show a profit—the big day when the bottom line proclaims you a success. Remember, that's the day you're working for.

Kitchen Check List

The list which follows details all the items you could possibly need. Use it to take inventory and to choose judiciously the items on which you'll spend your equipment allowance. Do not view it as a list of things you must have.

LARGE EQUIPMENT
- standard stove with four burners and one or two ovens
- countertop portable oven
- extra plug-in burners
- blender—three speeds
- food processor—four-cup capacity or one with continuous feed tube
- mixer on base with dough hook attachment

refrigerator (or two)
freezer—upright or chest type with baskets

ALL-PURPOSE TOOLS AND GADGETS

good carbon or stainless steel knives
sharpening stone
kitchen shears
poultry shears
hand can-opener
funnels—two sizes
colanders—two sizes
strainers—three sizes plus tea strainer
measuring cups—dry and wet, two sets of each
measuring spoons—two sets
ruler
thermometers—instant meat, candy/deep fry, freezer
vegetable parers—three
hand grater with four sides
salad spinner (optional)
melon baller
portable chopping surface
trussing needles
ball of heavy twine for trussing
scale
egg slicer (can also be used for mushroom caps)
lemon zester
citrus peel stripper
mushroom fluter
tongs, long and short
corers for fruits and vegetables
garlic press
assorted whisks
fruit juicer
cherry pitter
rolling mincer
aspic cutters
hand chopper
spatulas—wooden and rubber
wooden spoons
wooden paddles
assorted pastry bags and tips
rolling pins
small sifter
brushes
skewers (stick them into cork)
scallop shells
molds—hinged, fish, pudding, ice cream
terrines for pâtés
roasting pan and rack

SPECIAL BAKING NEEDS

pie weights
loose bottom tart tins—7, 8½, and 11 inches
individual tart tins—3½ and 4½ inches
flan forms
baking sheets
jelly roll pans
spring form pans—8½, 10½, 11, and 13 inches
cooling racks
bread pans—4×2×1½, 8×5½×2, and 9½×5½×2 inches
12-cup Bundt pan
angel cake pan with removable bottom
muffin tins—1½, 2, and 3 inches
cake pans with removable bottoms—8, 9, and 10 inches
biscuit and cookie cutter
brioche tins
charlotte molds

COOKING POTS AND PANS

skillets—assorted sizes
sauté pans
deep saucepans
kettles

fish poacher
electric skillet
crêpe pan
omelet pan

Serving Containers
paella pan
au gratin dishes—1, 1½, and 2 quarts
casseroles—1, 2, 3, and 4 quarts
soufflé dishes—½, 1, and 2 quarts
quiche dishes—8, 10½, and 12 inches
salad bowls—various sizes
enamelware
white pottery baskets

Miscellaneous and Optional
pressure cooker
coeur à la crème baskets or molds
madeleine pans
pasta scoop
Dutch oven
wok
"wonderball" (a useful gadget which holds bouquet garni or herbs for flavoring a casserole, for instance)

AFTERWORD

Catering is a business, and although it's personal and informal, it succeeds best when you approach it in a businesslike manner. But first and foremost, food is fun. Catering is a very creative enterprise, one you should enjoy. It is as exciting as the theater. There is showmanship and temperament; there are opening night jitters and—oh, joy—curtain calls. You're the writer, producer, and director of the show. You can probably arrange to be on stage, too, if you want to be: Some caterers cook omelets to order in front of the guests. Your artistic bent can find satisfaction in catering for years to come. Eating, after all, is here to stay.

Good luck!

SECTION IV

A Cookbook for Caterers

Introduction

Whether you choose to do traditional catering or to go "new wave," this cookbook will help you make the transition from cook to caterer. In fact, you could view it as a very extensive set of examples. The Packaged Frozen Foods segment, for instance, gives recipes for "fast food" that will help you get started as a new wave caterer. (But don't overlook the menus and recipes for traditional catering; you will find ideas there that you can adapt for your market.) The recipe segment includes recipes for the expensive, medium-priced, and economy menus listed in Chapters 3, 4, and 5. Those recipes and the procedures recommended in those chapters combine to give you a step-by-step blueprint for your first catering job, from the client's initial call to cleanup or delivery.

The cookbook begins with menus that are planned according to season, since food that is in season costs less, looks fresher, and tastes better. These menus meet the other criteria for menu-planning described in Chapter 3: They allow for appealing combinations of texture and color and for economic considerations. They also include ideas for social occasions. Thus, winter menus acknowledge the urge to stoke up on heartier fare—steak and kidney pie, finnan haddie, pork, and sausages. Grapefruit comes into its best season then, and in the East, during the holidays, fresh chestnuts are available to enhance the vegetable platter. The party menus range from a ski-lodge supper to a moderately sized cocktail party. Spring begins with asparagus and continues on to celebrate the season with strawberries, fresh peas, and watercress. For social occasions, there is a lunch, a brunch, and a buffet, as well as a theater party. Summer brings weddings and luncheons, outdoor parties and cold buffets. It's the time to use fresh garden produce and the fruits of the sea. Make the most of a brief season of cold salads, sandwiches, and molded desserts. Autumn's first chill is a sign for the beginning of formal dinners, pre-game brunches, and Thanksgiving weekend parties. Apples in many guises, heartier breads, and more solid dishes ranging from the informal simplicity of stuffed cabbage to roast veal and chicken Kiev enliven the menus of fall.

INTRODUCTION

Because these menus are seasonal, you may not always be able to prepare each dish in a given menu for lack of the ingredients. Fresh produce may not be available in your part of the country when it is abundant elsewhere. Asparagus is plentiful and reasonable in California long before it appears in New Jersey. Florida strawberries come into market earlier than Long Island strawberries do. If a set menu calls for a food not yet appearing in your market, or otherwise unavailable, utilize the powers of substitution also advocated in Chapter 3. Remember the feeling of the season and choose a food that will sustain it.

And feel free to use a given party menu for whatever occasion you have at hand. A pre-game brunch can be used for any informal noon gathering. Luncheons and dinners can be interchangeable, the buffet and cocktail parties enlarged or reduced. All of these menu suggestions are merely springboards to launch you. One of the aims of this cookbook is to inspire your innate creativity.

Another aim of the menu section is to help you answer a question you will hear over and over again from clients, "What goes well with this entrée? What can we have with it?" Studying these menus will develop your sense of which foods partner each other effectively, as well as your awareness of the aesthetic qualities that make a pleasing meal.

A special feature of the menu section is both a vegetarian dinner and a "diet" or low-calorie dinner, either of which today's customers might request. You'll also find a variety of picnics that can be prepared by both traditional and new wave caterers.

After the menus come recipes grouped in categories that proceed conventionally, starting with Appetizers and progressing more or less as a meal of several courses does. Thumb through these recipes to get ideas. (The page numbers of the recipes are also given with the menus for easy cross-reference.)

Notice that when you substitute one recipe for another in a given menu, you may have the problem of changing the quantity. Recipes are too individual to permit much generalization about this. Some rules of thumb for changing amounts were covered in Chapter 3. Refer to them, and note also that when you reduce a recipe, always allow at least one serving more than you need. When increasing, allow two servings extra. If you're in doubt, test your recipe.

The most important thing to remember is that recipes are your stock-in-trade. Pick out a few that you are willing to share and keep the rest to yourself. When you're asked for a special one, refuse the request politely but firmly. You must not give away the secrets of your success.

Your recipes should sell your business for you. You should have a good, varied, extensive repertoire, and it should change constantly. Collect and test recipes all the time, always updating your files. Use the recipes in this cookbook to start with, and then change them; improvise and invent until you have made them your own and created dishes that win your personal seal of approval.

And if, after all of this, you should decide that the catering business isn't for you, just use the cookbook and become the most popular hostess in town.

MENU SUGGESTIONS

SPRING

SEATED DINNER FOR EIGHT TO TEN
Asparagus Soup *129*
Veal and Carrot Roulade *141*
Amber Glazed Onions *162*
Rice Pilaf *157*
Cold Strawberry Soufflé *195*

•

BUFFET FOR TWENTY
Stuffed Edam Cheese *127*
Caviar Mold *118*
Shrimp Toast *120*
Turban of Chicken with Watercress Sauce *148*
Sautéed Cherry Tomatoes with Cucumbers *163*
Kasha with Mushrooms *159*
Rhubarb Crumble with Brandied Whipped Cream *212*

BRUNCH FOR SIXTEEN
Strawberries in Orange Juice and Champagne
Crêpes Florentine *179*
Sausages in White Wine *143*
Sally Lunn with Homemade Preserves *203*

•

LUNCHEON FOR FOURTEEN
Eggs Mollet Florentine *155*
Green Salad
Refrigerator Rolls with Sweet Butter *182*
Lemon Sponge Roll *201*

•

BEFORE THEATER PARTY FOR EIGHT
Fresh Pea Soup *130*
Crabmeat Pasties *135*
Coffee Macaroon Cream *193*

SUNDAY SUPPER FOR TWELVE

Chicken and Oyster Pie 153
Corn Soufflé 166
Green Salad
Meringue Cups with Lemon Curd 191

BRIDAL DINNER FOR FORTY

Coquilles Seviche 119
Chicken Breasts Duxelles 147
Baked Rice with Vegetables 158
Dacquoise 189

SUMMER

COLD BUFFET FOR THIRTY

Salmon or Striped Bass in Aspic 136
Poulet Vert 149
Cucumber Mousse 169
Brioche 180
Vegetables à la Grecque 164
Mango Mousse with Rum Sauce 189

WEDDING RECEPTION FOR SEVENTY-FIVE

Mushroom Turnovers 114
Tiny Cheese Strudels 126
Crab- and Shrimp-Filled Eclairs 119
Smoked Salmon Pâté Sandwiches 174
Curried Chicken Canapés 123
Dried Beef and Horseradish Sandwiches 174
Wedding Cake 206

COCKTAIL BUFFET FOR TWENTY

Garlic Popcorn 116
Barbecued Almonds 116
Crudités with Guacamole 113
Gougère Ring Filled with Ham 127
Tabbouli 172
Herbed Marinated Mushrooms 114
Curried Lamb Meatballs 124

DINNER FOR EIGHT TO TEN

Cold Zucchini Soup 128
Game Hens with Ginger Sauce 154
Rice with Raisins and Pine Nuts 158
Broiled Tomatoes Mayonnaise 164
Blueberry Charlotte 208

LUNCHEON FOR TWELVE TO FOURTEEN

Chicken Salad in Curry Ring *172*

Seafood Vinaigrette in Cucumber Ring *132*

Carrotes Râpées *168*

Buttermilk Biscuits *181*

Danish Cream Cake *200*

SUPPER FOR SIX

Caponata with Black Bread *113*

Country Captain *145*

Rice

Cucumber and Green Pepper Salad *169*

Poached Peaches with Raspberry Sauce *187*

•

BRUNCH FOR TEN

Seafood Crêpes *178*

Blueberry Muffins *181*

Broiled Tomatoes Parmesan *164*

Sliced Peaches in Honey and Brandy *186*

AUTUMN

DINNER FOR TEN TO TWELVE

Roast Veal with Apples in Orange Sauce *139*

Spinach Tart *167*

Brown Rice with Almonds *159*

Bread Pudding with Brandied Fruits *193*

BUFFET FOR TWENTY

Stuffed Cabbage *139*

Baked Green Noodles *156*

Glazed Apple Slices *185*

Chocolate Cream *192*

•

PRE-GAME BRUNCH FOR TWENTY-FOUR

Kedgeree *134*

Chicken Hash à la Ritz *152*

Hot Fruit Compote *187*

Sour Cream Pecan Coffee Cake *204*

Formal Dinner for Eight

Fish Timbales with
Sauce Aurore 121

Chicken Kiev 146

Puréed Broccoli and
Winter Squash 161

Julienne of Endive
and Watercress 170

Brie en Croûte with
Grapes and Pears 198

Post-Game Cocktail Buffet for Twenty-Five

Sausage en Brioche 124

Veal and Spinach Pâté 125

Vegetables à la Grecque 164

Baby Cheesecakes 199

Oatmeal Cookies 197

Thanksgiving Weekend Party for Sixteen

Lasagne Verde Bolognese 138

Salad Bar Salad 170

Herb Bread 185

Walnut Oatmeal Roll
with Whipped Cream 197

Sunday Supper for Twenty

Corn and Chicken Chowder 131

Assorted Breads and Cheeses

Pear Crunch Pie 210

Lemon Chess Tart 210

Sour Cream Apple Pie 212

WINTER

Dinner for Eight to Ten

Lady Curzon Soup 131

Steak and Kidney Pie 137

Puréed Spinach with Chestnuts 161

Irish Coffee Soufflé 194

Dinner for Six

Pork Olives with Yams
and Fruit Sauce 144

Mushroom Pie 167

Parslied Carrots 162

Floating Islands with
Caramel Sauce 190

MEN'S LUNCHEON FOR EIGHT

Finnan Haddie Roulade with Crabmeat *133*
Sautéed Cherry Tomatoes with Cucumbers *163*
Green Salad
Gingered Fruit *186*
Brownies *196*

•

COCKTAIL PARTY FOR THIRTY

Stuffed Mushrooms *115*
Tapenade with Crudités *117*
Brandade de Morue *118*
Stuffed Croissants *125*
Crispy Chicken Balls *123*
Grated Cheese Melba Toast *183*

LUNCHEON FOR TEN

Seafood Soufflé *133*
Grapefruit Ring with Watercress *171*
Tunnel Cake *205*

•

SKI LODGE SUPPER FOR TEN

Pork and Sausage Casserole *143*
Macaroni with Three Cheeses *157*
Green Bean Salad *170*
Carrot Cake *199*

•

HOLIDAY DINNER FOR EIGHT

Gnocchi *160*
Chicken Marengo *146*
Corn Timbales on Broccoli Purée *166*
Holiday Rum Raisin Cake *203*

OTHER OCCASIONS

LOW-CALORIE DINNER FOR SIX

Gazpacho
(167 calories per serving) 128
Chicken Marsala
(120 calories per serving) 151
Broiled Tomatoes Parmesan
(10 calories per serving) 164
Cold Rice Salad
(129 calories per serving) 171
Cold Strawberry Soufflé
(90 calories per serving) 195

VEGETARIAN DINNER FOR SIX

Apple-Blueberry Soup *129*
Crêpes Florentine *179*
Tabbouli *172*
Marinated Cucumbers and Tomatoes *163*
Baked Pear Crumble *211*

PICNICS

BOAT PICNIC FOR EIGHT

Potage Parmentier (with Carrots)
(Pour into thermoses; provide cups)
130

Stuffed Chicken Drumsticks
(Wrap individually and pack in basket) 154

Pan Bagna
(Wrap individually in plastic wrap) 175

Melon Crescents in Wine
(Pack in plastic container) 188

Shortbread
(Pack in cookie tin) 205

•

LUNCHEON PICNIC FOR EIGHT

Romaine Leaves Filled with Chicken Salad 173

Sardine Deviled Eggs 117

Cheese Bread Sticks 183

Fresh Fruit

Lemon Yogurt Pound Cake 201

(Pack each lunch separately in cardboard meat container lined with napkin; provide spoon)

TAILGATE PICNIC FOR SIX

Celery Root Remoulade 168

Pizza Rustica 175

Apples, Pears, and Grapes

Bourbon Balls 196

White Wine, Chicken Bouillon, and Clam Juice
(Mix equal parts together, heat, and pour into thermoses)

•

BRIDAL DINNER PICNIC FOR TWENTY-FOUR

Coquilles Seviche 119

Brioche 180

Onion Crêpes Filled with Smoked Salmon 178

Cold Rice Salad 171

Strawberries

Tiny Almond Tarts 196

Split of Champagne for Each Couple

(Pack individual picnics in baskets or on wicker trays lined with napkins)

APPETIZERS

CRUDITÉS WITH GUACAMOLE

Serves 20

- 3 large ripe avocados
- 1 tablespoon lemon or lime juice
- 1 tablespoon minced onion
- 1 clove garlic, mashed
- 2–3 canned green chiles, seeded and minced
- Salt and freshly ground black pepper
- Carrots
- Celery
- Asparagus spears
- Small green beans
- Sugar peas
- Broccoli, flowerets only

Peel and seed the avocados and mash them until they are smooth. Add the lemon or lime juice immediately. Blend in the minced onion, garlic, chiles, and salt and pepper to taste.

Place the guacamole in a bowl, cover tightly, and chill.

Cut the carrots, celery, and asparagus into strips. Arrange them on a platter with the uncooked green beans, sugar peas, and broccoli flowerets.

Serve the guacamole as a dip for the raw vegetables.

CAPONATA WITH BLACK BREAD

Serves 6

- 1 large eggplant
- 2 garlic cloves, crushed
- 1 onion, chopped fine
- 1 teaspoon salt
- Freshly ground black pepper
- 1 tablespoon drained capers
- 1 tablespoon pine nuts
- ¼ teaspoon ground cinnamon
- 1 tablespoon vinegar
- 3 tablespoons oil
- 1 tablespoon grated lemon rind
- 1 tablespoon lemon juice
- 1 tablespoon chopped mint

Preheat oven to 350°F.

Place the eggplant, whole, on a baking sheet and bake for 45 minutes until it is very soft. Peel the baked eggplant and chop it fine. Do not use a food processor.

In a large bowl add all the other ingredients to the chopped eggplant and mix well. Allow the mixture to stand for several hours.

When you are ready to serve, turn the eggplant "caviar" into a large pottery crock or bowl and serve it with a basket of dark bread.

HERBED MARINATED MUSHROOMS

Serves 20

- ¼ cup prepared mustard, preferably Dijon
- 6 tablespoons wine vinegar
- 1 teaspoon sugar
- 1 teaspoon salt
- Freshly ground black pepper
- 2 cups oil, half olive and half peanut oil
- ¼ cup minced shallots
- 3 pounds mushrooms, wiped clean and sliced thin
- ¼ cup minced parsley

Put the mustard, vinegar, sugar, salt, and pepper into the bowl of a food processor. Turn on the motor and slowly add the oil through the top. Process until the dressing is well blended. Add the shallots.

Toss the mushrooms with the dressing and marinate for 2 hours at room temperature.

Turn the mushrooms and marinade into shallow bowls and sprinkle with parsley. Chill.

MUSHROOM TURNOVERS

Makes about 200

PASTRY:
- 12 cups butter (6 pounds)
- 16 cups flour
- 4 egg yolks
- 1½ cups sour cream
- 2 teaspoons salt
- Egg wash: 1 egg yolk beaten with 1 tablespoon water

Mix all the ingredients, except the egg wash, together in a food processor or use an electric mixer. The mixing will have to be done in approximately 4 batches, depending upon the size of the machine. Wrap and chill the pastry.

FILLING:
- 2 pounds mushrooms, chopped fine
- 4 tablespoons chopped shallots
- 12 tablespoons butter
- ¾ cup flour
- ½–¾ cup heavy cream
- Salt and freshly ground black pepper to taste

Melt the butter in 2 large skillets. Add half the shallots and half the mushrooms to each skillet. Sauté them over medium heat until most of the moisture has evaporated.

Stir in the flour and cook for 3 minutes. Add enough cream to make a thick mixture and season with salt and pepper to taste. Cool the filling.

Preheat oven to 400°F.

Roll out the pastry to ⅛-inch thickness. Cut it into 3-inch rounds with a cookie cutter.

Place ½ teaspoon of the mushroom filling on each round. Fold the pastry into half-moons and crimp it around the edges with a fork.

Place the turnovers on baking sheets. Brush them with the egg wash and bake in the oven for 10 minutes.

NOTE: These turnovers may be made and frozen, uncooked. The unused pastry and mushroom filling may also be frozen.

STUFFED MUSHROOMS

Serves 14

COLD STUFFED MUSHROOMS:
- 50 mushrooms, medium-sized
- 8 ounces cream cheese
- 8 ounces blue cheese
- Brandy

Remove the stems from the mushrooms and save them for duxelles (see recipe, page 147). Wipe the caps clean, but do not peel them.

Beat together the cheeses with enough brandy to flavor them and make a creamy mixture. Put the mixture into a pastry tube and pipe the cheese filling into the mushroom caps. Chill the mushrooms and serve them cold.

HOT STUFFED MUSHROOMS:
- 50 mushrooms, medium-sized
- Butter for greasing

Stuff with:
½ pound sausage meat, cooked and mixed with ¼ cup minced pecans, 1 tablespoon grated onion, 2 tablespoons sherry, salt, pepper, and enough cream to bind mixture

or

1 cup chicken liver pâté (see recipe, page 122)

or

8 ounces cream cheese mixed with one 4½-ounce can crabmeat or shrimp

Preheat oven to 400°F.
Prepare the filling of your choice.
Remove the stems from the mushrooms and wipe the caps clean. Do not peel them. Place the mushrooms on a greased baking pan and bake them in the oven for 10 minutes. Stuff each mushroom with the filling and serve hot.

GARLIC POPCORN

Popcorn
Bacon fat
1 clove garlic, peeled and split
½ cup butter for every 1 quart popped corn
Coarse salt

Pop the popcorn according to the instructions for the corn popper or use a sturdy skillet with a tightly fitting lid. Substitute the bacon fat for the usual amount of cooking oil.

Place a peeled, split garlic clove in a saucepan with the desired amount of butter and heat until the butter is melted. Discard the garlic clove.

Toss the popcorn with salt and drizzle with the melted garlic butter. Serve the popcorn in baskets.

BARBECUED ALMONDS

Serves 20

3 tablespoons butter
3 tablespoons A-1 sauce or other bottled meat sauce
3 cups whole blanched almonds
1 teaspoon salt
4–5 drops Tabasco sauce

Melt the butter in a large iron skillet and add the A-1 sauce. Stir together.

Add the almonds and stir to coat the nuts with the butter sauce. Sprinkle the almonds with salt and Tabasco sauce and stir.

Place the skillet in a 325°F. oven for 15 to 20 minutes, stirring occasionally.

Drain the almonds on paper towels. Serve warm.

CUCUMBER-SHRIMP ROUNDS

Cucumber
Bread slices, crusts removed and cut into rounds
Mayonnaise
Canned shrimp
Paprika

Peel the cucumber and run a fork down the sides to make ridges. Cut the cucumber into thin slices.

Spread the rounds of fresh bread with mayonnaise.

Rinse the canned shrimp well in cold water.

Place a slice of cucumber on each round and top it with a tiny shrimp.

Sprinkle the cucumber-shrimp rounds with paprika.

SARDINE DEVILED EGGS

Makes 24 egg halves

12 eggs, small or medium-sized
Water
1 three-ounce tin sardines, drained
1 tablespoon grated onion
1 tablespoon lemon juice
3 tablespoons mayonnaise
½ teaspoon salt
Freshly ground black pepper
Garnish: Parsley or olives
Watercress

Place the eggs into a saucepan and cover them with cold water. Bring them to a boil, then turn off the heat and allow the eggs to sit for 15 minutes. Drain the eggs and cover them with cold water.

Remove the shells and cut each egg in half. Remove the yolks to a bowl, blender, or food processor.

Add the drained sardines, grated onion, lemon juice, mayonnaise, salt, and pepper. Mix until the egg mixture is very smooth and adjust the seasoning. If the mixture is too stiff, add more mayonnaise.

Fill a pastry bag and pipe the mixture into the egg whites.

Top each egg with a sprig of parsley or a round of olive.

Make a wreath of watercress around the edge of a platter and arrange the eggs in the center. Serve at room temperature.

TAPENADE WITH CRUDITÉS

Makes about 3 cups

2 tins anchovy fillets, drained
2 cups black olives, chopped
2 large cloves garlic
3 tablespoons drained capers
Juice of 1 lemon
4 tablespoons snipped parsley
1 teaspoon prepared mustard, preferably Dijon
1 cup olive oil
Crudités: Assorted raw vegetables

Into the container of a blender or food processor, put all ingredients, except the oil.

Turn on the motor and add the oil gradually until the mixture is thick and smooth.

Turn the tapenade into a bowl and chill in the refrigerator for 2 to 3 hours or overnight. Serve it at room temperature with crudités.

BRANDADE DE MORUE

Serves 50

2 pounds dried salt cod	4 cloves garlic
Water	1 cup olive oil
⅔ cup heavy cream	Fried Toast*

Soak the dried cod in cold water for 24 hours, changing the water 4 times.

Place the cod in a large saucepan with just enough simmering water to cover it. Simmer the fish until it flakes, about 30 minutes. Do not let the water boil.

Cut the cod into small squares.

Heat the cream.

Place half the cream, half the cod and 2 garlic cloves in the container of a food processor fitted with a metal blade. Turn on the processor and add half the oil through the feed tube. Process until the mixture is smooth. Remove the mixture and repeat the process with the remaining ingredients.

To serve, heat the mixture until it is just warm. Divide the brandade in half and make pyramid-shaped mounds on two serving platters, surrounded with triangles of fried toast.

CAVIAR MOLD

Serves 10

1 tablespoon plain gelatin	1 cup mayonnaise
¼ cup milk	1 cup heavy cream, whipped
2 tablespoons grated onion	1 four-ounce jar of black caviar
1 tablespoon lemon juice	Melba toast
1 teaspoon Worcestershire sauce	Garnish: Sieved egg yolk

Soften the gelatin in the milk. Liquefy the gelatin over a container of hot water. Cool.

Mix the onion, lemon juice, and Worcestershire sauce into the mayonnaise. Stir in the gelatin and the whipped cream. Fold in the caviar.

Turn the caviar mixture into an oiled 1-quart mold. Chill it overnight.

Unmold the caviar onto a serving platter and surround it with melba toast. Garnish the top of the mold with sieved egg yolk.

---

*To make fried toast, cut slices of bread into triangles. Sauté them in butter or oil until they are golden and crisp on both sides. Drain the toast on paper towels.

APPETIZERS / 119

COQUILLES SEVICHE

Serves 40

- 5 pounds bay or sea scallops
- 5 pounds firm white fish (bass, haddock, or flounder)
- 5 cups lime juice, fresh or frozen but not bottled
- 1¼ cups chopped onion
- 2½ cups oil
- 1½ cups chopped parsley
- 1 cup peeled canned green chiles
- 8 garlic cloves, peeled
- Salt and freshly ground black pepper to taste
- 4–5 dashes of Tabasco sauce
- Garnish: Parsley, finely chopped

If using sea scallops, cut them into quarters or eighths. Cut the fish into pieces of comparable size.

Put all the seafood into a large non-metal bowl and marinate it in the lime juice for 4 hours or overnight.

Place the oil, onions, parsley, chiles, and garlic cloves into a blender or food processor. Chop; do not purée. Add the salt, pepper, and Tabasco sauce, and mix well.

Drain the seafood and toss it with the dressing. Chill.

Serve the seviche in scallop shells or small ramekins sprinkled with chopped parsley. Small forks would be the best utensil.

NOTE: This dish may be prepared 1 day ahead. Refrigerate covered with plastic wrap, not foil.

CRAB- AND SHRIMP-FILLED ÉCLAIRS

Makes 75 éclairs

PASTRY:
- 6 tablespoons butter
- ½ cup milk
- ½ cup water
- 1 teaspoon salt
- 1 cup flour
- 4 eggs
- Egg wash: 1 egg yolk beaten with 1 tablespoon water.

Put the butter, milk, water, and salt into a saucepan. Bring to a boil. Remove from the heat and stir in the flour with a wooden spoon.

Return to the heat and stir for 2 minutes until the dough forms a ball and the bottom of the pan is slightly filmed.

Turn the dough into the bowl of a mixer or food processor. Add the eggs, one at a time, making sure each egg is thoroughly incorporated before adding the next one.

Preheat oven to 375°F.

Fit a pastry bag with a plain ½-inch tip and fill it with dough. Onto a lightly greased baking sheet press out 2-inch lengths of dough.

(Continued)

(Continued)

Brush the dough with egg wash and bake for 15 to 20 minutes until puffed and golden. Cool the éclairs on racks.

Makes 2 cups

SHRIMP FILLING:

- 1 four and one half-ounce can shrimp, drained and chopped fine
- 1 eight-ounce package cream cheese, softened
- 2 tablespoons chopped chives
- 1 tablespoon minced dill weed
- 1 hard-cooked egg, chopped fine
- Salt and freshly ground black pepper to taste

Mix all the ingredients together.

Makes 2 cups

CRAB FILLING:

- 1 four and one half-ounce can crabmeat, shredded
- 1 eight-ounce package cream cheese, softened
- 2-3 drops Tabasco sauce
- Grated rind of 1 lemon
- 2 tablespoons minced parsley
- Salt and freshly ground black pepper to taste
- Garnish: Parsley, watercress, or lemon wedges

Mix all the ingredients together.

To fill the éclairs, slit them along the side, lengthwise. Remove any uncooked dough inside. The fillings can be inserted with a spoon or pastry bag fitted with a wide tip.

Serve the éclairs on platters garnished with parsley, watercress, or lemon wedges dipped in chopped parsley.

SHRIMP TOAST

Makes 54 pieces

- 1½ pounds raw shrimp
- 18 water chestnuts
- 3 eggs
- 1 teaspoon salt
- 1½ teaspoons sugar
- 1 tablespoon dry sherry
- 3 tablespoons minced scallions
- 2½ tablespoons cornstarch
- 18 slices firm white bread, thinly sliced
- Peanut oil

Wash and shell the shrimp.

Finely chop the shrimp and water chestnuts together.

Beat the eggs, then beat in the shrimp mixture, salt, sugar, sherry, scallions, and cornstarch. This also can be done in a food processor with a metal blade.

Remove the crusts from the bread and cut each slice into 4 triangles.

Spread each triangle with the shrimp mixture. In a large skillet heat peanut oil 1 inch deep to 375°F. Put in the triangles shrimp side down and cook until they are lightly browned. Turn and cook until the toast is golden. Drain on paper towels.

Keep shrimp toast warm in a 200°F. oven until ready to serve.

NOTE: Shrimp toast may be made in advance and frozen. To serve, put frozen toasts in a 350°F. oven for 12 to 15 minutes.

FISH TIMBALES WITH SAUCE AURORE

Serves 8

- 4 small fillets of sole or flounder
- Butter
- Salted water
- 8 ounces frozen, shelled shrimp
- 1/3 cup chopped walnuts
- 1 small apple, peeled and cored
- 1 egg
- Salt and freshly ground black pepper to taste
- 1/2 teaspoon ground mace
- 2 tablespoons dry sherry
- Sauce Aurore (recipe follows)

Preheat oven to 375°F.

Split the fish fillets in half lengthwise and line the insides of well-buttered custard cups with the fillets.

Bring salted water to a boil in a saucepan and drop in the frozen shrimp. Remove the pan from the heat, cover it, and let it stand for 5 minutes.

Drain the shrimp and combine it with the walnuts and apple in a food processor. Process until the shrimp mixture is fairly smooth.

Remove the mixture to a bowl and blend in the egg, seasonings, and sherry. Fill the centers of the fish-lined cups with the shrimp mixture.

Set the cups in a pan of hot water and cover loosely with foil. Bake the timbales in the oven for 25 minutes.

Remove the cups to a rack for 5 minutes. Run a knife around the edges of the cups and unmold them onto a serving platter. Mop up the extra liquid on the platter with paper towels.

Spoon Sauce Aurore over and around the timbales.

Makes 2 cups

SAUCE AURORE:
- 3 tablespoons butter
- 4 tablespoons flour
- 1 cup milk
- 1/3 cup clam juice
- 1/2 cup heavy cream
- 2 tablespoons vermouth
- Salt and freshly ground black pepper to taste
- 1 tablespoon tomato paste

(Continued)

(Continued)

Melt the butter in a saucepan. Gradually add the flour, stirring, until the mixture is well blended, golden, and bubbly.

Add the milk and clam juice. Cook the sauce over medium-high heat, stirring, until it is thickened and smooth.

Add the cream and vermouth. Simmer, stirring occasionally, for 10 minutes.

Stir in salt and pepper to taste and tomato paste. Cook until the sauce is well blended and silken in texture.

CHICKEN LIVER PÂTÉ

Makes 2 cups

- 4 cups water
- 1 teaspoon salt
- 1 stalk celery
- 1 onion, peeled
- 2 chicken bouillon cubes
- 1 pound chicken livers
- 1 teaspoon ground ginger
- Salt and freshly ground black pepper to taste
- ¼ teaspoon ground cloves
- 1 teaspoon dry mustard
- 1 tablespoon chopped onion
- 8 tablespoons butter, melted
- 2 tablespoons brandy
- Garnish: Finely chopped parsley.
- Melba toast (see recipe, page 183)

Put 4 cups of water in a saucepan. Add 1 teaspoon of salt, the celery, peeled onion, and chicken bouillon cubes. Bring the water to a boil. Reduce the heat and simmer the stock for 10 minutes.

Trim the fat from the chicken livers and wash them. Put the livers into the simmering stock, cover, and cook them for 15 minutes. Drain the livers and place them in a blender or food processor.

Add the ginger, salt, pepper, cloves, mustard, and chopped onion. Start blending and gradually add the melted butter. Add the brandy. Blend until the mixture is perfectly smooth. If necessary, stop from time to time to scrape down the container's sides with a rubber spatula.

When the pâté is smooth, pack it into a crock and refrigerate it for 24 hours.

Before serving, sprinkle chopped parsley over the top. Serve the pâté with melba toast.

NOTE: This pâté cannot be frozen, but it can be made 3 to 4 days ahead and refrigerated.

CRISPY CHICKEN BALLS

Makes about 42

- 2 cups finely chopped cooked chicken (1 one-pound breast)
- 1 cup mashed potatoes
- 1 egg, separated
- Salt and freshly ground black pepper to taste
- 1 teaspoon curry powder
- 1–2 tablespoons heavy cream
- ½ cup fine bread crumbs
- ½ cup ground almonds
- Fat for frying

Mix together the cooked chicken, mashed potatoes, egg yolk, salt, pepper, curry powder, and enough cream to moisten the mixture. Shape the mixture into small balls.

Dip each ball into egg white, bread crumbs, and then the ground almonds. Chill the balls for 30 minutes or longer.

Heat fat to 375°F. Fry the balls for 2 minutes until they are crisp and golden.

Serve them immediately or keep them warm in a 200°F. oven.

NOTE: These can be fried ahead of time, cooled, and frozen. Before serving, reheat the frozen balls on a baking sheet in a 400°F. oven for 10 to 12 minutes.

CURRIED CHICKEN CANAPÉS

Makes 48

- 1 large whole chicken breast, halved, skinned, and boned
- Salt
- Lemon juice
- 1 eight-ounce package cream cheese
- 2 tablespoons chutney
- ½ teaspoon curry powder
- Bread slices, crusts removed and cut into rounds
- Slivered amonds

Preheat oven to 425°F.

Place the chicken breast on a baking sheet and sprinkle it with a little salt and lemon juice. Cover tightly and bake it for about 20 minutes until it is opaque and firm.

When the chicken is cool, cut it into large pieces and put it into a food processor with the cream cheese. Process the ingredients until the mixture is smooth.

Add the chutney and curry powder to the mixture and process it once more.

Spread the curried chicken mixture onto the bread rounds.

Top each round with a slivered almond.

CURRIED LAMB MEATBALLS

Serves 20

- 3 pounds lean ground lamb
- 2 eggs
- ½ cup dry whole wheat bread crumbs
- 1 teaspoon ground cumin
- 1 teaspoon ground cinnamon
- ¼ teaspoon hot pepper flakes
- 1 teaspoon salt
- 1 tablespoon grated ginger root
- 3 tablespoons oil
- 2 tablespoons minced onion
- 2 cloves garlic, minced
- 1 teaspoon curry powder or to taste
- 1 cup chicken bouillon
- 2 tablespoons wine vinegar
- 1 cup applesauce
- 3 tablespoons apricot jam

Mix the ground lamb with the eggs, bread crumbs, cumin, cinnamon, pepper flakes, salt, and ginger root. Shape the mixture into bite-sized balls.

Heat the oil in a skillet and brown the lamb balls.

Add the onion and garlic to the skillet and sauté until soft. Stir in the curry powder and cook for 3 to 4 minutes. Add the chicken bouillon, vinegar, and applesauce. Stir in the apricot jam.

Bring the liquid to a boil. Reduce the heat to a simmer and cook for 30 minutes, covered.

Turn the meatballs and sauce into a chafing dish and keep them hot over hot water, or serve them from a casserole placed on a hot tray.

SAUSAGE EN BRIOCHE

Serves 20 to 24

- 2 pieces smoked sausage, about 8 inches long and 2 inches in diameter
- Brioche (see recipe, page 180)
- 2 eggs, beaten

Prepare the brioche dough according to the recipe and allow it to rise once. Punch it down.

Preheat oven to 375°F.

Divide the dough in half and roll each half to ½-inch thickness. Brush the dough with beaten egg.

Place a sausage in the center of each piece of dough and wrap it up neatly, tucking in the ends. If necessary, glue the dough together on the seams with egg.

Place the rolls seam side down on a greased baking sheet. Use cutouts made from scraps of dough to decorate the tops of the rolls, if desired. Glue them on with egg.

Brush the rolls with the beaten egg. Let them stand for 10 minutes.

Bake for 35 to 40 minutes until the dough is golden. Cool the rolls slightly before slicing.

NOTE: These sausage rolls can be baked in advance, refrigerated, and warmed slightly before serving. The rolls will keep up to 3 days before use. Do not freeze them.

STUFFED CROISSANTS

Makes 48

3 (eight ounces each) packages crescent dinner rolls (in a tube)
Chicken liver pâté (see recipe, page 122)
Egg wash: 1 egg yolk beaten with 1 tablespoon water

Unroll the crescent dough as instructed on the package and cut each triangle in half.

Spread the triangles with pâté and roll them up into small crescents. Chill for 1 hour.

Brush each crescent with egg wash and bake at 375°F. for 10 to 12 minutes until the croissants are puffy and golden.

NOTE: These croissants can be made ahead and frozen. When ready to serve them, reheat at 400°F. on a baking sheet loosely covered with foil.

VEAL AND SPINACH PÂTÉ

Serves 20 to 24

2 pounds ground veal
1 pound ground pork fat
2 eggs
¼ cup brandy
½ cup heavy cream
½ cup Madeira
1 teaspoon thyme
Salt and freshly ground black pepper to taste
2 (10 ounces each) packages frozen leaf spinach
4 large mushrooms
1 tablespoon butter
1 tablespoon flour
⅓ cup light cream
½ teaspoon nutmeg
½ cup pine nuts
1 pound bacon
Garnish: Watercress

(Continued)

(Continued)

Preheat over to 300°F.

Mix together the veal, pork fat, and eggs. Stir in the brandy, cream, and Madeira. Season the veal mixture with thyme, salt, and pepper.

Cook the spinach, drain, squeeze it dry and set it aside.

Wash and chop the mushrooms and sauté them in butter over high heat for 5 minutes. Stir in the flour and cook for 3 minutes. Add the light cream and cook the mushroom sauce until it is smooth and thick.

Combine the spinach and mushroom sauce. Season the spinach mixture with nutmeg, salt, and pepper. Mix in the pine nuts.

Line 2 eight-cup molds with slices of bacon. Put one-quarter of the veal mixture in each. Spread half of the spinach mixture over the veal in each mold. Fill the molds with the remaining veal mixture.

Cover the tops of the molds with bacon slices and seal the molds with foil. Place them in pans of water and bake for 2 hours.

Remove the molds from the oven and place heavy cans or bricks on top of them. Let them stand overnight in a cool place. Remove the weights and turn out the pâtés. Wrap them well and refrigerate.

Before serving, remove the bacon slices. Place the pâtés on long platters and slice 2 to 3 pieces from the ends. Garnish the platters with watercress.

NOTE: These pâtés will keep up to a week.

TINY CHEESE STRUDELS

Makes about 36 pieces

1 three-ounce package cream cheese	1 tablespoon cream
¼ pound feta cheese	½ cup minced parsley
½ cup small curd creamed cottage cheese	1 tablespoon chopped fresh dill
1 tablespoon grated Parmesan cheese	Pinch of salt
1 egg	½ pound Phyllo pastry sheets (not frozen)
	½ cup melted butter

In a bowl mix the cheeses, the egg, and cream into a smooth paste. Stir in the parsley, dill, and salt.

Cut the Phyllo sheets crosswise and lengthwise, making four pieces from each sheet, and pile the sheets on top of each other. Cover them with a damp towel to prevent drying.

Take one Phyllo sheet from the pile and place it in front of you. Brush the entire surface with butter. Place a teaspoonful of the cheese mixture on the pastry. Roll it up into a cigarette shape or fold it in a triangle as you would fold a flag.

When all the sheets are used, brush the strudels with butter. Place them on an ungreased sheet and chill for 20 minutes.

Bake at 350°F. for 20 to 25 minutes until golden.

NOTE: These freeze well.

STUFFED EDAM CHEESE

Serves 10

1 one-pound whole Edam cheese
¾ cup unsalted butter
2 tablespoons brandy
2 drops Tabasco sauce
1 teaspoon Worcestershire sauce
Crackers

Cut off the top of the cheese and hollow it out, leaving a ½-inch shell. Cut the butter into small pieces.

Put pieces of the cheese into a food processor with the pieces of butter, the brandy, and the Tabasco and Worcestershire sauces. Process the mixture until it is smooth and creamy.

Using a pastry bag with a star tube, pipe the cheese into the Edam shell. Chill.

Before serving, bring the cheese to room temperature. Arrange it on a platter surrounded by plain toasted crackers.

NOTE: This stuffed cheese is best when made 2 days in advance.

GOUGÈRE RING FILLED WITH HAM

Serves 8

6 tablespoons unsalted butter
1 cup beer
½ teaspoon salt
1 cup flour
4 eggs
½ cup ground ham
1 cup grated Gruyère cheese
Egg wash: 1 egg yolk beaten with 1 tablespoon water

Preheat oven to 375°F.

In a saucepan over high heat bring the butter, beer, and salt to a full boil.

Remove the pan from the heat and with a wooden spoon stir in the flour all at once. Return the pan to the heat and stir for about 2 minutes until dough forms a smooth ball and a film forms on the bottom of the pan.

Turn the dough into the bowl of a mixer or food processor. With the machine running, add the eggs one at a time, making sure each egg is thoroughly incorporated before adding the next one.

(Continued)

(Continued)

Beat in the ground ham and half the cheese.

Lightly grease a baking sheet. Fill a pastry bag fitted with a plain ½-inch tip with dough. Squeeze out large puffs of dough in a 9-inch circle. The puffs should be touching each other, the whole forming a wreath. Brush the dough with egg wash and sprinkle with the remaining cheese.

Bake for 45 minutes until the ring is puffed and brown. Cool on a rack.

NOTE: This ring may be frozen. To reheat, place it on a baking sheet and cover loosely with foil. Place in a 375°F. oven for 30 minutes.

SOUPS

GAZPACHO

Serves 6

3 cucumbers
3 ripe tomatoes
1 small onion
1 clove garlic
1 small green pepper
4 cups tomato juice
Juice of 1 lemon
6 tablespoons vegetable oil
Salt and freshly ground
black pepper to taste
2 tablespoons chopped chives

Peel the cucumbers and tomatoes and chop them fine. Remove them to a bowl.

Chop the onion, garlic, and green pepper fine. Add them to the cucumbers and tomatoes.

Stir in the tomato juice, lemon juice, and oil. Season with salt and pepper.

Chill the soup and serve it sprinkled with chopped chives.

COLD ZUCCHINI SOUP

Serves 8

3 medium zucchini
4 tablespoons butter
1 onion, chopped
2 stalks celery, chopped
6 cups chicken bouillon
1 teaspoon curry powder
1 cup milk
¼ teaspoon ground ginger
Salt and freshly ground
black pepper to taste
1 cup heavy cream
3 tablespoons minced parsley

Slice the unpeeled zucchini into ½-inch rounds.

Melt the butter in a large saucepan. Add the zucchini, chopped onion, and celery. Sauté the vegetables, stirring, for 3 to 4 minutes.

Add the chicken bouillon and bring to a boil. Cover and simmer until the vegetables are tender.

Remove the vegetables and liquid to a processor, purée, and then pour the soup into a saucepan.

Dissolve the curry powder in the milk and add it to the soup. Season with ginger, salt, and pepper. Bring the soup to a boil.

Purée the soup again, then chill it overnight.

Before serving, stir in the cream. Garnish with parsley.

APPLE-BLUEBERRY SOUP

Serves 6

2 cups fresh blueberries
4 cups apple juice

Lemon yogurt

In a blender purée the blueberries with the apple juice. Strain and chill the liquid. Serve the soup in soup bowls with a spoonful of lemon yogurt.

ASPARAGUS SOUP

Makes about 9 cups

1½ pounds asparagus
Water
5 cups chicken bouillon
2 tablespoons minced onion
2 cups half-and-half
Salt and freshly ground
black pepper to taste
½ cup sour cream

Wash the asparagus and break off the ends. Place the asparagus in a large skillet; add enough salted water to cover them.

Cover the skillet and bring the water to a boil. Cook until the asparagus tops are barely tender.

Remove the asparagus and reserve the liquid. Cut off the tips, chop them and set them aside.

Cut the stalks into 1-inch pieces and place them in a saucepan with the chicken bouillon and 1 cup of the reserved asparagus water. Add the minced onion.

Bring the stalks to a boil and cook until they are very tender.

Purée the asparagus stalks with their liquid in a blender.

Return the asparagus purée to the saucepan and add the half-and-half. Bring to the boiling point.

(Continued)

(Continued)

Season with salt and freshly ground pepper to taste.

Serve in soup cups or mugs, topping each serving with a tablespoon of sour cream and a sprinkling of the chopped asparagus tips.

NOTE: The purée can be made in advance and frozen. Thaw the purée and heat it. Then add the half-and-half, season, and serve.

POTAGE PARMENTIER (WITH CARROTS)

Serves 8

- 2 leeks, white part only
- 3 carrots
- 2 small potatoes
- 2 tablespoons butter
- 1 tablespoon vegetable oil
- 6 cups chicken bouillon
- Salt and freshly ground black pepper to taste
- ½ teaspoon ground ginger
- 2 cups light cream or half-and-half
- 2 tablespoons chopped chives

Chop the leeks and carrots in a food processor using a metal blade. Peel and chop the potatoes.

Melt the butter and oil in a heavy saucepan and add the vegetables. Cook the vegetables, stirring, over medium-high heat for 3 minutes. Add the chicken bouillon and bring it to a boil. Reduce the heat. Cover the pan and simmer until the vegetables are tender, about 20 minutes.

Put the mixture into the container of a blender or food processor in 2 or 3 batches and purée it.

Return the purée to the saucepan and season it to taste with salt, pepper, and ginger. Add the cream and heat it to just under the boiling point. Serve with a sprinkling of chives in each cup.

FRESH PEA SOUP

Serves 8

- 2 tablespoons butter
- 1 large leek, white part only, chopped
- 2 (ten ounces each) packages frozen tiny peas
- 6 cups chicken bouillon
- 2 tablespoons flour
- 2 teaspoons chopped fresh mint
- 1 teaspoon chopped fresh tarragon or ¼ teaspoon dried thyme
- 2 cups heavy cream
- ½ teaspoon salt

Melt the butter in a large saucepan and add the leek and peas. Sauté, breaking up the frozen peas, for 5 minutes.

Add the chicken bouillon and simmer, covered, for 10 minutes.

Purée the mixture in a blender in 2 or 3 batches, adding the flour and herbs.

Return it to the saucepan and add 1½ cups cream. Bring the soup just to the boiling point but do not boil.

Whip the remaining ½ cup cream, adding ½ teaspoon salt. Serve the soup in bowls with a spoonful of whipped cream on each.

NOTE: The purée can be frozen. To serve, thaw it, add the cream, and heat.

CORN AND CHICKEN CHOWDER

Serves 20

½ pound salt pork, diced
5 large onions, thinly sliced
6 potatoes, peeled and diced
10 cups chicken bouillon
5 (ten ounces each) packages frozen corn kernels
10 cups diced cooked chicken
10 cups whole milk
Salt, freshly ground black pepper, and paprika

In a large saucepan cook the salt pork until it is crisp. Set the salt pork aside. Pour off all but 3 tablespoons of fat.

Add the onions to the pan and sauté until they are just limp. Add the potatoes and chicken bouillon. Bring to a boil. Reduce the heat and simmer, covered, until the vegetables are tender, about 20 minutes.

Add the corn and cook 5 minutes longer.

Add the chicken and milk and heat to the boiling point. Season with salt, pepper, and paprika to taste.

Turn the chowder into 2 or 3 soup tureens and sprinkle them with the salt pork. Keep the tureens warm on hot trays. Serve the chowder in heated soup bowls or mugs.

NOTE: This chowder can be made in advance and refrigerated. Reheat it slowly, without boiling it, before serving.

LADY CURZON SOUP

Serves 10

4 apples, cored and quartered
4 onions, quartered
8 cups beef bouillon
2 cups heavy cream
¼ cup Scotch whiskey, or 2 teaspoons curry powder
Salt and freshly ground black pepper to taste

(Continued)

(Continued)

Place the apples, onions, and beef bouillon in a large saucepan. Bring to a boil, reduce the heat, and simmer, covered, for 1 hour or until the apples and onions are very soft.

Strain the bouillon, discarding the vegetables.

Return the liquid to the saucepan and add the cream mixed with the Scotch whiskey or curry, choosing whichever of these two flavorings is preferred. Bring the soup to the boiling point and season to taste with salt and pepper.

Serve the soup very hot in small cups either at the table or in the living room before dinner.

NOTE: Lady Curzon soup can be made a day or two ahead.

ENTRÉES

SEAFOOD VINAIGRETTE IN CUCUMBER RING

Serves 8

- 1½ packages plain gelatin
- 1 cup water
- ½ cup white vinegar
- ½ cup sugar
- 3 tablespoons lime juice
- ½ teaspoon salt
- 2 medium cucumbers, peeled, seeded, and chopped fine
- ¾ cup chopped celery
- ½ cup chopped cabbage
- ¼ cup chopped green pepper
- 1 tablespoon grated onion

Soften the gelatin in ¼ cup of water.

Add the vinegar and sugar to the remaining water and heat, stirring to dissolve the sugar. Dissolve the gelatin in the hot vinegar mixture. Stir in the lime juice and salt.

Add the cucumbers and the rest of the vegetables and pour the mixture into a 6-cup ring mold that has been rinsed in cold water. Chill the mold overnight.

Unmold the ring and fill the center with the seafood vinaigrette. Arrange the remaining seafood around the edge of the cucumber ring.

SEAFOOD VINAIGRETTE:
- 2 cups water
- ½ cup white wine or vermouth
- 1 tablespoon lemon juice
- 1 pound firm white fish (halibut, cod, bass), cut into 1-inch pieces
- 1 pound sea or bay scallops
- 1 pound fresh shrimp, shelled
- Vinaigrette dressing (see recipe, page 173)
- Garnish: Fresh dill weed, snipped

Put the water, wine, and lemon juice into a large non-aluminum pan.

Bring the liquid to a boil and add the white fish. Lower the heat to a simmer. Cook the fish until opaque, about 15 minutes. Remove the fish with a slotted spoon.

If using sea scallops, cut them in quarters. Add the shrimp and scallops to the liquid and cook until firm, about 7 minutes. Remove the seafood and discard the liquid.

Toss the fish and seafood with vinaigrette dressing. Sprinkle the seafood salad with snipped dill. Chill.

SEAFOOD SOUFFLÉ

Serves 10

- 1 pound Gruyère cheese, diced
- 8 slices buttered bread, cubed
- 2 cups cooked shrimp or crabmeat, carefully picked over
- 6 eggs
- 3 cups milk
- 1 teaspoon salt
- Freshly ground black pepper to taste
- 2 tablespoons grated onion
- 2 tablespoons minced parsley
- 1 teaspoon prepared mustard, preferably Dijon

Toss together the cheese and buttered bread cubes, and turn the mixture into 2 buttered 1½-quart soufflé dishes.

Arrange 1 cup of seafood on top of the cheese mixture in each dish.

Beat together the eggs, milk, salt, pepper, onion, parsley, and mustard and pour half of the mixture into each dish. Refrigerate for at least 3 hours or overnight.

Preheat oven to 350°F. Bake for 45 to 55 minutes until the seafood soufflé is puffy and browned.

FINNAN HADDIE ROULADE WITH CRABMEAT

Serves 8

- 1 pound finnan haddie fillet
- 5 eggs
- Salt and freshly ground black pepper to taste
- ½ teaspoon ground nutmeg
- 3 tablespoons butter
- 3 tablespoons flour
- 1½ cups milk
- ½ cup sour cream
- 2 cups canned or fresh crabmeat, picked over well
- 2 tablespoons lemon juice
- 2–3 drops Tabasco sauce

(Continued)

(Continued)

Preheat oven to 350°F.

Place the finnan haddie in a baking dish and add water halfway up the sides of the dish. Cover with foil. Bake for 20 to 30 minutes until the fish flakes easily. The length of time depends on the quality of the fish. Remove the fish from the water, cool, and flake the fish.

Place the fish in the bowl of a food processor and with a metal blade work until the fish is finely chopped, not puréed. Add the eggs and seasonings to the bowl and process until the ingredients are just mixed.

Grease a 10- × 15-inch jelly roll pan. Line it with waxed paper and grease the paper.

Spread the fish mixture evenly in the pan.

Bake for 20 to 25 minutes at 350°F. The fish mixture should be puffed and firm to the touch. Turn it out onto a clean towel. Remove the pan and let the fish stand for 5 minutes. Strip off the waxed paper carefully. Roll up the fish mixture. Unroll it and cool.

Meanwhile, melt the butter in a saucepan. Stir in the flour and cook, stirring, until it is bubbling. Add the milk and cook, stirring, until the mixture is thick and smooth. Remove from the heat and stir in the sour cream, crabmeat, lemon juice, and Tabasco sauce. Season the mixture with salt and pepper.

Spread two-thirds of the mixture over the fish. Roll it up and place it on an ovenproof serving platter. Cover the roulade with remaining sauce mixture.

Reheat in a 325°F. oven for 20 minutes.

KEDGEREE

Serves 24

1½ pounds salmon fillets	8 hard-cooked eggs
1½ pounds haddock or scrod fillets	6 cups cooked rice
Water	2–3 teaspoons curry powder
Juice of 1 lemon	Freshly ground black pepper
¼ cup vermouth	1½ cups heavy cream
1 teaspoon salt	¼ cup minced parsley

Preheat oven to 350°F.

Place the salmon and haddock in a baking pan. Pour in water halfway up the fish. Add the juice of 1 lemon, ¼ cup vermouth, and 1 teaspoon salt. Cover the pan.

Poach the fish in the oven for 20 to 30 minutes until the fish flakes but does not disintegrate. Remove the fish from the liquid and cool.

Chop the whites and yolks of the eggs separately.

Flake the fish and toss it gently with the rice and chopped egg whites. Season the kedgeree with curry powder and salt and pepper. Stir in the cream.

To serve, divide the mixture between two shallow serving dishes. Sprinkle each with the chopped egg yolks and minced parsley. Set the dishes on hot trays. This dish can also be served in chafing dishes over hot water.

CRABMEAT PASTIES

Serves 8

PASTRY:

- ¾ cup butter
- 8 tablespoons vegetable shortening
- 3¾ cups flour
- 1 tablespoon lemon juice
- 3 tablespoons ice water
- 1 teaspoon salt

Using a food processor or mixer, quickly blend all the ingredients into a pastry dough. If the dough is too dry, add another tablespoon of ice water. Divide it into 2 parts, wrap it, and chill it for 30 minutes or longer.

FILLING:

- 2 tablespoons flour
- 2 tablespoons butter
- ½ cup clam juice
- ½ cup milk
- 1 tablespoon brandy
- Salt and freshly ground black pepper to taste
- Dash of Tabasco sauce
- ½ teaspoon prepared mustard, preferably Dijon
- 1 tablespoon lemon rind
- 1 pound fresh crabmeat, or 2 cans (6½ ounces each), picked over well
- ½ cup cooked rice
- 1 egg, beaten
- 1 tablespoon water

Melt the butter in a saucepan. Gradually add flour, stirring until smooth. Add the clam juice and milk, and cook until the mixture is thick and smooth.

Add the brandy, the salt and pepper to taste and the other seasonings. Simmer for 5 minutes.

Mix the sauce with the crabmeat and rice.

Remove the chilled pastry from the refrigerator and roll it out to ¼-inch thickness on a floured board or between waxed paper. Cut twelve 5-inch circles, using a saucer or can as a guide.

On one half of each circle, spread 3 or 4 tablespoons of filling. Turn the other half of the pastry over the filled portion making a crescent shape. Seal the edges with a fork.

(Continued)

(Continued)

Place the crabmeat pasties on baking sheet and chill.

Preheat oven to 375°F. Before baking, brush each pastry with the beaten egg, mixed with 1 tablespoon of water. Bake for 30 minutes or until golden.

NOTE: These crabmeat pasties can be made ahead, refrigerated, then reheated. When reheating, cover loosely with foil so they don't overbrown.

SALMON OR STRIPED BASS IN ASPIC

Serves 30

2 (seven or eight pounds each) salmon or striped bass, gutted and cleaned with heads and tails left on or 3 fish, five pounds each	Juice of 4 lemons Juice of 4 oranges Juice of 4 limes

Using two fish poachers, place the fish on the poaching trays and lower them into the poachers. Fill with water about two-thirds up the sides of the container. Remove the tray with the fish.

Add to each poacher the juices of 2 lemons, 2 oranges, and 2 limes.

Bring the liquid to a boil, reduce the heat, and lower the fish gently into the poachers. Maintain an even simmer; never boil. Partially cover the containers and simmer for 40 minutes for large fish, and 30 minutes for smaller fish. Test for doneness. Fish should be still firm but flaking when done.

Remove the fish from the liquid and let it stand at room temperature until cool.

Remove the top skin from the fish and place them on separate serving platters.

ASPIC:

2 quarts of strained fish stock plus clam juice to make up the difference 2 cups tomato juice 8 envelopes plain gelatin 4 egg shells, crushed 4 egg whites	¼ cup white wine Garnish: Cucumbers, thinly sliced DRESSING: 3 cups mayonnaise thinned slightly with cream and white wine

In a large saucepan, combine the fish stock, tomato juice, gelatin, egg shells, and egg whites.

Bring the liquid to a boil over medium heat, stirring, until it boils up. Remove from the heat and let the liquid settle. Bring to a boil a second time. Remove from the heat and add the wine.

Line a sieve with cheesecloth and pour the liquid through it into a bowl. Chill until the aspic is the consistency of egg whites. Spoon it over the poached fish.

Decorate the fish with thin slices of cucumber to resemble scales. Chill the fish.

Coat the fish with 3 layers of aspic, chilling between each application. Chill any leftover aspic.

Before serving, chop the remaining aspic and use it as garnish with sprays of dill and watercress leaves dipped in oil. Serve the fish with mayonnaise dressing.

STEAK AND KIDNEY PIE

Serves 10

- ½ pound veal kidneys
- 4 pounds lean beef, top round, or sirloin, cut into 1-inch cubes
- ½ cup flour
- ½ teaspoon ground mace
- 1 teaspoon salt
- Freshly ground black pepper
- 3 tablespoons butter
- 2 tablespoons oil
- 2 cups beef bouillon
- 1 cup Port wine
- 2 tablespoons Worcestershire sauce
- ½ pound mushrooms, sliced
- 3 hard-cooked eggs
- Basic pie pastry, 1 nine-inch crust (see recipe, page 207)
- Egg wash: 1 egg yolk beaten with 1 tablespoon water

Trim the kidneys, removing the membrane and fat. Cut them in half, remove the white membrane in the center, and dice.

Dredge the beef and kidneys in flour seasoned with mace, salt, and pepper.

Heat the butter and oil in a heavy skillet and sauté the meat and kidneys until they are brown on all sides. Remove them to a deep 3-quart baking dish. Choose a dish without a lip to make it easier to fit on the crust.

Pour the beef bouillon and Port into a skillet and bring it to a boil. Pour the liquid over the meat. Stir in the Worcestershire sauce. Add the mushrooms.

Cover the dish and bake in a 300°F. oven for 2 to 3 hours until the meat is very tender. If the gravy is too thin, thicken it with a beurre manié of 2 tablespoons of flour and 2 tablespoons of shortening. Cool.

Slice the hard-cooked eggs and place them in rows on top of the meat.

Roll out the pastry and place it over the top, gluing it to the edge of the dish with the egg wash. Cut out designs from the pastry trimmings, glue them to the crust with egg, and brush the entire top with egg wash.

(Continued)

(Continued)

Bake at 400°F. for 30 to 40 minutes until the pastry is golden and the dish is bubbling.

NOTE: This dish can be put together the day before it is needed and refrigerated. The flavor is best if it is baked just before serving or baked and kept warm on a hot tray.

LASAGNE VERDE BOLOGNESE

Serves 16

- 1 pound ground sausage
- 2 pounds lean ground beef
- 2 onions, chopped
- 1 cup tomato purée
- 1 teaspoon salt
- 1 tablespoon sugar
- ½ teaspoon ground nutmeg
- ¼ teaspoon ground cloves
- ¾ cup butter
- 12 tablespoons flour
- 6 cups milk
- Salt and freshly ground black pepper to taste
- Boiling salted water
- 1 pound green spinach lasagne, cooked until just tender
- 2 cups grated Parmesan cheese
- ¼ cup chopped parsley

Preheat oven to 375°F.

Brown the sausage in a skillet. Pour off the fat, and set the sausage aside.

Brown the ground beef. Add the onion and cook until the onion is soft. Stir in the tomato purée and the salt, sugar, nutmeg, and cloves. Cook over low heat for 15 minutes. Stir in the sausage.

Meanwhile, make a cream sauce with the butter, flour, and milk. Season the sauce to taste with salt and pepper.

In boiling salted water, cook the lasagne noodles until they are just "al dente."

Arrange the cooked lasagne across the bottoms of two 9- × 12-inch baking dishes. Alternate with a layer of meat sauce, cream sauce, and grated cheese, making two layers in each dish. Sprinkle the top layer with parsley.

Bake the lasagne for 20 to 30 minutes until it is bubbling.

NOTE: This lasagne can be assembled and baked in advance. It freezes nicely.

ENTRÉES / 139

STUFFED CABBAGE

Serves 20

40 large cabbage leaves
4 cups cooked rice
4 pounds (total weight) beef, veal, and pork, ground together
3 onions, grated
2 tablespoons Worcestershire sauce
2 eggs
Salt and freshly ground black pepper to taste
Bacon fat or butter
6 cups tomato sauce
Juice of 1 lemon
2 tablespoons sugar
1 tablespoon instant coffee
12 gingersnaps, crushed

Preheat oven to 350°F.

Place the cabbage leaves in a large bowl and pour boiling water over them. Let them stand for 5 minutes until they wilt. Pat the leaves dry.

Mix together the rice, meat, onion, Worcestershire sauce, eggs, salt, and pepper.

Place some of the mixture on each leaf. Roll up each leaf, tucking in the sides to make a neat package. Secure the rolls with a toothpick or tie with a string.

Brown the rolls lightly in bacon fat or butter and place them in single layers in baking pans.

Combine the tomato sauce with the lemon juice, sugar, and instant coffee. Pour the sauce over the rolls and cover the pans with foil.

Bake for 1 hour. Remove the rolls to serving dishes.

Add the crushed gingersnaps to the tomato sauce in the pans and blend well. Pour the sauce over the rolls. Refrigerate the stuffed cabbage until ready to reheat and serve.

ROAST VEAL WITH APPLES IN ORANGE SAUCE

Serves 10 to 12

4 tablespoons butter
1 tablespoon oil
1 large stalk celery, chopped
1 apple, peeled and diced
2 shallots, minced
Salt and freshly ground black pepper to taste
1 teaspoon ground ginger
1 five- to six-pound veal roast
2 tablespoons brandy
2 cups chicken bouillon
1 cup dry white wine
2 tablespoons cider vinegar
1 tablespoon arrowroot
3 tablespoons orange liqueur
Garnish: 2 navel oranges peeled and sliced
Watercress

(Continued)

(Continued)

Heat 2 tablespoons of butter and 1 tablespoon of oil in a large skillet. Add the celery, apple, and shallots and sauté them until they are soft. Place them in a deep casserole.

Rub the salt, pepper, and ginger into the veal roast. Brown the roast on all sides in the fat remaining in the skillet. Add more fat if necessary. Heat the brandy, pour it over the veal in the skillet and set it aflame. Put the veal on top of the vegetables in the casserole.

Pour the chicken bouillon into the skillet and bring it to a boil, scraping up browned bits from the bottom of the pan. Pour it over the veal. Pour the wine and vinegar into the casserole.

Cover and bake the roast at 325°F. for 15 minutes per pound or until it is tender all through. Remove the veal to a serving platter.

Put the contents of the casserole into a blender or food processor and purée. Pour it into a saucepan and bring it to a boil over high heat. Boil until the liquid is reduced to 2 cups. Dissolve the arrowroot in the orange liqueur and stir it into the hot sauce. Cook, stirring, until it is thickened.

Melt the remaining butter and sauté the orange slices until they are glazed.

Slice the veal roast and arrange the slices in overlapping rows on a serving platter. Cover the veal with sauce and garnish the platter with the glazed orange slices and watercress.

NOTE: This dish may be prepared ahead and reheated, before slicing and garnishing it.

VEAL RAGOÛT

Serves 10

- 6 tablespoons bacon fat
- 5 pounds veal for stew, well trimmed of fat, cut into 1-inch cubes
- 2 tablespoons butter
- 2 large onions, chopped
- 3 (ten ounces each) cans cream of mushroom soup
- ½ cup white wine
- 1 cup heavy cream
- 1 cup sour cream
- Salt and freshly ground black pepper to taste
- 1½ pounds mushrooms
- 6 tablespoons butter
- 2 tablespoons chopped parsley

Preheat oven to 300°F.

Heat the bacon fat in a large heavy skillet. Add the veal, turning the pieces until they are browned on all sides. Do not put too many pieces in the pan at once or the veal will stew without browning. Remove the browned pieces to a large casserole.

When all veal is browned, add 2 tablespoons of butter to the skillet. Cook the onions, stirring, until they are soft, about 10 minutes.

Add the cream of mushroom soup and the wine to the skillet and cook, stirring, until the soup is liquid and smooth. Add the cream and sour cream to the soup and cook until the mixture is well blended. Season to taste with salt and pepper.

Pour the sauce over the veal in the casserole. Cover the casserole and bake it in the oven for 2 hours.

Remove the stems from the mushrooms and wipe the caps clean.

Just before serving, melt 6 tablespoons of butter in a large skillet. Sauté the mushroom caps over high heat for about 5 minutes until they are just golden but not soft.

To serve the veal ragoût, arrange mushroom caps on top of the stew and sprinkle it with parsley.

NOTE: This stew can be made a day in advance. To serve, reheat in a 325°F. oven for 30 to 40 minutes.

VEAL AND CARROT ROULADE

Serves 10

- 2 one-pound chicken breasts, uncooked, skinned and boned
- 1 pound uncooked ground veal
- 2 eggs
- ½ cup fine bread crumbs
- 1 small onion, minced
- 2 teaspoons prepared mustard, preferably Dijon
- 2 teaspoons salt
- Freshly ground black pepper to taste
- 1½ pounds carrots
- Water
- 2 teaspoons sugar
- 1 teaspoon freshly ground nutmeg
- 3 tablespoons finely chopped parsley
- ¼ cup melted butter
- 1 tablespoon lemon juice
- Garnish: 1 cup seedless grapes

Preheat oven to 350°F.

Grind the chicken breasts in a food processor.

In a large bowl mix together the ground chicken and veal, the eggs, bread crumbs, and the minced onion. Blend in the mustard, 1 teaspoon of salt and freshly ground black pepper to taste.

Divide the meat mixture in half. Place each half on a piece of waxed paper and pat or roll each portion into a rectangle.

Wash and scrape the carrots, then dice them. Cook them in a saucepan of boiling salted water until they are tender. Drain well. Purée the

(Continued)

(Continued)

carrots in a blender or food processor, a portion at a time. If the carrots are too moist, dry them out in a saucepan over low heat.

Mix the puréed carrots with the sugar, the remaining teaspoon of salt, pepper, nutmeg, and parsley. Spread half of the carrot mixture over each rectangle of meat.

Starting on the long sides, lift the waxed paper and carefully roll up the meat. Roll the roulades onto buttered baking sheets.

Bake for 45 minutes. Cool.

Cut the roulades into 1-inch slices and arrange them on a serving platter. Garnish with grapes.

NOTE: This dish can be prepared a day ahead and the unsliced roulades refrigerated until needed. To reheat, place them on a baking sheet and pour the melted butter and lemon juice over the roulades. Cover them loosely with foil. Bake at 325°F. for 35 to 40 minutes until hot.

BUTTERFLIED LEG OF LAMB

Serves 8

- 3 cups dry white wine
- 1 cup vegetable oil
- 1 onion, chopped
- 1 clove garlic
- ½ cup chopped parsley
- 1 bunch fresh dill
- 1 teaspoon salt
- Freshly ground black pepper
- 1 (seven- to eight-pound) leg of lamb, boned and butterflied

Combine the wine, oil, onion, garlic, herbs, and seasonings in a blender or food processor. Blend well.

Place the lamb leg in a shallow, non-aluminum container, and pour the marinade over it. Let the lamb stand for 24 hours in the refrigerator. Turn the meat occasionally. If desired, the lamb can be put into a large plastic bag with marinade, and frozen for future use.

Have ready a grill whose coals are gray, not red. Dry the lamb and place it over the coals about 5 to 6 inches above the heat.

Grill the meat about 12 minutes on each side for pink meat, basting it often with the marinade.

To serve, slice the meat thin.

ENTRÉES / 143

SAUSAGES IN WHITE WINE

Serves 16

36 bratwurst or veal sausages
Water
4 tablespoons butter
Seasoned flour
3 cups dry white wine

In a large skillet put as many sausages as will lie flat in one layer. Fill the skillet halfway up with water.

Cover and cook the sausages at a simmer for 15 minutes. Do not boil or the sausages will split. Remove them to paper towels and repeat with the remaining sausages.

Drain the skillet, add butter and heat it to bubbling. Roll the sausages in the seasoned flour and brown them on all sides. Remove them to a chafing dish.

Add the wine to the skillet and bring it to a boil, scraping up the brown bits from the bottom of the pan. Boil for 5 minutes until the wine is slightly reduced.

Pour the wine over the sausages and keep them warm in a chafing dish over a pan of boiling water which is placed over a flame. If 1 chafing dish will not accommodate all the sausages, use 2 or put the remainder in a baking dish.

Serve this dish with good mustards.

PORK AND SAUSAGE CASSEROLE

Serves 10

2 tablespoons butter
2 tablespoons oil
3 pounds lean pork, cut into 1-inch cubes
1 pound smoked sausage, cut into 1¼-inch slices (kielbasi type)
1 cup chopped onion
1 clove garlic, minced
1 bottle stout or dark ale
2 cups plum tomatoes, drained
Salt and freshly ground black pepper
2 tablespoons chopped parsley
2 bay leaves
2 one-pound cans pinto beans
Garnish: Finely chopped parsley

Preheat oven to 350°F.

Heat the butter and oil in a large skillet. Sauté the pork cubes and sausage pieces until they are browned on all sides. Remove them to a deep 4-quart casserole.

If necessary, add more fat to the skillet and sauté the onion and garlic until they are soft.

(Continued)

(Continued)

Pour the stout into the skillet and bring it to a boil. Pour it over the meat. Add the tomatoes to the dish, breaking them up with a fork. Season the casserole with salt and pepper and add the parsley and bay leaves.

Rinse the pinto beans under cold water in a colander, then add them to casserole, stirring them in.

Cover and bake the casserole for 1 hour or until the pork is tender. Sprinkle with additional chopped parsley before serving.

NOTE: This dish can be made in advance and reheated. The casserole also can be frozen without the beans, which should be added after it has thawed and is being reheated.

PORK OLIVES WITH YAMS AND FRUIT SAUCE

Serves 6

- 2 pounds boneless pork loin
- 1 teaspoon ground ginger
- 2-3 tablespoons orange juice or orange liqueur
- Grated rind of 1 orange
- 2 tablespoons melted butter
- 1 cup cooked mashed yams
- Salt and freshly ground black pepper to taste
- ½ cup flour seasoned with salt and pepper
- 2 tablespoons butter
- 1 tablespoon oil
- 3 tablespoons brandy
- 1 cup apple cider
- ½ cup chicken bouillon
- 1 cup sugar
- 1½ cups red wine
- 2 cups cranberries
- 1 tablespoon cornstarch or arrowroot mixed with 1 tablespoon water
- Garnish: Lemon slices
- Finely chopped parsley

Cut the pork into slices ¼ inch thick. Pound each slice between waxed paper until it is ⅛ inch thick.

Beat the ginger, orange juice and rind, and melted butter into the yams. Season with salt and pepper to taste. The mixture should be fairly thick.

Spread the yam mixture onto the pork slices, roll up the slices, and tie them. Dredge the pork rolls in the seasoned flour. Heat the butter and oil in a large skillet and brown the pork rolls.

Heat the brandy and flame the pork rolls. Add the cider and chicken bouillon to the skillet. Cover and simmer for 45 minutes until the pork is tender.

Meanwhile, put the sugar and wine into a saucepan and bring to a boil. Add the cranberries and cook them until they pop. Remove the cranberries from the liquid.

Remove the pork and cut off the strings. Place the rolls on a serving platter.

Add the wine from the cranberries to the liquid in the skillet and bring it to a boil. Boil until it is reduced to 2 cups. Stir in the cornstarch mixture and cook until the sauce is thick and smooth. If mixture is not thick enough, add more cornstarch.

Pour the sauce over the pork rolls and garnish them with the cooked cranberries.

With a lemon stripper, cut strips of peel off the lemon from top to bottom, so that the lemon slices will have a notched effect. Arrange around platter and sprinkle parsley over everything.

COUNTRY CAPTAIN

Serves 6 to 8

- ½ cup flour
- 1 teaspoon salt
- Freshly ground black pepper
- 2 three-pound frying chickens, cut into serving pieces
- 3 tablespoons butter
- 1 tablespoon oil
- 3 onions, chopped
- 2 green peppers, chopped
- 2 cloves garlic, minced
- 2 teaspoons curry powder
- 1 teaspoon dried thyme
- 2 tablespoons chopped parsley
- 3 cups canned Italian plum tomatoes
- ½ cup raisins
- ½ cup slivered almonds

Preheat oven to 300°F.

Combine the flour, salt, and pepper. Dredge the chicken pieces in the seasoned flour.

Heat the butter and oil in a large skillet and brown the chicken on all sides. Remove the chicken to baking dishes.

Sauté the onions, peppers, and garlic in the skillet, adding more fat if necessary. When the vegetables are soft, stir in the curry powder. Cook for 2 minutes. Stir in the thyme and parsley. Add the tomatoes. Bring the sauce to a boil and pour it over the chicken.

Cover the baking dishes and bake for 1½ hours. Add the raisins 15 minutes before the chicken is done. Sprinkle the chicken with the slivered almonds just before serving.

CHICKEN MARENGO

Serves 8

- 10 puff pastry fleurons (see recipe, page 207)
- 1 frying chicken, cut into 8 pieces
- 1 whole chicken breast, split and cut into 4 pieces
- 3 tablespoons butter
- 1 tablespoon oil
- Salt and freshly ground black pepper to taste
- 1 clove garlic, minced
- 2 sprigs parsley
- 1 bay leaf
- ½ teaspoon dried thyme
- ¼ cup brandy
- 1 cup chicken bouillon
- ¼ cup tomato paste
- 12 uncooked shrimp, shelled and deveined
- 12 mushroom caps

Make the fleurons.

Wash and dry the chicken pieces. Heat the oil and butter in a large skillet and sauté the chicken until it is brown on all sides. Season it with salt and pepper and add the herbs. Add the brandy and chicken bouillon.

Cover and simmer for 40 minutes, until the chicken is tender. Remove the chicken to a serving platter and keep it warm.

Bring the liquid in the skillet to a boil. Add the tomato paste and boil until it is slightly reduced. Add the shrimp, then turn off the heat. Let the sauce stand for 5 minutes until the shrimp are pink and firm.

Meanwhile, sauté the mushroom caps quickly until they are browned but firm.

Garnish the chicken with shrimp, mushrooms, and fleurons. Pour sauce over all.

NOTE: This dish is better when made a day ahead.

CHICKEN KIEV

Serves 8

- 6 whole chicken breasts, halved, skinned, and boned
- Brandy
- ¾ cup cold butter (1½ sticks)
- 2 tablespoons chopped chives
- 1 tablespoon fresh tarragon or 1 teaspoon dried tarragon
- Salt and freshly ground black pepper
- 1 cup flour
- 2 eggs, beaten
- 1–1½ cups bread crumbs
- 1 pound vegetable shortening

Pound the chicken breasts between sheets of waxed paper until they are thin. Brush each half breast with brandy.

Cut the butter into 12 fingers. Place 1 finger in the center of each breast and sprinkle it with ½ teaspoon chives, ¼ teaspoon tarragon, salt, and pepper. Roll up the breast, tucking in the sides. Make neat packages with the butter completely enclosed.

Dip each roll first in the flour, then in the beaten eggs and crumbs. Place them on a baking sheet and refrigerate for at least 1 hour.

To cook, heat the shortening to 375°F. at a depth of 1 to 1½ inches. If you do not have an electric french fry machine, use an electric skillet as it is essential to keep the temperature even. Fry the chicken rolls about 4 minutes on each side.

Place them on a heated platter, garnished with watercress.

NOTE: Serve this dish as soon as possible. The Chicken Kiev will stay warm in a low oven for 15 minutes without the butter seeping out.

CHICKEN BREASTS DUXELLES

Serves 40

- 4 pounds mushrooms
- 16 large shallots
- 2 cups butter
- 1 cup flour
- Heavy cream
- 30 whole chicken breasts, boned and skinned
- Salt and freshly ground black pepper to taste
- Lemon juice
- Sauce Suprême (recipe follows)
- Garnish: 60 mushroom caps, sautéed

Wipe the mushrooms with a damp towel. Peel the shallots, put them into the container of a food processor, and chop fine. Remove them to a bowl.

Chop the mushrooms, 8 to 10 at a time, in a food processor using a metal blade. Remove the mushrooms to a bowl. Mix them with the shallots.

In a large skillet melt ½ cup butter. Add about one quarter of the mushroom-shallot mixture. Sauté until the ingredients are dark in color and the moisture has evaporated. Sprinkle with ¼ cup flour and cook 2 to 3 minutes longer.

Add enough cream to make a thick mixture. Cook another 2 to 3 minutes. Remove to a bowl and continue this process with the remaining ingredients.

Split the chicken breasts in half and pound them between sheets of waxed paper until they are thin and flat.

Spread each half breast with 1 to 1½ tablespoons of the mushroom mixture. Roll up the breast, tucking in the sides. No skewer is necessary to keep it rolled.

Place the rolled breasts in a single layer in baking pans. Sprinkle the

(Continued)

(Continued)

breasts slightly with salt, pepper, and lemon juice (1 tablespoon to every 8 half-breasts). Cover the pan tightly with foil.

Bake at 425°F. for 20 minutes until breasts are opaque and no longer pink. Remove the chicken breasts to ovenproof serving platters or casseroles.

Pour the liquid from the pans into a measuring cup and prepare the Sauce Suprême.

SAUCE SUPRÊME:

- 1 cup butter
- 1½ cups flour
- 4 cups of liquid from pans plus chicken bouillon, if necessary
- 3 cups light cream
- 1 cup dry white wine
- 2 tablespoons brandy
- Salt and freshly ground white pepper to taste

Melt the butter in a deep heavy saucepan. Add the flour and heat, stirring the mixture with a whisk until it is smooth and bubbling.

Pour in the broth, cream, and wine. Bring the sauce to a boil, stirring, and cook until it is thick and smooth. Add the brandy and cook for 2 to 3 minutes.

Taste and, if sauce is harsh in flavor, add a little more cream and cook over low heat 5 to 10 minutes longer. Season to taste with salt and white pepper.

Spoon the sauce over the chicken breasts.

Just before serving, garnish the chicken with mushroom caps that have been very quickly sautéed in hot butter. Arrange bunches of watercress that have been sprinkled with oil at either end of the baking dishes.

NOTE: Casseroles can stand at room temperature for 1 hour, then be reheated at 325°F. The mushrooms cannot stand long or they will become limp.

TURBAN OF CHICKEN WITH WATERCRESS SAUCE

Serves 6

- 7 chicken breast halves, skinned and boned
- Butter
- 2 egg whites
- ½ cup heavy cream
- 1 teaspoon salt
- Freshly ground black pepper
- ½ teaspoon ground nutmeg
- ¼ pound prosciutto ham in one piece
- 20 whole pistachio nuts, shelled
- 12 whole mushrooms
- Watercress Sauce (recipe follows)

Pound 4 of the chicken breast halves between sheets of waxed paper until thin. Butter a 5- to 6-cup ring mold and line it with the flattened chicken, completely covering the inside of the mold.

Put the 3 remaining chicken breast halves in a food processor with a metal blade. Process until the meat is finely ground. Add the egg whites, cream, and seasonings. Process until the mixture is smooth.

Place half of the mixture into the lined ring mold.

Dice the ham into ¼-inch pieces. Sprinkle the nuts and diced ham over the chicken mixture.

Pile the mold lightly with remaining chicken mixture. The mixture will not come to the top, but it will expand. Cover with foil.

Place the mold in a pan of hot water. Bake at 350°F. for 40 minutes.

Remove the mold from the water and let it stand for 5 minutes. Pour off excess liquid from the mold. Turn it out onto a serving platter. Pour some of the Watercress Sauce over the ring and serve the remaining sauce in a sauceboat. If desired, garnish the ring with puff pastry fleurons.

Wash the mushrooms, remove the stems and sauté the caps in butter. Fill the center of the mold with sautéed mushroom caps.

NOTE: Ring may be made ahead and reheated, loosely covered with foil. Triple this recipe to serve 20.

WATERCRESS SAUCE:
- 3 tablespoons butter
- 3 tablespoons flour
- 1 cup chicken bouillon
- ½ cup milk
- ½ cup heavy cream
- 1 teaspoon brandy
- Salt and freshly ground black pepper to taste
- 1 cup chopped watercress leaves

Melt the butter in a saucepan. Add the flour, stirring constantly, until the mixture is bubbly, add the chicken bouillon and milk. Cook, stirring, until the sauce is thick and smooth.

Add the cream. Reduce the heat to simmer and cook for 15 minutes. Add the brandy and seasonings. Stir in the watercress leaves.

NOTE: Double this recipe for 3 turbans.

POULET VERT

Serves 30

- 25 whole chicken breasts, split, skinned, and boned
- ½ cup lemon juice
- Salt
- 1 one-pound bag fresh spinach
- 4 bunches watercress
- 1 bunch parsley
- ¾ cup tarragon vinegar
- 2 flat anchovy fillets
- ¾ cup oil
- ¾ cup sour cream
- 3 cups mayonnaise
- Garnish: Cherry tomatoes

(Continued)

(Continued)

Remove pieces of fat from the chicken breasts and wash them. Place the chicken in one layer in baking pans. Sprinkle with lemon juice and with salt lightly. Cover the pans tightly with foil.

Place them in a preheated 425°F. oven and bake for 15 minutes. If the breasts are done, they will be opaque with no pinkness and will be springy to the touch. Remove the pans from the oven and cool.

Meanwhile, remove the stems from the spinach, watercress, and parsley. Put all the remaining ingredients, including the greens, into the container of a blender or food processor and blend well. This will have to be done in 2 or 3 batches. Do not process too long or the sauce will be too liquid.

Arrange the chicken breasts on platters and spoon the sauce over them. Chill, covered with plastic wrap. Serve at room temperature garnished with cherry tomatoes.

CHICKEN FLORENTINE

Serves 10

- 4 whole chicken breasts (1 pound each), skinned and boned
- ½ teaspoon salt
- 1 tablespoon lemon juice
- 4 (ten-ounces each) packages frozen chopped spinach
- ½ pound noodles, medium-width
- 1½ cups canned tomato sauce
- 3 tablespoons chopped chives
- 4 tablespoons butter
- 4 tablespoons flour
- 2 cups canned chicken broth
- 1 cup heavy or medium cream
- ½ teaspoon salt
- Freshly ground black pepper to taste
- ½ teaspoon ground nutmeg
- ¼ cup grated Parmesan cheese

Preheat oven to 425°F.

Place the chicken in a baking pan and sprinkle with the salt and lemon juice. Cover the pan tightly with foil. Bake for 25 minutes.

When the chicken is cool, cut it with a scissors into 1½-inch pieces.

Cook the spinach according to the package directions. Drain it well in a colander and squeeze it dry with the hands.

Cook the noodles according to the package directions. Drain them in colander and rinse them under hot water. Place the noodles in a bowl and mix in the tomato sauce and chives.

In a saucepan melt the butter over low heat and add the flour, stirring with a whisk, until they are bubbling. Pour in the chicken broth. Cook, stirring, until the sauce is thick and smooth. Add the cream. Reduce the heat and simmer for 10 minutes longer. Season the cream sauce with salt, pepper, and nutmeg. Mix ½ cup of cream sauce into the spinach.

ENTRÉES / 151

To assemble the Chicken Florentine, butter a 9- × 12-inch baking dish and spread the creamed spinach over the bottom. Cover the spinach with noodles in tomato sauce. Place the chicken pieces on top and pour the remaining cream sauce over all. Sprinkle the top with the Parmesan cheese.

Bake the casserole in a 350°F. oven for 45 minutes until it is hot.

NOTE: The casserole can be assembled and frozen before baking. To serve, thaw it completely before putting it in the oven.

CHICKEN MARSALA

Serves 4

- 1 tablespoon butter
- 1 tablespoon vegetable oil
- 1 clove garlic, minced
- 2 shallots, minced
- 4 half chicken breasts, skinned, boned, and with fat removed
- ½ cup Marsala wine
- Salt and freshly ground black pepper to taste

Heat the butter and oil in a skillet. Add the garlic and shallots and sauté them for 2 minutes.

Add the chicken breasts, season with salt and pepper, and sauté them for 2 minutes on each side, until the breasts turn color. Add the Marsala.

Cover the pan, reduce the heat, and cook for 10 minutes, or until the chicken is done. Remove the chicken to a warm serving platter.

Raise the heat under the liquid and boil until it is reduced and syrupy. Pour the sauce over the chicken.

TARRAGON CHICKEN WITH ARTICHOKES

Serves 8

- 2 (ten ounces each) packages frozen artichoke hearts
- 2 cups dry white wine
- 6 whole chicken breasts, 1 pound each, skinned and boned
- 4 cups chicken bouillon
- 2 teaspoons salt
- ½ teaspoon dried tarragon
- 4 sprigs parsley
- 3 stalks celery with leaves, cut in half
- 1 leek, cleaned and tops split from the bulb
- 2 tablespoons tarragon vinegar
- 4 tablespoons butter
- ½ cup minced onion
- ½ cup flour

(Continued)

(Continued)

1½ cups heavy cream	Juice of 1 lemon
Salt and freshly ground black pepper to taste	½ pound mushroom caps
	4 tablespoons minced parsley
3 egg yolks	

Cook the frozen artichokes according to package directions until they are barely tender, about 5 minutes. Drain the artichokes and place them in a bowl with the wine. Let them stand for 2 hours or longer at room temperature.

Cut the chicken breasts into 1-inch pieces.

Combine the chicken with the bouillon, salt, herbs, celery and leek tops, and vinegar in a saucepan. Cover the pan and simmer until the meat is tender, about 35 minutes.

Drain the chicken and keep it warm. Reserve the liquid, strain it, and boil it down until it is reduced to 2 cups. Set aside.

Mince the white part of the leek and combine it in a saucepan with the butter and minced onion. Cook the vegetables until they are soft. Stir in the flour and cook until the ingredients are smooth. Add the reserved broth and the cream. Cook, stirring, until the sauce is smooth. Season to taste with salt and pepper.

Drain the artichoke hearts and reserve the wine.

Beat the egg yolks into the wine and add the lemon juice. Stir the mixture into the sauce over low heat.

Sauté the mushroom caps.

To serve, place the chicken in the center of a deep, ovenproof dish. Arrange the artichokes and sautéed mushroom caps around the chicken. Pour about half the sauce over the chicken. Sprinkle the dish with parsley. Serve remaining sauce separately.

CHICKEN HASH À LA RITZ

Serves 24

2 green peppers, chopped	4 tablespoons chopped parsley
4 tablespoons butter	4 cups béchamel sauce (see recipe, page 180)
16 cups cooked, skinned, boned, and chopped chicken	½ pound bacon, cooked and crumbled
2 tablespoons chopped chives	Buttered toast

Sauté the green pepper in butter until it is soft. Combine it with the cooked chicken. Mix in the chives and parsley. Fold in the béchamel sauce.

Turn the chicken mixture into 2 or 3 shallow baking dishes. Sprinkle the tops with crumbled bacon.

Heat the dishes at 350°F. for 20 minutes. Serve with triangles of buttered toast.

NOTE: This dish can be made ahead and reheated in a 325°F. oven for 30 minutes before serving.

CHICKEN AND OYSTER PIE

Serves 6 to 8

- 1 cup oyster liquor and chicken bouillon
- ½ cup light cream
- 2 tablespoons chopped parsley
- 1 tablespoon butter
- 3 hard-cooked egg yolks
- ½ cup bread crumbs
- 3 tablespoons dry sherry
- ½ teaspoon salt
- Freshly ground black pepper
- ½ teaspoon ground nutmeg
- 1 pint shucked oysters
- 2 cups diced cooked chicken
- 1 egg white
- Egg wash: 1 egg yolk beaten with 1 tablespoon water
- Pastry for one 9-inch top crust (use basic pie crust or puff pastry)

Preheat oven 375°F.

Put the oyster liquor mixed with the chicken bouillon to make 1 cup, cream, parsley, and butter into a saucepan and bring to a boil. Remove from the heat.

Mash the egg yolks with the crumbs and sherry in a bowl. This also can be done in a food processor. Stir the egg mixture slowly into the hot liquid. Return it to the heat and cook until it is thickened. Season with salt, pepper, and nutmeg.

Place the oysters and cooked chicken into a 9-inch pie dish. Pour the liquid mixture over all. Cool.

Fit the pastry crust over the top of the dish, making a fluted edge with your fingers or a fork. Use pastry trimmings to make decorative cutout shapes. Glue the cutouts on the pie crust with the egg white. Brush the entire top crust with the egg wash.

Place the pie dish on a baking sheet. Bake for 30 minutes until the crust is brown and the interior is bubbling.

NOTE: You can double this recipe and make 2 pies to serve 12. The pie can be made a day ahead and reheated.

STUFFED CHICKEN DRUMSTICKS

Serves 8 to 10

8–10 chicken drumsticks, uncooked
½ pound seasoned sausage meat
2 slices whole wheat bread
1 egg
2 tablespoons chopped parsley
Salt and freshly ground black pepper to taste
Oil
Paprika

Slit the uncooked drumsticks down one side and remove the bone by scraping the meat away from the bone. Lay the meat flat and pound until the skin covers the meat evenly.

Sauté the sausage meat until it is no longer pink. Place the sausage meat in the container of a food processor. Add the bread slices and egg. Process with a metal blade until the mixture is smooth. Add the parsley. Mix in the salt and pepper.

Spread the filling equally over the flattened meat of the drumsticks. With a needle and thread sew drumsticks into their original shape, skin side out, tucking in the sides.

Brush each drumstick with oil and place it in an oiled baking pan. Sprinkle the drumsticks with paprika.

Bake at 350°F. for 40 minutes until the drumsticks are golden. Drain them on paper towels. Chill.

Serve at room temperature.

GAME HENS WITH GINGER SAUCE

Serves 10

10 game hens, fresh if possible
¼ cup melted butter
2 tablespoons oil
1½ cups orange juice
1½ cups Port wine
¾ cup ginger marmalade
Grated rind of 2 oranges
1 cup heavy cream
1 teaspoon salt
1 teaspoon paprika
Garnish: Orange sections
Watercress

Split the game hens lengthwise. Place them flat on baking sheets, skin side down. Combine the melted butter and oil and brush over the hens. Broil until they are golden.

Turn the hens, brush again with the butter-oil mixture and broil until golden.

Combine the orange juice, Port wine, marmalade, and orange rind to make a sauce. Heat the mixture, stirring occasionally, until the marmalade is melted. Continue to cook the sauce until it is thickened slightly. Add the cream and seasonings and bring the sauce to a boil. Cook for 2 to 3 minutes.

Place the broiled game hens in baking dishes. Pour the sauce over them. Cover and bake for 30 minutes.

Serve the game hens garnished with orange sections and watercress.

EGGS MOLLET FLORENTINE

Serves 14

Water
16 large eggs, at room temperature
5 (ten ounces each) packages frozen leaf spinach
¼ cup butter
4 tablespoons flour
1 cup chicken bouillon
½ cup milk
½ cup cream
Salt and freshly ground black pepper
1 tablespoon grated onion
1 teaspoon ground nutmeg
1 cup grated Gruyère cheese

Bring a large pan of water to a rolling boil. Gently lower the eggs into the water. If you have a lettuce basket, put the eggs in it and place the basket in the pan of boiling water. Lower the heat and simmer the eggs for exactly 6 minutes.

Drain, then submerge the eggs in cold water for 8 minutes. Remove them and crack their shells all over. Peel and set the eggs aside.

Cook the spinach according to instructions on the package. Drain, squeeze dry, then chop the spinach.

Melt the butter in a saucepan and add the flour, stirring constantly until they are well blended. Add the chicken bouillon and the milk. Cook, stirring, until the mixture is smooth and thickened. Stir in the cream. Cook the cream sauce over low heat for 10 minutes. Season the sauce with the salt, pepper, grated onion, and nutmeg. Stir ½ cup of the grated cheese into the sauce.

Mix the cream sauce into the spinach. Spread the creamed spinach over the bottom of a greased 9- × 13-inch baking dish. (The dish should be oval or rectangular and not too deep.) Arrange the whole eggs on top, pushing them down slightly into the spinach. Sprinkle the remaining ½ cup of cheese over the eggs and spinach. Reheat the assembled dish at 325°F. for 20 minutes.

SIDE DISHES

BAKED GREEN NOODLES

Serves 20

Water
1½ pounds green noodles
1 cup melted butter
1½ cups cottage cheese
6 egg yolks
Salt and freshly ground black pepper to taste
1½ cups heavy cream, whipped
1 cup buttered bread crumbs*

Preheat oven to 350°F.

Cook the noodles in a large amount of boiling salted water until they are just tender. Drain.

Put the butter, cottage cheese, and egg yolks into a blender. Blend until smooth.

Combine the noodles with the egg mixture and season to taste with salt and pepper. Fold in the whipped cream. Turn the noodles into 2 large baking dishes and sprinkle them with bread crumbs.

Bake for 20 to 30 minutes until hot.

NOTE: This casserole can be assembled ahead, refrigerated, then baked before serving.

NOODLES IN GREEN SAUCE

Serves 10

1 pound noodles, medium width
¼ small onion, chopped
2 tablespoons drained capers
2 cloves garlic
1 anchovy fillet
2 cups snipped parsley
2 teaspoons fresh basil or ½ teaspoon dried basil
⅔ cup olive oil
2 tablespoons lemon juice
1 teaspoon salt
Freshly ground black pepper to taste

Cook the noodles according to the package directions. Drain them in a colander and rinse well under lukewarm water.

While the noodles are cooking, put all the remaining ingredients into the container of a blender or food processor. Blend until the mixture is smooth.

In a large bowl toss the noodles with the sauce. Let them stand for 2 to 3 hours at room temperature.

---

*Butter 2 slices of bread. Grate them in a food processor.

MACARONI WITH THREE CHEESES

Serves 10

- 6 tablespoons butter
- ½ cup minced onion
- 6 tablespoons flour
- 2 cups heavy cream
- 1 cup white wine
- Salt and freshly ground black pepper to taste
- 1 cup ricotta cheese
- 1 cup grated Gruyère cheese
- 1 pound macaroni, cooked and drained
- 1 cup grated Parmesan cheese

Melt the butter and sauté the onion until it is soft but not browned. Sprinkle the flour over the onion and cook for 3 minutes longer.

Add the cream and wine and cook, stirring, until the sauce is thick and smooth. Season with salt and pepper to taste. Stir in the ricotta, Gruyère, and ½ cup of Parmesan cheese.

Combine the cheese mixture with the macaroni and turn it all into a 3-quart baking dish. Sprinkle the remaining Parmesan cheese over the top.

Bake the casserole at 350°F. for 30 minutes until it is bubbling.

NOTE: This dish can be prepared in the morning of the day it is needed and baked before serving.

RICE PILAF

Serves 16

- 1½ cups butter
- 1½ cups thin vermicelli noodles, broken into small pieces
- 6 cups white rice
- 2 teaspoons salt
- Freshly ground black pepper to taste
- 12 cups water or beef or chicken bouillon

It is best to cook this recipe in 2 pans. Melt half the butter in each pan and divide each of the following steps between the two pans.

Brown the vermicelli in the melted butter, being careful not to overbrown it.

(Continued)

(Continued)

Add the rice. Cook until the rice is opaque. Season the pasta and rice with salt and pepper.

Add the water or bouillon. Bring to a boil. Reduce the heat and simmer, covered, for 30 minutes. If the water has been absorbed, remove the pans from the heat and fluff the pilaf with a fork. If the liquid is not yet absorbed, cook until the mixture is dry.

NOTE: To reheat, turn the pilaf into 2 large baking dishes. Cover loosely and place them in a 300°F. oven.

BAKED RICE WITH VEGETABLES

Serves 40

½ cup butter
5 cups long grain rice
10 cups chicken bouillon
Salt
3 cups chopped celery
2 cups chopped green pepper
2 cups chopped red pepper
2 cups chopped black olives
Freshly ground black pepper to taste

Preheat oven to 350°F.

Melt the butter in a large skillet and sauté the rice until opaque, about 5 minutes. Stir to coat all the grains. Turn the rice into baking dishes.

Heat the bouillon and pour it over the rice. Sprinkle the rice with salt.

Cover the baking dishes tightly and bake for 40 minutes, or until the rice is tender and all the liquid is absorbed.

Meanwhile, steam the celery and peppers over hot water until they are just tender, but still crunchy.

When the rice is done, fluff it with a fork and stir in the steamed vegetables and chopped olives. Season the pilaf with salt and pepper.

NOTE: This dish can be made a day ahead. To reheat, pour a little broth into each dish to moisten it and place in a 325°F. oven for 30 minutes, uncovered. Check to make sure the rice is not drying out.

RICE WITH RAISINS AND PINE NUTS

Serves 10

⅓ cup chicken bouillon
1 cup golden raisins
Water
½ cup butter
½ cup pine nuts
6 cups cooked rice

Heat the chicken bouillon in a saucepan.

In a small bowl, soak the raisins in water to cover them for 15 minutes, then drain and set them aside.

Melt 2 tablespoons butter in a large skillet or saucepan and sauté the pine nuts for 5 minutes.

Add the remaining butter, the cooked rice, and raisins. Stir them all together and simmer for 10 minutes.

Turn the pilaf into a warm serving dish.

NOTE: This dish can be kept warm in a low oven, loosely covered.

BROWN RICE WITH ALMONDS

Serves 10 to 12

¼ cup butter
¼ cup finely chopped onion
2 cups brown rice
5 cups chicken bouillon
Freshly ground black pepper to taste
1 cup slivered almonds

Preheat oven to 350°F.

Melt 2 tablespoons of butter in a heavy skillet. Sauté the onion until it is soft but not browned, about 7 minutes. Add the rice and sauté it, stirring, until the rice is opaque.

Turn the rice into a 2-quart baking dish. Pour in the chicken bouillon and add the pepper.

Cover the dish and bake for 45 minutes until the rice is tender and all the liquid is absorbed.

Five minutes before serving, stir in the slivered almonds and the remaining butter.

NOTE: This dish can be made ahead, including the addition of the almonds, and refrigerated. Reheat, loosely covered with foil. Add additional chicken bouillon if the rice is dry.

KASHA WITH MUSHROOMS

Serves 20

2 extra large eggs
3 cups kasha (bulgar wheat)
½ cup butter
Salt and freshly ground black pepper
6 cups chicken bouillon
2 pounds mushrooms, sliced
3 cups sour cream
2 cups cottage cheese
Finely chopped parsley

(Continued)

(Continued)

Break the eggs into a large skillet and beat them with a fork. Stir the kasha into the eggs and cook over medium heat, stirring, until the kasha grains are well coated with egg and beginning to take on a roasted appearance.

Stir in the butter and seasoning. Add the pepper liberally. Add the chicken bouillon. Cover the pan and cook over low heat until the kasha is tender and all the liquid absorbed, about 20 to 30 minutes.

Sauté the sliced mushrooms in butter very briefly until tender but firm.

Stir the sour cream, cottage cheese, and mushrooms into the kasha. Heat through but do not boil.

Turn the kasha into chafing dishes or baking dishes. Sprinkle with chopped parsley.

GNOCCHI

Serves 8

1½ cups water	½ cup butter
1½ cups milk	2 cups Parmesan cheese
Salt	3 eggs, well beaten
1 cup Cream of Wheat cereal	

Combine the water, milk, and 1 teaspoon of salt in a saucepan. Bring the liquid to a boil. Gradually stir in the Cream of Wheat. Cook it over medium heat, stirring constantly, until it is very thick.

Remove it from the heat and stir in half of the butter and ½ cup of Parmesan cheese. Stir in the beaten eggs, mixing well.

Spread the mixture ½ inch thick on a baking sheet. Smooth the top with a wet spatula. Chill it overnight.

With a 1- to 2-inch round cutter, cut the batter into circles. Arrange the circles in a buttered shallow baking dish in overlapping circles. Sprinkle them with butter and the remaining Parmesan cheese.

Bake the gnocchi at 350°F. for 20 minutes, until they are golden.

NOTE: This dish can be prepared ahead of time and baked just before serving. It will stand on a hot tray.

VEGETABLES

PURÉED BROCCOLI AND WINTER SQUASH

Serves 8

BROCCOLI:
- 3 (ten ounces each) packages frozen broccoli
- 6 tablespoons melted butter
- Sour cream
- Salt and freshly ground black pepper to taste
- ½ teaspoon ground nutmeg

Cook the broccoli in boiling salted water until it is very soft.

Purée it in a blender or food processor, adding butter and enough sour cream to make a moist but not runny mixture. Season the broccoli with salt, pepper, and nutmeg. The purée should have some texture, so do not make it too smooth.

Place the mixture in a pastry bag with a star tip and pipe it into rounds about 3 inches in diameter onto a buttered serving platter.

WINTER SQUASH:
- 3 (ten ounces each) packages frozen butternut squash
- 6 tablespoons melted butter
- 1 teaspoon ground ginger
- Salt and freshly ground black pepper to taste
- 2 tablespoons brown sugar

Cook the squash until it is soft. Put it into the container of a blender or food processor with the melted butter. Purée until the mixture is smooth. Season the purée with ginger, salt, and pepper. Stir in the brown sugar. Put the mixture into a pastry bag with a star tip. Pipe 3-inch rounds onto a serving platter, alternating them with the broccoli.

NOTE: This vegetable dish can be done ahead and warmed in a 325°F. oven.

PURÉED SPINACH WITH CHESTNUTS

Serves 10

- 1½ pounds chestnuts
- Water
- 4 (ten ounces each) packages frozen leaf spinach
- ¾ cup butter
- ¼ cup heavy cream
- 1 teaspoon ground nutmeg
- Salt and freshly ground black pepper to taste
- 2-3 tablespoons sugar

Place the chestnuts in a deep saucepan and cover them with cold water. Cover the pan and bring the water to a boil. Boil for 10 minutes or until the chestnuts are tender. Test them with the point of a knife.

(Continued)

(Continued)

Remove the pan from the heat but leave the chestnuts in hot water. With a sharp knife peel off both the outer and inner skins. Try to leave the nuts whole or in halves.

Cook the spinach, drain well, and chop it fine in a food processor.

Melt ½ cup of butter with the cream and beat it into the spinach. Season with nutmeg, salt, and pepper.

Melt the remaining butter in a large skillet and sauté the chestnuts, sprinkling them with sugar, until they are shiny and glazed. Keep them warm.

Turn the spinach into a shallow 1½-quart serving dish and heat. Garnish the puréed spinach with the chestnuts.

PARSLIED CARROTS

Serves 6

2 pounds carrots
Chicken bouillon
2 tablespoons butter
Salt and freshly ground
black pepper to taste
¼ cup finely chopped parsley
¼ teaspoon ground nutmeg

Scrub or peel the carrots and slice them into ¼-inch rounds. Put the carrot slices into a saucepan and barely cover them with chicken bouillon. Cover the pan and cook the carrots until they are just tender.

Uncover the pan, raise the heat, and add the butter. Boil the carrots until almost all the liquid has evaporated.

Sprinkle the sliced carrots with salt, pepper, parsley, and nutmeg and serve immediately.

AMBER GLAZED ONIONS

Serves 8 to 10

6 large or 12 medium-sized
yellow onions
¼ cup butter
2 tablespoons honey
4 tablespoons bottled chili
sauce
1 tablespoon paprika

Preheat oven to 350°F.

Peel the onions and, if large, cut them in half crosswise. If they are medium-sized, peel them and cut off the tops to make a flat surface.

Heat together the butter, honey, chili sauce, and paprika until the mixture is smooth and well blended.

Place the onions in a baking dish flat side up and spoon over them.

Cover the onions and bake them for 45 minutes until they are tender but not shapeless.

MARINATED CUCUMBERS AND TOMATOES

Serves 6

4 ripe tomatoes
2 large cucumbers
1 cup vinaigrette dressing (see recipe, page 173)
1 tablespoon chopped chives
1 tablespoon fresh chopped basil

Peel and cut the tomatoes into thin slices.

Using a vegetable peeler, strip off narrow pieces of peel down the length of each cucumber to give a striped effect. Slice the cucumber into thin rounds.

Pile the cucumber rounds in the center of a platter and surround them with tomato slices.

Pour vinaigrette dressing over the tomatoes and cucumbers and sprinkle them with the chives and basil. Let the vegetables marinate at room temperature for 2 to 3 hours.

Serve at room temperature.

SAUTÉED CHERRY TOMATOES WITH CUCUMBERS

Serves 20

1 quart cherry tomatoes
¼ cup vegetable oil
4 firm cucumbers, peeled, seeded, and diced
1 tablespoon chopped fresh basil
1 tablespoon chopped chives
2 tablespoons chopped parsley
Salt and freshly ground black pepper to taste

Peel the tomatoes by plunging them into boiling water for the count of 5, then slipping off the skins.

Heat the oil in a large skillet. Add the diced cucumbers and sauté them for 5 to 7 minutes, until they are glazed.

Add the tomatoes and continue to sauté, stirring, for 5 minutes. Do not overcook the vegetables or they will lose their shape.

Turn the cucumbers and tomatoes into a warm serving dish and sprinkle them with the herbs and seasonings.

CATER FROM YOUR KITCHEN

BROILED TOMATOES MAYONNAISE

Serves 10

12 ripe tomatoes, medium-sized
Salt and freshly ground black pepper to taste
1½ cups mayonnaise
4 tablespoons grated onion
¼ cup grated Parmesan cheese
1 teaspoon prepared mustard, preferably Dijon

Peel the tomatoes and cut them in half across.

Mix together the remaining ingredients and spread the cut sides of the tomato halves with the mayonnaise mixture, forming mounds.

Place the tomatoes on a baking sheet. Broil for 5 minutes until they are puffy and golden.

Serve immediately.

BROILED TOMATOES PARMESAN

Serves 4

1 tablespoon prepared mustard, preferably Dijon
4 tablespoons grated Parmesan cheese
1 tablespoon chopped fresh basil, or 1 teaspoon dried
2 large tomatoes, peeled and halved

Combine the mustard, Parmesan cheese, and basil in a bowl. Place the tomatoes on a broiler pan. Spread the cheese mixture over the tomato halves. Broil them until they are bubbling and golden.

VEGETABLES À LA GRECQUE

Serves 30

3 pounds asparagus
3 (ten ounces each) packages frozen broccoli flowerets
3 (ten ounces each) packages frozen artichoke hearts
2 pounds carrots
2 heads cauliflower
2 pounds green beans, topped and tailed
2 quarts water
Juice of 2 lemons
1 cup olive oil
1 teaspoon salt
8 peppercorns
Garnish: Tomatoes
  Radish flowers

Wash and break the asparagus stalks to remove the tough ends and peel the stems up to the tips. Run hot water through the packages of frozen vegetables until they separate. Trim and scrape the carrots and quarter them. Separate the cauliflower heads into flowerets and trim the stalks.

Bring to a boil with 2 quarts of water, the lemon juice, olive oil, salt, and pepper. Cook each vegetable separately by lowering the vegetable in a colander or lettuce basket into the boiling liquid. Remove when done; cool.

To serve, arrange the vegetables on large platters and sprinkle them with chopped parsley and chives. For color, you can garnish with tomato slices, cherry tomatoes, or radish flowers.

SUMMER POTPOURRI

Serves 16

- 3 tablespoons butter
- 3 tablespoons olive oil
- 8 zucchini, cut into ½-inch rounds
- 2 large sweet onions, sliced thin
- 4 green peppers, sliced in thin strips
- 12 ears fresh corn
- 6 tomatoes, peeled and chopped coarsely
- Salt and freshly ground black pepper to taste
- 3–4 drops Tabasco sauce
- 1 tablespoon chopped fresh basil
- 2 tablespoons chopped parsley
- 2 tablespoons chopped chives

In a skillet, heat the butter and oil, and sauté the zucchini slices until they are lightly browned and transparent. Remove the zucchini to two 3-quart baking dishes.

Add the onions and green peppers to the skillet, and sauté them until they are limp.

Cut the corn from the cob.

Add the tomatoes and corn to the skillet. Season the vegetables with salt, pepper, and Tabasco sauce. Stir all the vegetables together and simmer them for 5 minutes.

Stir in the herbs and pour the vegetables over the zucchini in the baking dishes. Cover the dishes and bake for 30 minutes at 325°F.

Uncover, and cook longer until most of the liquid has been absorbed. Check the seasonings; the mixture should be quite peppery.

Serve the potpourri at room temperature.

CORN TIMBALES ON BROCCOLI PURÉE

Makes 12

1 (ten-ounce) package frozen corn kernels
4 eggs
1½ cups heavy cream
1 teaspoon prepared mustard, preferably Dijon
½ teaspoon salt
1 teaspoon sugar
Freshly ground black pepper
3 drops Tabasco sauce
Butter for greasing muffin tins
Hot water
3 cups broccoli purée (see recipe, page 161)
Garnish: Strips of pimiento

Preheat oven to 350°F.

Place the frozen corn in a colander and run hot water through it until the kernels separate.

Put the corn, eggs, cream, mustard, and seasonings into a blender or food processor and purée. The mixture will not be completely smooth.

Pour it into well-greased 2½-inch glass custard cups or muffin tins. Put the cups into a pan of hot water and cover it with foil.

Bake for 30 to 35 minutes until the timbales are firm to the touch. Remove them from the water pan and let them stand for 10 minutes.

Remove the timbales from the cups and place them on a bed of broccoli purée. Garnish the platter with strips of pimiento.

NOTE: This dish can be partially prepared ahead of time. Make the timbales and broccoli purée and refrigerate them. Before serving, reheat them separately and assemble the dish following the directions above.

CORN SOUFFLÉ

Serves 12

4 eggs
3 cups milk
3 cups uncooked corn kernels
¼ cup flour
2 tablespoons melted butter
2 tablespoons sugar
1 teaspoon salt
Freshly ground black pepper

Preheat oven to 350°F.

Beat together the eggs and milk with a whisk. Beat in the corn kernels and flour. Mix well. Stir in the melted butter and seasonings.

Turn the mixture into two 1½-quart buttered soufflé dishes. Bake for 45 minutes until the soufflés are firm and puffy.

NOTE: These soufflés will stand on a hot tray for 1 to 2 hours.

MUSHROOM PIE

Serves 6

- 7 tablespoons butter
- 2 shallots, minced
- 1½ pounds mushrooms, sliced
- 6 tablespoons flour
- 1 cup chicken bouillon
- ⅔ cup heavy cream
- ⅓ cup Madeira
- 2 egg yolks
- Salt and freshly ground black pepper
- ½ teaspoon ground nutmeg
- ½ cup buttered bread crumbs*

Preheat oven to 350°F.

Melt 3 tablespoons of butter in a large skillet and sauté the shallots and mushrooms over high heat until they are just tender. The mushrooms should be still firm.

In a saucepan melt the remaining 4 tablespoons of butter with the flour. Cook until bubbling.

Add the chicken bouillon and ⅓ cup of cream. Cook until the sauce is thick and smooth. Add the Madeira and cook 5 minutes longer.

Beat the egg yolks with the remaining ⅓ cup of cream and beat them into the hot sauce. Remove the sauce from the heat and season it with salt, pepper, and nutmeg.

Fold the mushroom mixture into the sauce and turn it all into a shallow 9-inch baking dish. Sprinkle the top with buttered bread crumbs.

Bake for 30 minutes and serve hot.

NOTE: Mushroom pie may be prepared a day ahead and heated before serving.

SPINACH TART

Serves 12

- 5 (ten ounces each) packages frozen leaf spinach
- 4 eggs
- ½ pound ricotta cheese
- 3 tablespoons butter
- ½ cup chopped onion
- 2 shallots, chopped
- ½ pound feta cheese
- ½ cup light cream
- 1 teaspoon salt
- ½ teaspoon ground nutmeg
- Freshly ground black pepper to taste
- ½ cup grated Parmesan cheese

Preheat oven to 375°F.
Cook the spinach, drain, and chop it fine.
Beat together the eggs and ricotta cheese.

---

*1 slice of buttered bread grated in a food processor.

(Continued)

(Continued)

Melt the butter and sauté the onion and shallots in it for 5 minutes.

Combine the spinach with the onion mixture and the feta cheese. Combine the ricotta mixture with the spinach mixture and moisten it with cream. Season with the salt, nutmeg, and pepper.

Turn the mixture into 2 buttered quiche dishes. Sprinkle Parmesan cheese over the tops. Bake for 20 to 30 minutes until firm and puffed.

SALADS

CARROTES RAPÉES

Serves 12

- 4 cups coarsely grated carrots
- ¾ cup mayonnaise
- ¾ cup sour cream
- Juice of 1 lemon
- 1 teaspoon prepared mustard, preferably Dijon
- 1 teaspoon salt
- Freshly ground black pepper to taste
- 3 tablespoons minced parsley

Combine all the ingredients except the carrots in a bowl. Beat them together with a wire whisk.

Toss the dressing with the grated carrots and place the rapée in a glass bowl.

NOTE: Prepare this dish 2 hours in advance and serve it at room temperature.

CELERY ROOT REMOULADE

Serves 6

- 1 large or 2 medium celery roots
- Salted water
- 1 cup mayonnaise
- 1 tablespoon ground cardamom
- 1 teaspoon prepared mustard, preferably Dijon

Peel the celery root and cut it into julienne strips. Soak the strips in salted water for 30 minutes.

Mix together the mayonnaise, cardamom, celery seed, and mustard. Dry celery root well and mix it with the dressing. Chill.

CUCUMBER AND GREEN PEPPER SALAD

Serves 6

- 2 cucumbers
- 2 green peppers
- 1 cup plain yogurt
- 2 tablespoons vinegar
- 2 teaspoons sugar
- 1 teaspoon salt
- 1 teaspoon grated onion
- 2 tablespoons chopped fresh mint

Peel and seed the cucumbers, then cut them into 4-inch strips. Wash and seed the peppers and cut them into similar strips.

Mix together the yogurt, vinegar, sugar, salt, and onion.

Arrange the cucumber and pepper strips decoratively on a platter and pour the dressing over them. Sprinkle the salad with mint.

CUCUMBER MOUSSE

Serves 30

- 8 large cucumbers
- 6 packages plain gelatin
- ⅓ cup water
- ⅓ cup lime juice
- 3 cups mayonnaise
- 1 cup sour cream
- 2 cups heavy cream
- Tabasco sauce to taste
- 2 teaspoons salt
- Garnish: Watercress
  Cucumber slices
  Lime slices

DRESSING: 1½ cups mayonnaise
1½ cup sour cream

If cucumbers are garden fresh with unwaxed skins, do not peel them. If not, remove the peels. Cut them in half lengthwise, scoop out the seeds, and cut into chunks. Place the cucumbers in the container of a blender or food processor. Blend them to a pulp.

Soften the gelatin in the water and lime juice. Set the container of gelatin in a pan of simmering water until it is clear and liquid.

Turn the cucumber pulp into a bowl and mix in the gelatin, mayonnaise, sour cream, Tabasco sauce, and salt. Beat the cream until stiff and fold it into the cucumber mixture.

Rinse three 5- to 6-cup ring molds in cold water. Fill them with the mousse and chill overnight or longer. Unmold the rings onto round serving plates and fill their centers with watercress. Surround the rings with alternate slices of cucumbers and limes. Serve with the mayonnaise-sour cream dressing.

JULIENNE OF ENDIVE AND WATERCRESS

Serves 8

- 4 heads endive
- 2 bunches watercress
- 1 hard-cooked egg yolk, sieved
- 1 cup vinaigrette dressing, with 1½ teaspoons prepared mustard, preferably Dijon stirred in (see recipe, page 173)

Slice the endive lengthwise into very thin strips.

Cut off the watercress stems and save them for garnishing soups.

Arrange the endive around the edge of a fairly deep glass salad bowl. Place the watercress leaves in the center. Sprinkle the sieved egg yolk over the watercress.

Just before serving, toss the salad with vinaigrette dressing.

GREEN BEAN SALAD

Serves 10

- 4 (ten ounces each) packages frozen tiny whole green beans
- Salted water
- ⅓ cup vinaigrette dressing (see recipe, page 173)
- ½ cup chopped radishes
- ½ cup sliced onion rings (use small white onions)

Place the frozen beans in a colander and run hot water through them until they are separated. Cook them briefly in a small amount of salted water until they are barely tender. Drain and dry them on paper towels.

Toss the beans with vinaigrette dressing and let them stand at room temperature for 2 to 3 hours. Arrange the salad on a shallow platter and garnish it with radishes and onion rings.

SALAD BAR SALAD

Serves 30

- 1 head lettuce for every 5 people
- 1 bunch watercress for every 3 people
- 3 cups croutons
- 4 red onions, cut in rings
- 4 cucumbers, sliced
- 3 cups canned garbanzo beans, rinsed and drained
- 1 quart cherry tomatoes, halved
- 4 green peppers, cut in strips

Parmesan cheese, grated
1 quart vinaigrette dressing (see recipe, page 173)
1 quart blue cheese dressing

Tear up the greens and mix them in a very large salad bowl.

Put out bowls of the other ingredients and allow the guests to make their own salad combinations.

GRAPEFRUIT RING WITH WATERCRESS

Serves 10

3 packages plain gelatin
2 cups grapefruit juice
2 cups ginger ale
2 pink grapefruit, peeled and sectioned
2 white grapefruit, peeled and sectioned
2 cups grapes, halved and seeded
Watercress
1 ripe avocado
½ cup mayonnaise
Juice of 1 lemon
Salt to taste

Soften the gelatin in 1 cup of grapefruit juice.

Heat the remaining cup of grapefruit juice and add the first cup of grapefruit juice to it to dissolve the gelatin. Add the grapefruit juice to the ginger ale.

Arrange the grapefruit sections and grapes in two 5- to 6-cup ring molds. Pour the gelatin mixture over them. Chill for several hours until the molds are firm.

Turn the rings out onto round serving platters and surround them with watercress.

Mash the avocado and mix it with the mayonnaise and lemon juice. Season to taste with salt. Turn the avocado mixture into small bowls and place them in the center of the grapefruit rings.

COLD RICE SALAD

Serves 4

3 quarts salted water
1 cup rice
¼ cup vinaigrette dressing (see recipe, page 173)
4 tablespoons chopped parsley
4 tablespoons chopped chives
½ cup chopped cucumber
½ cup chopped green pepper
½ cup chopped raw zucchini
Salt and freshly ground black pepper

Bring 3 quarts salted water to a boil. Add the rice and cook it over high heat, uncovered, for exactly 12 minutes. Drain the rice and turn it into a bowl.

(Continued)

(Continued)

Stir in the vinaigrette dressing.

When the rice is cool, mix in the remaining ingredients. Season the salad to taste with salt and pepper.

TABBOULI

Serves 6 to 8

- 1¼ cups water
- 1 teaspoon salt
- 1 cup bulgar wheat
- 1 cup cooked, drained lentils
- ¼ cup finely chopped fresh mint
- 1½ cups finely chopped parsley
- 1 tomato, peeled and chopped
- ½ cup finely chopped scallions
- ½ cup oil
- ¼ cup lemon juice
- Salt and freshly ground black pepper

Bring 1¼ cups water and 1 teaspoon of salt to a boil in a saucepan. Add the bulgar wheat. Cover the pan and remove it from the heat. Let the wheat stand for 30 minutes until all the liquid is absorbed. Fluff with a fork.

Combine the wheat with the remaining ingredients and mix them together well.

Let the tabbouli stand at room temperature for at least 2 hours before serving it on a bed of salad greens.

CHICKEN SALAD IN CURRY RING

Serves 10

CURRY RING:
- 1½ teaspoons curry powder or to taste
- 2 packages plain gelatin
- ½ cup cold water
- 4 cups chicken bouillon
- Juice of 1 lemon
- 10 hard-cooked egg yolks

So as not to waste the egg whites, separate the eggs and drop the yolks into boiling salted water. When they are firm, scoop them out and drain them on paper towels.

Soften the gelatin in cold water. Heat the chicken bouillon with the lemon juice and stir in the gelatin. Remove from the heat when the gelatin is dissolved.

In a food processor mash the cooked yolks with the curry powder. Blend in the chicken bouillon. This will have to be done in two batches.

Pour the mixture into a 6-cup ring mold that has been rinsed in cold water. Refrigerate the ring overnight.

Unmold the curry ring onto a serving platter and fill the center with chicken salad. Arrange the remaining salad around the edge of the ring.

CHICKEN SALAD:
- 2 tablespoons chutney, chopped
- 1 cup mayonnaise
- 4 cups cooked diced chicken
- 2 firm apples, cored and diced
- 1 small bunch seedless grapes, halved

Mix the chutney with the mayonnaise. Toss the chicken and fruit with the mayonnaise. Chill.

ROMAINE LEAVES FILLED WITH CHICKEN SALAD

Serves 8 to 10

- 3 whole chicken breasts, halved, skinned, and boned
- 1 tablespoon lemon juice
- ½ teaspoon salt
- ½ cup vinaigrette dressing (see recipe, below)
- 1 cup mayonnaise
- 2 teaspoons chopped fresh tarragon leaves
- Grated rind of 1 lemon
- 1 head romaine lettuce

Preheat oven to 425°F.

Place the chicken in a baking pan in a single layer. Sprinkle it with the lemon juice and salt. Cover the pan tightly with foil and bake for 25 minutes.

When the chicken is cool, cut it into small pieces.

Marinate the chicken in the vinaigrette dressing for 2 to 3 hours at room temperature. Drain and combine the chicken with the mayonnaise, tarragon, and lemon rind.

Wash and dry the romaine and, using 8 to 10 leaves as "boats," fill each with a portion of the chicken salad.

Wrap each leaf separately in plastic.

VINAIGRETTE DRESSING

Makes 1 cup

- 1 teaspoon salt
- ½ teaspoon freshly ground black pepper
- 1 teaspoon dry mustard
- 1 clove garlic, split
- ¼ cup vinegar
- ¾ cup oil, olive and peanut oil mixed
- Herbs: Chives, basil, or parsley, optional

(Continued)

(Continued)

Put all the ingredients into a jar and shake them well.

Always add a handful of chopped parsley and a grinding of black pepper to a salad before tossing it with the dressing.

NOTE: Make sure the salad greens are completely dry before adding the dressing. If they are damp, the dressing will not stick to the leaves.

SANDWICHES

SMOKED SALMON PÂTÉ SANDWICHES

Makes about 100 sandwiches

- ½ cup finely chopped, peeled and seeded cucumber
- ¾ pound smoked salmon
- 4 (eight ounces each) packages cream cheese
- 3 drops Tabasco sauce
- 1 tablespoon lemon juice
- Salt and freshly ground black pepper to taste
- 2 loaves melba-thin-sliced white bread

Put all the ingredients, except the bread, in a food processor or blender and process until the mixture is smooth.

Season to taste and mix in the cucumber.

Trim the crusts from the bread and cut each slice in two. Spread the bread slices with the salmon pâté.

DRIED BEEF AND HORSERADISH SANDWICHES

Makes about 200 sandwiches

- 4 (eight-ounces each) packages of cream cheese
- 2 large 5-ounce jars dried beef
- 2 tablespoons horseradish or to taste
- 2 tablespoons grated onion
- 4 loaves melba-thin-sliced whole wheat bread

Soften the cream cheese.

Tear apart the dried beef. Put half of the cream cheese and dried beef into a food processor with half of the horseradish and onion. Process until the mixture is smooth. Repeat with the remaining ingredients. Cut the crusts off the bread slices and spread them with the mixture. Cut the sandwiches into thirds. Place them on trays and cover tightly with plastic wrap. Cover the plastic wrap with damp towels to prevent the sandwiches from drying out.

NOTE: The filling can be made ahead and frozen for 2 weeks.

SANDWICHES

PAN BAGNA

Serves 8 to 10

8–10 round crusty sandwich rolls
⅓–½ cup olive oil
4 tomatoes, sliced
8–10 anchovy fillets
2 red onions, thinly sliced
3 green peppers, cut in strips
2 cucumbers, thinly sliced
4–5 hard-cooked eggs, sliced
2 tablespoons drained capers
16 olives, halved, either green pimiento-stuffed or black pitted
½ cup finely chopped parsley

Split the rolls and sprinkle the insides lightly with olive oil.
Layer the rolls with the remaining ingredients.
Press the two halves of each roll together and wrap it tightly in plastic. Refrigerate.

NOTE: The longer the rolls stand, the better they are. They will keep for 2 days. They are supposed to be soft.

PIZZA RUSTICA

Serves 6

Basic pie pastry for 1 nine-inch crust (see recipe, page 207)
2 teaspoons prepared mustard, preferably Dijon
4 eggs
1 cup ricotta cheese
1 tablespoon minced parsley
½ cup prosciutto ham, diced small
½ cup salami, diced small
¼ cup grated Parmesan cheese

Preheat oven to 425°F.
Line a pie pan with the pie pastry, making a decorative edge. Brush the shell with the mustard and prick it with a fork.
Bake the pastry on the center shelf of the oven for 10 minutes. Do not turn off the oven. Remove and cool the pastry.
Beat together the eggs, ricotta cheese, and parsley. Fold in the diced ham and salami.
Turn the mixture into the pastry. Sprinkle it with Parmesan cheese.
Reduce heat to 325°F. and bake for 30 minutes, until the filling is firm and puffy. Cool before cutting.

CRÊPES AND BREADS

CRÊPES CANNELLONI

Makes 75 filled crêpes

CRÊPES*:
- 3 eggs
- 1 cup flour
- 1¼ cups milk
- 2 tablespoons melted butter
- ½ teaspoon salt
- 2 tablespoons brandy (optional)

Put all the ingredients into a blender, food processor, or mixer and beat until the mixture is very smooth. Pour the batter into a pitcher and refrigerate it for 1 hour.

Have ready your crêpe pan, a small container of melted butter and a brush, the pitcher of crêpe batter, a knife or small spatula, a plate, and a paper towel.

Heat the pan over medium-high heat until a drop of water dances on its surface. Brush the pan with butter. Pour in a small amount of batter and tilt the pan so that the batter covers the whole surface. If there is too much batter in the pan, pour it back into the pitcher of batter. With the knife or spatula, cut away the batter that sticks to the edge of the pan and put it into the paper towel.

Allow the crêpe to cook for 1 minute. As soon as it is firm, lift it with the spatula and turn it over. Cook this side until it just starts to brown. Slide the crêpe out onto the plate.

Brush the pan with butter before making each crêpe.

As soon as the crêpes are cool, stack them with a piece of waxed paper between each one. They can now be refrigerated for 2 to 3 days or put into a plastic bag and frozen. If frozen, allow them to thaw for about 1 hour before using them.

FILLING:
- 9 whole chicken breasts (about 9 pounds)
- Salt to taste
- Lemon juice to taste
- 6 (ten ounces each) packages frozen chopped spinach
- 1 cup butter
- 1¼ cups flour
- 5 cups chicken broth
- 3 cups milk
- Freshly ground black pepper to taste
- 1 teaspoon ground nutmeg
- 2 teaspoons prepared mustard, preferably Dijon
- 3 cups canned tomato sauce
- 1½ cups grated Parmesan cheese

---

*This crêpe recipe makes 24 crêpes and must be tripled to make approximately 75 crêpes.

Preheat oven to 425°F.

Split the chicken breasts in half. Spread as many as possible out in one layer on a baking pan. Cook the rest of the breasts in batches. Sprinkle the breasts with 1 teaspoon salt and lemon juice. Cover the pan tightly with foil. Bake the chicken for 20 minutes, or until it is firm and white. Cool. Put the cooked breasts in a large bowl and repeat the baking process with the remaining breasts until all are cooked.

When the chicken is easy to handle, strip the meat from the bones and chop it very fine.

Meanwhile cook the spinach according to the directions on the package. Drain the spinach in a colander. When it is cool, squeeze it until it is dry.

Melt the butter in a large saucepan. Add the flour, stirring, until they are well blended and bubbling. Add the chicken broth and milk. Cook, stirring, until the sauce is thick and smooth.

Stir in salt and pepper to taste and the nutmeg and mustard. Simmer the sauce for 10 minutes, then pour it into a bowl.

To assemble the cannelloni, mix the spinach and chicken together with as much sauce as you need to make a very moist mixture. It should not be too dry, but neither should it be the consistency of gravy.

Place about 2 tablespoons of this mixture in the center of each crêpe and roll it up, cigar-fashion. Place the crêpes in one layer in a shallow buttered baking dish.

Pour the remaining cream sauce over the crêpes. Be sure to leave the ends of the crêpes uncovered so you can see them. Over the cream sauce pour a ribbon of tomato sauce about 3 inches wide. Sprinkle the Parmesan cheese over the tomato sauce.

To serve, heat in a 325°F. oven until they are hot and bubbling, about 30 minutes. Do not overheat or the cannelloni will dry out.

To prepare the crêpes cannelloni in advance, make the crêpes and freeze them. Prepare the spinach-chicken filling in the cream sauce and freeze it. Thaw both the crêpes and the filling and put casserole together with the tomato sauce and Parmesan cheese. Bake for 30 minutes and serve.

NOTE: For all the crêpe recipes in this section, the basic crêpe recipe makes 24 crêpes. If the crêpes are to be used for an appetizer or dessert, allow 2 crêpes per person, for an entrée allow 3 crêpes per person.

Always make the crêpes long before you will need them for two reasons: They are too much trouble to make the day of the party, and they are better if they are not too fresh.

ONION CRÊPES FILLED WITH SMOKED SALMON

Makes 24 filled crêpes

CRÊPES*:
- 3 eggs
- ½ cup water
- ½ cup milk
- 1 cup flour
- ½ teaspoon salt
- 2 tablespoons melted butter
- 2 tablespoons brandy
- 1 tablespoon chopped onion
- 1 tablespoon chopped chives

Place all the ingredients into the container of a blender or food processor and purée. If the mixture is too thick, thin it with water. Pour the batter into a pitcher and chill it for 1 hour.

Follow the instructions on page 176 for cooking the crêpes.

SMOKED SALMON FILLING:
- 4 tablespoons finely minced, peeled and seeded cucumber
- ½ pound smoked salmon
- 1 eight-ounce package cream cheese
- Dash of Tabasco sauce
- 1 tablespoon lemon juice
- Salt and freshly ground black pepper to taste

Put all the other ingredients into the container of a blender or food processor and blend until the mixture is smooth.

Season the mixture to taste with salt and pepper and mix in the cucumber.

Spread the filling on the crêpes and roll them up, browned side out. Serve the crêpes at room temperature.

SEAFOOD CRÊPES

Makes 40 filled crêpes

CRÊPES**:
- 3 eggs
- ½ cup water
- ½ cup milk
- 1 cup flour
- ½ teaspoon salt
- 2 tablespoons melted butter
- 2 tablespoons brandy
- 1 tablespoon grated onion
- 2 tablespoons snipped dill weed

---

*Double the crêpe recipe and the filling to make 48 crêpes, enough to serve 24.
**This crêpe recipe makes 24 crêpes and must be doubled to make 40 crêpes.

Combine all the ingredients in the container of a blender or food processor. Blend the batter until smooth.

Pour it into a pitcher and refrigerate for 1 hour. Follow the instructions on page 176 for cooking the crêpes.

SEAFOOD FILLING:
- 4 tablespoons butter
- 4 tablespoons flour
- 1 cup clam juice or fish stock
- 1 cup milk
- 1 cup sour cream
- Juice of 1 lemon
- Dash of Tabasco sauce
- Salt and freshly ground black pepper to taste
- 5 cups mixed cooked seafood (crabmeat, shrimp, scallops)
- Paprika

Heat the butter and flour together until they are smooth and golden. Add the clam juice and milk and cook, stirring, until the mixture is smooth.

Remove the sauce from the heat and stir in the sour cream. Season to taste with lemon juice, Tabasco sauce, and salt and pepper.

Combine the seafood with enough sauce to hold the mixture together.

Fill each crêpe with 2 to 3 tablespoons of seafood. Roll up the crêpes, put in one layer in shallow baking dishes, and cover them with the remaining sauce. Sprinkle with paprika.

Heat at 325°F. for 20 to 25 minutes until the crêpes are bubbling but not dried out.

CRÊPES FLORENTINE

Makes 48 filled crêpes

CRÊPES*:
- 1 cup flour
- ½ cup water
- ¾ cup milk
- ½ teaspoon salt
- 3 eggs
- 2 tablespoons melted butter
- 2 tablespoons brandy

Put all the ingredients into a food processor or blender. Blend until the batter is smooth. Pour the batter into a pitcher and refrigerate for 1 hour or longer.

Follow the instructions on page 176 for cooking the crêpes.

---

*Double this crêpe recipe to make 48 crêpes.

(Continued)

(Continued)

FILLING:

- 2 (ten ounces each) packages frozen chopped spinach, cooked and well drained
- 4 cups béchamel sauce made with half chicken bouillon and half milk
- Salt and freshly ground black pepper
- 2 cups sliced mushrooms, sautéed
- 2 cups ricotta cheese
- 2 eggs
- 2 cups grated Gruyère cheese

Mix the spinach with a small amount of béchamel sauce, about 1 cup, just to moisten and thicken it. Season to taste with salt and black pepper. Set aside.

Mix the mushrooms with the ricotta, eggs and enough béchamel sauce to make a thick mixture. Season again to taste.

Spread the cheese and mushroom mixtures on the crêpes alternately in layers with the spinach mixture, making about 4 stacks of crêpes.

Place them in ovenproof dishes. Pour the remaining béchamel sauce over the crêpes and sprinkle them with the grated Gruyère.

Bake at 375°F. for 20 to 30 minutes.

NOTE: Crêpes can be filled and stacked ahead. Cover them with sauce and grated cheese just before heating.

BÉCHAMEL SAUCE:

- ½ cup flour
- ½ cup butter
- 2 cups chicken bouillon
- 1½ cups milk
- Salt and freshly ground black pepper to taste

Melt the butter in a saucepan. Gradually add flour, stirring until smooth. Add the chicken bouillon and milk and cook, stirring, until the mixture is thick and smooth.

Season the sauce with salt and pepper to taste.

BRIOCHE

Makes about 30

- 1 tablespoon yeast
- ¼ cup lukewarm water
- 4½ cups flour
- 1 teaspoon sugar
- 1 teaspoon salt
- 4 eggs
- 2 cups unsalted butter
- Egg wash: 1 egg yolk beaten with 1 tablespoon water

Dissolve the yeast in the lukewarm water. Let it stand for 5 minutes. Put 2 cups of flour in the mixer bowl with the sugar, salt, and eggs. Beat until blended.

Add the yeast and the remaining 2½ cups of flour. Beat until the dough is well mixed and no longer sticky.

Add the butter by the tablespoon while beating, incorporating each piece before adding the next. When the dough is well beaten, it should be smooth and buttery. If it is sticky, beat in a little more flour. It will not be as heavy as bread dough and will be too soft to knead.

Cover the bowl and let the dough stand until it is light and well risen. Punch it down and refrigerate overnight.

Butter well thirty to thirty-six 3-inch brioche tins. Shape round balls of dough to fill the tins about halfway up. With a floured finger, punch an indentation in the tops of the balls and fill them with smaller balls of dough. Cover the pans and let the dough rise until it is light.

Brush the brioche with egg wash and bake at 375°F. for 25 to 30 minutes, until golden. Cool on racks.

NOTE: These freeze well.

BLUEBERRY MUFFINS

Makes about 20 muffins

2 cups flour
2 teaspoons baking powder
½ teaspoon salt
⅓ cup sugar
2 eggs
6 tablespoons melted butter
¾ cup milk
2 cups blueberries
Grated rind of ½ lemon

Preheat oven to 400°F.

Combine the flour, baking powder, salt, and sugar in a bowl. Quickly stir in the eggs, melted butter, and milk. Fold in the blueberries and lemon rind.

Fill greased 2-inch muffin tins two-thirds full of batter. Sprinkle additional sugar over the tops.

Bake for 20 to 25 minutes until the muffins have risen and are golden. Serve them hot with butter.

NOTE: Blueberry muffins will freeze well.

BUTTERMILK BISCUITS

Makes about 24

2 cups flour
½ teaspoon baking soda
1 teaspoon cream of tartar
½ teaspoon salt
¼ cup shortening
¾ cup buttermilk

(Continued)

(Continued)

Preheat oven to 425°F.

Place the flour, baking soda, cream of tartar, and salt in a bowl. Cut in the shortening. Add only enough buttermilk to form a soft dough.

Turn the dough out onto a floured board and knead it briefly. Roll it out to ½-inch thickness. Using a biscuit cutter, cut the dough into 1½-inch biscuits.

Bake them on an ungreased baking pan for 12 to 15 minutes. Before serving, split the biscuits and butter them.

NOTE: These biscuits can be made ahead and frozen.

REFRIGERATOR ROLLS

Makes about 48

1 cup milk
1 cup butter
½ cup sugar
1 teaspoon salt
2 packages yeast
1 cup lukewarm water
2 eggs
7–8 cups flour
Melted butter or egg wash
(1 egg yolk beaten with 1 tablespoon water)

In a saucepan, heat the milk with the butter until the butter has melted. Remove the pan from the heat and stir in the sugar and salt. Let the mixture stand until it is lukewarm.

Dissolve the yeast in 1 cup of lukewarm water.

Beat the eggs and half the flour into the milk mixture. Beat in the yeast.

Add the remaining flour gradually, beating until the dough is soft and no longer sticky. The dough should not be as stiff as bread dough.

Let the dough rise, covered, in a warm place until it is doubled. Punch it down and refrigerate overnight.

Shape the dough into rolls and place them in greased muffin tins. Cover and let them rise until they are light.

Preheat oven to 400°F. Brush the rolls with melted butter or egg wash. Bake the rolls for 20 minutes.

NOTE: This dough will keep in the refrigerator after one rising for 3 to 4 days. The rolls freeze well.

CHEESE BREAD STICKS

Makes 30 sticks

2–2½ cups unbleached flour	2 tablespoons vegetable oil
½ cup grated Parmesan cheese	Dash of Tabasco sauce
1 teaspoon salt	Egg wash: 1 egg yolk beaten with 1 tablespoon water
2 tablespoons yeast	Coarse salt
1 cup lukewarm water	
2 tablespoons olive oil	

Preheat oven to 325°F.

Into the bowl of a mixer put 1 cup of flour, the Parmesan cheese, salt, yeast, and 1 cup of lukewarm water. Beat until the mixture is well blended. Add the oils and Tabasco and beat. Add 1 more cup of flour and beat well to make a smooth, non-sticky dough. Beat in the remaining flour, if necessary.

Turn the dough out onto a floured board and knead briefly. Divide the dough into 30 equal pieces. Roll each piece into a long stick.

Place the sticks on oiled baking sheets, rolling them to cover all sides with oil. Cover and let the dough rise in a warm spot until it is puffy, about 30 minutes.

Brush the sticks with the egg wash. Sprinkle them with salt.

Bake the bread sticks for 20 to 30 minutes, until they are firm and glazed.

NOTE: To freeze the cheese bread sticks, wrap them tightly in plastic wrap.

MELBA TOAST

Makes 120 pieces

1 large loaf thin-sliced whole wheat bread	1 large loaf thin-sliced white bread

Preheat oven to 225°F.

Remove the crusts from the bread. Cut the bread into three fingers to a slice or into rounds.

Place the bread on a baking sheet.

Bake for 30 to 45 minutes, until the toast is very lightly browned, crisp, and completely dried out.

NOTE: As a variation, the bread may be brushed with melted butter and sprinkled with grated cheese *before baking*.

Place the melba toast in plastic bags and freeze.

FRENCH BREAD

Makes 3 loaves to serve 24

2 cups water
2 tablespoons shortening
1 tablespoon sugar
1 tablespoon salt
1 package yeast

6 cups unbleached or bread flour
2 teaspoons cornstarch
¼ cup cold water

Combine 2 cups of water, with the shortening, sugar, and salt in a saucepan. Stir the ingredients over medium heat until the shortening is melted. Pour the mixture into the bowl of a mixer and let it stand until it is lukewarm.

Sprinkle the yeast into the bowl. Add 3 cups of flour and beat it well. Then add 2½ cups of flour and beat it into the dough.

Turn the dough out onto a board or counter sprinkled with the remaining ½ cup of flour. Knead the dough until it is smooth and no longer sticky. The dough will have "blisters" like moon craters on the surface.

Place the dough in a greased bowl and cover it with a towel. Let it stand in a warm place until it is doubled in size. Test to see if the dough is ready by putting two fingers into it. If two holes remain and the dough does not spring back into shape, it is ready.

Cut the dough into three equal pieces with a sharp knife. Roll each piece into a long loaf, fatter in the middle than at the ends. Place the loaves on a greased baking sheet, not touching each other. Cover them with towels and let them rise for 30 minutes.

Preheat oven to 375°F.

With a scissors make 4 cuts along the top of each loaf, each about ½ inch deep.

Dissolve the cornstarch in ¼ cup of cold water and brush each loaf with it.

Place the loaves in the oven and bake them for 15 minutes. Remove the loaves and brush them again with the cornstarch mixture. Return them to the oven for another 15 minutes. Brush them once more with the cornstarch mixture.

Bake the loaves 10 minutes longer. They now should be golden and crusty. Remove them from the oven and cool them on racks.

NOTE: To freeze the bread, wrap it in plastic wrap and secure with rubber bands.

HERB BREAD

One loaf serves 8

2 packages yeast	2 tablespoons chopped chives
1/3 cup lukewarm water	2 teaspoons salt
2 cups cottage cheese	1/2 teaspoon soda
2 tablespoons grated onion	2 tablespoons melted butter
1 clove garlic, minced	2 eggs
1 tablespoon snipped dill	2 cups whole wheat flour
2 tablespoons chopped parsley	3–3 1/2 cups unbleached flour

Soak the yeast in 1/3 cup lukewarm water until it is bubbly, about 5 minutes. Set the yeast aside.

In a large mixer bowl combine the cottage cheese, onion, garlic, herbs, salt, soda, melted butter, and eggs. Beat the ingredients together.

Beat in the yeast and whole wheat flour. Beat in the remaining flour, adding enough flour to make a smooth, soft dough.

Turn the dough out and knead it for 2 to 3 minutes. Put the dough into a greased bowl. Cover the bowl and let the dough rise until it is doubled.

Turn the dough out again and punch it down. Divide the dough in half and shape each half to fit a 9-inch round pan. Grease the pan, pat the dough into it and cover. Let the dough rise until it reaches the top of the pan.

Bake at 350°F. for 40 to 50 minutes until the bread is golden and done. To test for doneness, remove the loaf from the pan and tap it on the bottom. If the loaf sounds hollow, it is done. Cool the bread on a rack.

DESSERTS

GLAZED APPLE SLICES

Serves 20

10 large firm cooking apples (not MacIntosh)	1 teaspoon vanilla extract
1/2 cup butter	1/4 cup sugar mixed with 1 teaspoon ground cinnamon

Preheat oven to 400°F.

Wash, core, and cut the apples into 1/2-inch slices.

Put 1/4 cup of butter and 1/2 teaspoon of vanilla into a baking pan and heat it in the oven until the butter is melted.

(Continued)

(Continued)

Arrange half of the apple slices in the pan. Bake the apples for 10 to 15 minutes until they are tender.

Turn the slices over, sprinkle them with cinnamon-sugar, and glaze them under the broiler.

Remove the slices and repeat with the remaining butter, vanilla, and apples. Arrange the apple slices in overlapping rows on shallow platters.

NOTE: Length of cooking time depends on how ripe and firm the apples are. This dish should be served slightly warm.

GINGERED FRUIT

Serves 8

- 5–6 cups assorted fresh or frozen fruits (strawberries, pineapple, papaya, peaches, cherries, melon)
- 1 tablespoon grated fresh ginger root
- 1 tablespoon grated lemon rind
- 2 tablespoons grated orange rind
- ½ cup Port wine

Wash, hull, and stem the fresh fruit. Defrost and drain the frozen fruit. Combine all the fruit in a bowl.

Mix the ginger, citrus rinds, and Port with the fruit.

Chill for 2 to 3 hours. Remove the fruit from refrigerator 1 hour before serving.

SLICED PEACHES IN HONEY AND BRANDY

- 1 peach per serving
- Honey
- Brandy
- Garnish: Chopped fresh ginger

Dip the peaches in boiling water for the count of 5 and slip off their skins. Slice them into individual bowls.

Heat equal parts of honey and brandy together until well blended. Toss the peaches in the honey-brandy mixture. Cover the bowls tightly with plastic wrap and chill.

Before serving, sprinkle each bowl with chopped fresh ginger.

NOTE: This dessert can be prepared 2 to 3 hours ahead of time.

POACHED PEACHES WITH RASPBERRY SAUCE

Serves 6

6 ripe peaches
1½ cups water
1 cup sugar
Juice of 1 lemon
Raspberry Sauce (recipe follows)

Peel the peaches by dipping them into boiling water for the count of 5. The skins will come off easily. Bring the sugar, 1½ cups water, and lemon juice to a boil. Reduce the liquid to a simmer and add the peaches. Poach them for 10 minutes until flesh can be pierced easily. Remove them to a bowl. Cover the peaches with the syrup they were poached in and refrigerate. Drain the chilled peaches and serve them with raspberry sauce.

RASPBERRY SAUCE:
2 boxes frozen raspberries
Kirsch to taste

Garnish: Fresh raspberries

Purée the raspberries and strain them to remove the seeds. Add the kirsch to taste. Pour the sauce over the peaches in a serving bowl and garnish with fresh raspberries.

HOT FRUIT COMPOTE

Serves 24

1 pound pitted prunes
1 pound dried apricots
1 pound dried peaches or pears
Water
6 navel oranges, peeled and sectioned
6 grapefruits, peeled and sectioned
5 bananas, peeled and cut into ¼-inch slices
3 (eight ounces each) cans pineapple chunks in natural juice
1½ cups light brown sugar
2 teaspoons ground nutmeg

Simmer the prunes, apricots, and peaches or pears in water until they are soft. Drain the fruit.

In two or three buttered shallow baking dishes arrange all the fruit, except the pineapple, in the following order: oranges and grapefruit sections in overlapping rows around the outside edge, bananas in an inner row, and the dried fruit in the center.

Drain the pineapple chunks, reserving the juice. Sprinkle the chunks over all the fruit. Pour about 1 cup of the pineapple juice on each dish.

Sprinkle the sugar and nutmeg all over the top. Glaze the topping

(Continued)

(Continued)

under the broiler, making sure the sugar does not burn. Serve the compote hot.

NOTE: This compote can be assembled in advance and refrigerated. Sprinkle with sugar and nutmeg, and glaze it under the broiler just before serving.

MELON CRESCENTS IN WINE

Serves 8

1 large honeydew melon
Rhine wine

Chopped mint

Quarter the melon. With a sharp knife, remove the rind. Cut the melon into thin crescents. Place the crescents in a large bowl and barely cover them with wine. Let the melon stand at room temperature for 2 hours.

Remove the crescents to a serving platter or dessert plates and sprinkle them with chopped mint.

FROZEN COFFEE MOUSSE

Serves 10

¾ cup cold strong coffee
1 envelope plain gelatin
1 cup sugar
3 eggs, separated
1 tablespoon coffee liqueur or vanilla extract
2 cups heavy cream
Garnish: ½ cup chopped walnuts

Put ¼ cup of coffee into a cup, add the gelatin and stir. Let it stand until it is firm.

Heat remaining ½ cup of coffee with the sugar. Stir until the sugar is dissolved. Add the firm gelatin to the hot coffee and stir until the gelatin is dissolved.

Beat the egg yolks until they are very light and lemon-colored. Beat the coffee mixture into the yolks. Beat in the coffee liqueur or the vanilla.

Beat the egg whites until they are stiff. Without washing the beater, beat the cream to stiff peaks.

Fold the cream into the coffee mixture. Fold in the egg whites.

Turn the mixture into a 2-quart serving or soufflé dish. Place it in the freezer overnight.

One hour before serving, remove the mousse from the freezer to the refrigerator. Sprinkle the mousse with ½ cup chopped walnuts.

NOTE: The mousse will keep for a week in the freezer.

MANGO MOUSSE WITH RUM SAUCE

Serves 24

10 ripe mangoes
Juice of 2 lemons
Rind of 1 lemon, grated
Rind of 1 orange, grated
Sugar
5 cups heavy cream
Garnish: Fresh mint leaves
Rum Sauce (recipe follows)

Peel the mangoes, scrape the pulp off the skin, and seed them. Put the pulp into a blender or food processor and purée. Turn it into a bowl and add the lemon juice, grated rinds, and sugar to taste.

Beat the cream until stiff and fold it into the mango mixture. Turn the mango mousse into four 5-cup molds that have been rinsed in cold water. Cover and refrigerate overnight.

Unmold by dipping the molds into hot water and turning them out onto serving platters. Garnish with fresh mint leaves and serve with bowls of rum sauce.

RUM SAUCE:
4 cups sugar
1 cup dark rum
½ cup butter
Grated rind of 2 oranges and 1 lemon
1 cup orange juice
¼ cup lemon juice

Combine all the ingredients and heat, stirring, until the sugar is dissolved, the butter melted, and the sauce is thickened. Serve hot.

DACQUOISE

Serves 8

5 egg whites
⅛ teaspoon salt
1¼ cups superfine sugar
1 teaspoon vanilla extract
1 cup ground almonds
2 tablespoons flour
2 tablespoons cornstarch
Butter
Mocha Butter Cream Icing (see recipe, page 202)

Preheat oven to 325°F.

Beat the egg whites with the salt until frothy. Add the sugar by tablespoonfuls until the whites are stiff. Beat in the vanilla.

(Continued)

(Continued)

Combine the ground almonds with the flour and cornstarch. Fold the almond-flour mixture into the egg whites.

Line baking sheets with parchment paper. Stick the paper to the baking sheets with dots of butter. Draw three 8-inch circles on the paper. Spoon meringue onto the circles and smooth it with a spatula.

Bake for 50 to 60 minutes until the meringues are dry and crisp. Cool and strip the meringues from the paper.

Spread a layer of meringue with mocha butter cream icing flavored with orange liqueur. Top with a second layer of meringue. Spread the second layer with icing. Top with the third meringue layer. To decorate, pipe rosettes of icing on the top layer.

NOTE: You will need 5 of these to serve 40, but the whole dessert completed freezes very well.

FLOATING ISLANDS WITH CARAMEL SAUCE

Serves 8

- 3 egg whites
- 1/4 teaspoon salt
- 3/4 cup superfine sugar
- 4 egg yolks
- 2/3 cup sugar
- 2 cups milk
- 1 teaspoon vanilla extract or 1 tablespoon orange liqueur
- Caramel Sauce (recipe follows)

Preheat oven to 225°F.

Beat the egg whites with the salt until foamy. Gradually add the superfine sugar, beating until the whites are very stiff.

Grease sixteen 2½- to 3-inch muffin tins. Fill the tins with the meringue.

Bake the meringue 40 to 45 minutes until it is dry. Cool, remove from the muffin tins, and place the meringues upside down on a rack.

Beat the egg yolks with 2/3 cup of sugar until they are light.

Heat the milk to the boiling point. Pour the milk into the yolks, while beating.

Turn the mixture into a saucepan and cook over medium heat, stirring constantly until the mixture coats the back of a spoon. Test this by running your finger down the back of the spoon; if it leaves a definite path, the custard is done.

Pour the custard into a bowl and set it over ice. When it is cold, add the vanilla or orange liqueur.

Turn the custard into a shallow 10- to 12-inch serving dish. Place the meringues, top-side up, over the custard. Drizzle the caramel sauce over the top.

CARAMEL SAUCE:

⅓ cup sugar

Put the sugar into an 8-inch heavy skillet over medium heat. The sugar will slowly become liquid and syrupy. Shake the pan occasionally but do not stir the sugar. As the sugar browns, roll the pan around to include the uncooked sugar.

When the sugar is dark brown and smoking, pour it over the dessert. Caramel can be kept liquid by placing the skillet in hot water.

NOTE: This dessert can be prepared in the morning or you can make all the parts separately the day before and put it together shortly before serving. The caramel sauce will soften with standing. If you want it hard and crunchy, pour the caramel sauce on at the last moment. Serve each person two meringue islands and spoon the sauce around them.

MERINGUE CUPS WITH LEMON CURD

Serves 8

6 egg whites at room temperature
¼ teaspoon salt
1½ cups superfine sugar
1 teaspoon vanilla extract
Lemon Curd (recipe follows)
1 pint fresh strawberries

Preheat oven to 200°F.

To bring chilled eggs to room temperature, put them unbroken in a bowl of very warm water for 10 minutes. Separate the eggs. Put the egg whites and salt in the bowl of a mixer. Beat until they are foamy.

Gradually add the sugar by spoonfuls, beating constantly until 1¼ cups of the sugar has been added. Beat until the meringue is not grainy to the touch. Fold the remaining ¼ cup of sugar and the vanilla into the meringue.

Fill a pastry bag fitted with a star tube with meringue. Pipe the meringue onto lightly greased baking sheets, forming cups about 1¼ inches deep.

Bake for 1 hour until the meringue is completely dry. Remove the meringue cups to racks to cool.

Fill each cup with lemon curd and top with a fresh strawberry.

NOTE: Meringue shells may be made in advance and frozen.

Lemon Curd

Makes 1 cup

    Rind of 1 lemon
    2 tablespoons unsalted butter
    ⅔ cup sugar
    2 eggs
    ⅓ cup lemon juice

Place strips of lemon rind into the container of a food processor with a metal blade and chop fine. Scrape the rind into a heavy enamelware saucepan.

Put the butter, sugar, eggs, and lemon juice into the food processor container. Beat the ingredients until they are well mixed. Empty the mixture into the saucepan with the lemon rind.

Over medium heat cook, stirring, until the mixture is a thick, smooth custard. Turn the custard into a bowl and cover with plastic wrap. Cool, then chill in the refrigerator.

NOTE: Use as a filling for meringue cups or as a tart or cake filling. The lemon custard will keep in the refrigerator for 2 weeks, but do not freeze it.

CHOCOLATE CREAM

Serves 10

    1 pound sweet German chocolate, broken up
    ½ cup unsalted butter
    ¼ cup light corn syrup
    1½ tablespoons instant coffee
    ¾ cup plus 2 tablespoons heavy cream
    ½ cup orange juice
    4 eggs, separated
    ½ cup orange liqueur
    Salt
    1 teaspoon gelatin

In a saucepan combine the chocolate, butter, corn syrup, and instant coffee. Stir the ingredients over medium heat until the chocolate and butter are melted and well blended. Stir in the cream and orange juice.

Remove the pan from the heat and beat in the egg yolks. Beat the mixture until it is thick and creamy. Stir in the orange liqueur. Cool.

Beat the egg whites with a pinch of salt until they are stiff. Fold the whites into the chocolate mixture.

Turn the mixture into a 1½-quart soufflé or serving dish. Chill well.

Whip the remaining ½ cup of heavy cream with 1 teaspoon of gelatin. Turn the whipped cream into a strainer lined with cheesecloth. Set the strainer over a bowl and refrigerate. The whipped cream will hold for 2 to 3 hours.

Garnish the dessert with whipped cream, piped through a pastry bag.

NOTE: This dessert, with the exception of the whipped cream garnish, can be made a day ahead and refrigerated until ready to serve. Double this recipe for 20 people.

COFFEE MACAROON CREAM

Serves 8

1½ tablespoons gelatin	½ teaspoon almond extract
¼ cup amber or dark rum	1 teaspoon vanilla extract
2 cups strong coffee	1½ cups heavy cream
⅓ cup sugar	1 cup macaroon crumbs

Soften the gelatin in the rum.

Heat the coffee with the sugar and almond and vanilla extracts. Add the gelatin and rum and stir until the gelatin is dissolved.

Pour enough of this mixture into a 5- to 6-cup ring mold to cover the bottom. Chill until jelled.

Whip the cream and fold 2 cups of it into the remaining coffee mixture along with the macaroon crumbs. Turn the cream mixture into the mold over the jellied coffee. Chill until firm.

Unmold the ring onto a serving platter. Pipe the remaining whipped cream into the center of the ring.

NOTE: This dessert can be made a day ahead, and refrigerated.

BREAD PUDDING WITH BRANDIED FRUITS

Serves 10

2 cups mixed dried fruits (pitted prunes, apricots, peaches)	¾ cup heavy cream
	1 cup sugar
	4 eggs
½ cup brandy	3 egg yolks
10 slices French bread	1 teaspoon vanilla extract
Butter	Confectioners' sugar
3 cups milk	

Combine the dried fruits and brandy in a bowl and let them stand overnight.

Preheat oven to 375°F.

Butter the bread slices on one side.

Combine the milk and cream in a saucepan, bring them to a boil, then remove from the heat. Stir in the sugar until it is dissolved. Beat in

(Continued)

(Continued)

the eggs and the egg yolks. Add the vanilla. Drain the fruit and add its liquid to the egg-cream mixture.

Arrange the fruit in the bottom of a buttered shallow baking dish, approximately 13 × 9 inches. Arrange the bread, buttered sides down, over the fruit. Pour the custard over all.

Place the dish in a pan of hot water. Bake for about 40 minutes, until the pudding is set. Cool.

Before serving, sprinkle the pudding with confectioners' sugar; run it under the broiler to produce a glazed top.

IRISH COFFEE SOUFFLÉ

Serves 6

2½ packages plain gelatin
¼ cup cold water
1½ tablespoons instant coffee
½ cup boiling water
6 eggs, separated
¾ cup sugar
½ cup Irish Mist liqueur
1¼ cups heavy cream

Garnish: ½ cup heavy cream, whipped with 1 tablespoon Irish Mist liqueur and 2 tablespoons confectioners' sugar
2 tablespoons chopped walnuts

Prepare a 1½-quart soufflé dish by attaching a collar of waxed paper around the upper edge. The collar should stand 3 inches higher than the top of the dish.

Soften the gelatin in ¼ cup of cold water until it is firm.

Stir the instant coffee into ½ cup of boiling water. Stir the softened gelatin into the coffee.

Beat the egg yolks, adding the sugar slowly. Beat the coffee mixture and liqueur into the egg yolks. Cool until the mixture starts to congeal.

Beat the egg whites until they are stiff. Beat the cream into stiff peaks. Fold the egg whites into the whipped cream and fold them both into the coffee mixture.

Turn the coffee soufflé mixture into the prepared soufflé dish.

Oil a glass tumbler and push it, closed side down, into the center of the soufflé dish. This will force the soufflé mixture up into the collar.

Refrigerate the soufflé for several hours or overnight.

To serve, remove the collar. Remove the tumbler and fill the center with whipped cream flavored with Irish Mist liqueur. Allow the whipped cream to come out of the top in in a large pouf. Sprinkle it with 2 tablespoons of chopped walnuts.

DESSERTS

COLD MOCHA SOUFFLÉ

Serves 8

½ cup strong coffee
½ pound sweet chocolate
4 eggs, separated
⅓ cup coffee liqueur
¼ cup sugar
1½ cups heavy cream
Marrons in syrup (brandied chestnuts)

In a saucepan, heat the coffee and add the chocolate. When the chocolate is melted, remove the pan from the heat and cool it slightly. Stir in the egg yolks and coffee liqueur.

Beat the egg whites, adding the sugar gradually, until they are stiff.

Beat 1 cup of cream into stiff peaks.

Fold the whipped cream into the chocolate mixture. Fold in the egg whites.

Turn the soufflé into a 1½-quart soufflé dish. Chill it overnight.

Before serving, beat the remaining cream until it is stiff. Put it into a pastry bag and pipe rosettes of cream on top of the soufflé. Place a marron on each rosette.

COLD STRAWBERRY SOUFFLÉ

Serves 6

2 cups fresh or 1 (10-ounce) package frozen strawberries
1 envelope gelatin
¼ cup cold water
1 cup skim milk
3 eggs, separated
½ teaspoon vanilla extract
2 tablespoons fruit-flavored brandy or liqueur
Garnish: 6 whole strawberries

Purée the strawberries by placing the fresh strawberries, washed, hulled, and cut in half, or the thawed frozen strawberries, in a food processor. Process for 3 seconds.

Soften the gelatin in ¼ cup cold water.

In a saucepan scald the milk. Beat the egg yolks in a bowl. Dissolve the gelatin in the scalded milk. Pour the milk over the egg yolks while beating.

Return the egg-milk mixture to the saucepan and cook it over medium heat, stirring, until the mixture thickens. Remove it from the heat and cool.

Add the puréed strawberries and flavorings.

Beat the egg whites until they are stiff and fold them in.

Turn the soufflé into a 1-quart soufflé dish. Chill.

TINY ALMOND TARTS

Makes 24 tarts

Basic pie pastry (see recipe, page 207)
1 cup chopped almonds
4 hard-cooked egg yolks
2 tablespoons brandy
½ cup sugar
¼ cup apricot preserves
6 tablespoons butter
Garnish: Slivered almonds

Using a 3-inch round cookie cutter, cut circles of pastry and fit them into 2-inch muffin or tart tins. Prick the pastry and chill it.

Preheat oven to 400°F. Bake the tart shells for 8 to 10 minutes until they are golden and crisp. Cool. Remove the shells from the tins.

Place the remaining ingredients in a blender or food processor and blend until the mixture is smooth.

Fill the tart shells with the almond filling, topping each tart with 2 slivered almonds.

BOURBON BALLS

Makes about 24

1 cup vanilla wafer crumbs
1 cup finely chopped pecans
½ cup bourbon whiskey
1½ tablespoons light corn syrup
2 tablespoons cocoa
Confectioners' sugar

Mix all the ingredients together. This can be done in a food processor.

With hands dusted in confectioners' sugar, form walnut-sized balls of dough. Roll them in confectioners' sugar.

NOTE: Let the balls mellow 24 hours before serving.

BROWNIES

Makes 16 brownies

½ cup butter
2 squares unsweetened chocolate
2 eggs
1 cup sugar
½ cup flour
½ teaspoon salt
1 tablespoon vanilla extract
1 cup chocolate bits

Preheat oven to 350°F.

Heat together the butter and chocolate until they melt.

Beat the eggs with the sugar until the eggs are light in color. Beat the chocolate mixture, flour, salt, and vanilla into the eggs. Stir in the chocolate bits.

Turn the batter into a greased and floured 9- × 9-inch pan.

Bake the brownies for 30 minutes until the brownies shrink from the sides of the pan and are shiny and cracked on top. Cut them into squares while warm. When the brownies cool, remove them from the pan to a rack.

NOTE: Brownies can be made in advance and frozen unwrapped. After they are completely frozen, store them in plastic bags.

OATMEAL COOKIES

Makes 48 cookies

- 1 cup butter
- 1½ cups sugar
- 1 egg
- ¾ cup flour
- ¾ cup wheat germ
- 1 teaspoon baking soda
- 1 teaspoon ground cinnamon
- 1½ cups regular oats
- ¾ cup raisins
- ¾ cup chopped walnuts or pecans
- 1 teaspoon vanilla extract

Preheat oven to 350°F.

Cream the butter and sugar together thoroughly. Beat in the egg.

Combine the flour, wheat germ, baking soda, and cinnamon. Add the flour to the creamed mixture and mix together well.

Stir in the oats, raisins, nuts, and vanilla. Blend well.

Drop the cookie batter by spoonfuls onto greased baking sheets. Flatten the mounds with a spatula.

Bake for 10 to 15 minutes. Cool the cookies on racks.

NOTE: These oatmeal cookies freeze well.

WALNUT OATMEAL ROLL WITH WHIPPED CREAM

Serves 8

- 7 eggs, separated
- 1 cup walnuts
- ½ cup regular oats
- ¾ cup sugar
- 1 teaspoon baking powder
- 2 cups heavy cream
- Confectioners' sugar
- Garnish: Chopped walnuts or glazed walnut halves

(Continued)

(Continued)

Preheat oven to 350°F.

Grease a 10- × 15-inch jelly roll pan. Line it with waxed paper, letting the paper extend 1 inch over the ends. Grease the paper.

Beat the whites until they are stiff.

Put the nuts and oats in a blender or food processor and grind them until they are fine.

Without washing the egg beater, beat the yolks gradually adding the sugar until they are pale and thick. Beat in the baking powder and nut mixture. Fold in the egg whites.

Spread the batter in the prepared baking pan. Bake for 18 minutes.

Turn the cake out onto a towel. Remove the pan. Let the cake rest for 5 minutes, then strip off the waxed paper. Roll up the cake, then unroll it. Cool.

Beat the cream with confectioners' sugar to taste until it is stiff.

Spread the cake with whipped cream. Roll up the cake and cover it with whipped cream. Sprinkle the roll with additional nuts or garnish it with glazed walnut halves. (To glaze the walnuts, dip them in lightly beaten egg white, then in sugar. Dry them in a 300°F. oven.)

NOTE: This roll can be frozen. Let it come to room temperature before serving.

BRIE EN CROÛTE

Serves 8

1 eight-ounce wheel of ripe Brie cheese	1 egg, separated
Puff pastry (see recipe, page 207)	Grapes Pears

Preheat oven to 375°F.

Roll out the puff pastry to ⅛-inch thickness. Cut out 2 circles of pastry ½ inch larger than the wheel of cheese.

Put the cheese on 1 circle of pastry and turn up the edge all the way around. Glue the pastry to the cheese with egg white.

Place the remaining pastry circle over the cheese and shape it to fit.

Roll out the pastry trimmings and cut out decorative shapes. Glue the shapes to the top of the pastry-wrapped cheese with egg white.

Place the pastry on a baking sheet and brush it with egg yolk.

Bake in the oven for 30 to 40 minutes, until it is puffed and golden. Let it stand 20 to 30 minutes before cutting.

Surround the Brie en croûte with grapes and sliced or whole pears.

BABY CHEESECAKES

36 cakes

1 cup graham cracker crumbs
1 cup plus 2 tablespoons sugar
2 eight-ounce packages cream cheese
3 eggs, separated
Grated rind of 1 lemon
1 teaspoon vanilla extract
½ teaspoon almond extract
1 cup sour cream

Preheat oven to 350°F.

Combine the graham cracker crumbs with ¼ cup of sugar. Sprinkle the crumbs into buttered 1½-inch muffin tins, covering the bottoms and sides.

Beat together the cream cheese, ¾ cup sugar, egg yolks, lemon rind, and flavorings until light. Beat the egg whites until they are stiff and fold them in.

Fill the muffin tins with the cheese mixture. Bake for 15 to 20 minutes until the cheese is set and puffy. Remove the tins from the oven and turn the heat up to 400°F.

Combine the sour cream with 2 tablespoons of sugar. Spread sour cream over the top of each cheesecake.

Return them to the oven for 5 to 7 minutes. Cool.

NOTE: These baby cheesecakes can be baked in advance and frozen.

CARROT CAKE

Serves 10

1½ cups oil
2 cups sugar
4 eggs
2 cups flour
2 teaspoons baking soda
1 teaspoon salt
2 teaspoons ground cinnamon
1 teaspoon ground ginger
½ teaspoon ground nutmeg
2 teaspoons vanilla extract
3 cups finely grated carrots
Cream Cheese Icing
(recipe follows)

Preheat oven to 325°F.

Beat together the oil, sugar, and eggs. Combine the flour, baking soda, salt, cinnamon, ginger, and nutmeg and add them, beating well. Add the vanilla and grated carrots and blend well.

Turn the batter into 3 greased and floured 8-inch cake tins. Bake for 45 minutes until the layers test done.

Turn them out onto racks and cool.

Cover the tops of the first and second layers with cream cheese icing. Stack up all three layers and frost the top and sides of the cake with the

(Continued)

(Continued)

remaining icing. After frosting the cake, place about ½ cup of frosting into a pastry bag and pipe decorations on top of the cake.

CREAM CHEESE ICING:

- ½ cup butter
- 1 eight-ounce package cream cheese
- 1 box confectioners' sugar
- 2 teaspoons vanilla extract

Beat together the butter and cream cheese. Beat in the sugar and vanilla until the icing takes on a spreading consistency.

DANISH CREAM CAKE

Serves 10

- 1 cup heavy cream
- 2 eggs, beaten
- 1 cup sugar
- 1½ cups flour
- 2 teaspoons baking powder
- ½ teaspoon salt
- ¼ teaspoon almond extract
- ½ teaspoon vanilla extract

Preheat oven to 350°F.

Whip the cream into soft peaks. Blend in the eggs and sugar.

Combine the flour, baking powder, and salt, and sift over the cream mixture. Fold the dry ingredients in with the flavorings.

Turn the batter into a greased and floured 9-inch round cake pan with a removable bottom.

Bake for 45 minutes until a toothpick inserted in the middle of the cake comes out clean. The cake is then done.

While the cake is baking, prepare the topping.

DANISH CREAM TOPPING:

- 6 tablespoons butter
- 2 tablespoons heavy cream
- ½ cup sugar
- 1½ tablespoons flour
- ⅓ cup slivered almonds

Combine all the ingredients in a small saucepan. Cook and stir them over medium heat until the mixture is smooth and well blended.

Spread the topping over the cake and return the cake to the oven for 10 minutes until the topping is golden and bubbling.

LEMON SPONGE ROLL

Serves 8

4 eggs, separated
¾ cup sugar
1 teaspoon lemon extract
¾ cup flour
1 teaspoon baking powder
½ cup heavy cream, whipped to make 1 cup

2 cups lemon curd (see recipe, page 192)
Garnish: Crushed sour lemon candies

Preheat the oven to 375°F.

Grease a 10- × 15-inch jelly roll pan. Cover the pan with a strip of waxed paper long enough to hang over each end. Grease the waxed paper.

Beat the yolks until light, gradually adding the sugar and lemon extract.

Combine the flour and baking powder in a sifter.

Beat the egg whites until stiff. Rapidly fold one-third of the whites into the yolks.

Sift the flour over the yolks and fold it in while folding in the remaining whites. The easiest way to do this is with your hand.

Turn the batter into the prepared pan, making sure you spread it evenly into the corners. Bake for 12 minutes until the cake is golden and springy to the touch.

Turn it out of the pan onto a clean towel, but do not remove the paper. Let stand 5 minutes, then strip off the paper. Roll up the cake roll while warm. Unroll it immediately and allow it to cool.

Combine 1 cup of whipped cream with 2 cups of lemon curd. Spread about two-thirds of this mixture over the roll and roll it up onto a serving platter.

Frost the top and sides with the remaining lemon curd mixture. Sprinkle crushed sour lemon candies over the top.

LEMON YOGURT POUND CAKE

Serves 12 to 16

6 eggs, separated
Pinch of salt
2 cups sugar
1 cup butter
Grated rind of 1 lemon

3 cups flour
1 teaspoon baking powder
½ teaspoon ground mace
1 cup lemon yogurt

Preheat oven to 350°F.

Beat the egg whites with a pinch of salt into soft peaks. Gradually
(Continued)

(Continued)

beat in ½ cup of sugar until the whites are stiff and shiny. Set the beaten egg whites aside.

Cream the butter with the remaining sugar until it is light. Beat in the egg yolks. Add the lemon rind.

Combine the flour, baking powder, and mace. Add the flour mixture and the yogurt to the creamed mixture alternately.

Rapidly stir in one-third of the beaten whites. Fold in the remaining whites gently.

Turn the batter into a greased and floured 13- × 9- × 2-inch pan. Bake for 45 to 55 minutes until the cake tests done.

Place the pan on a rack until cool. Cut the cake into squares.

FIVE-LAYER MOCHA TORTE

Serves 8

1 sixteen-ounce frozen pound cake
3 squares unsweetened chocolate
2 cups ricotta cheese
⅓ cup sugar
¼ cup coffee liqueur
½ teaspoon ground cinnamon
Mocha Butter Cream Icing (recipe follows)

Partially thaw the pound cake. Cut it lengthwise into five slices.

Place the chocolate in the container of a food processor and grate it coarsely with an on-off motion. If you do not have a food processor, grate the chocolate in a blender or on a grater.

Add the remaining ingredients to the container and blend quickly to make a smooth mixture.

Spread each layer of the cake, except the top, with the chocolate-cheese mixture. Wrap the torte in plastic wrap and refrigerate until it is firm.

MOCHA BUTTER CREAM ICING:

2 egg yolks
½ cup butter
½ cup margarine
1 six-ounce package chocolate bits
1 tablespoon instant coffee
1 tablespoon vanilla extract
Hot water
3 cups confectioners' sugar

In the bowl of a mixer beat the egg yolks, butter, and margarine together until they are smooth.

Meanwhile, place the chocolate bits, instant coffee, and vanilla in a small bowl. Put the bowl inside a larger pan of hot water over medium heat. When chocolate has melted, stir the mixture and set it aside until cool.

Beat the chocolate mixture into the butter mixture. Beat in the sugar, stirring until the frosting is completely smooth and well blended.

Cover the cake completely with frosting. Put the remaining frosting into a pastry bag and decorate the top of the cake with rosettes and a border.

NOTE: This cake freezes well.

HOLIDAY RUM RAISIN CAKE

Serves 8

- 1 sixteen-ounce frozen pound cake
- ½ cup raisins
- ¼ cup rum
- 1 cup granulated sugar
- ½ cup slivered almonds
- 2 cups heavy cream
- 2 teaspoons plain gelatin
- ½ cup confectioners' sugar
- 2 egg yolks
- Garnish: Additional whipped cream and toasted slivered almonds

When the cake is partially thawed, cut it into 5 lengthwise slices. Soak the raisins in rum for 20 minutes.

Put the granulated sugar into a heavy skillet and place it over medium heat. The sugar will slowly turn caramel-colored. Shake the skillet occasionally. When the sugar is brown, syrupy, and smoking, add the slivered almonds. Turn the caramel out onto foil. Let it harden. Break it up and crush it in a blender or food processor.

Beat the cream until it is stiff, gradually adding the gelatin. Beat in the confectioners' sugar and egg yolks. Fold in the raisins and crushed caramel.

Layer the cake slices with the whipped cream mixture. Cover the sides as well.

Freeze the cake overnight. Before serving, pipe ribbons of whipped cream over the top and decorate the cake with toasted slivered almonds.

NOTE: This cake can be made ahead and frozen for 5 to 6 days. Remove it to the refrigerator 1 hour before serving.

SALLY LUNN

Serves 8

- 2 tablespoons yeast
- ¼ cup lukewarm water
- 1 tablespoon sugar
- 2 cups milk
- 4 cups flour
- 2 eggs
- ¼ cup melted butter
- 1 teaspoon salt

(Continued)

(Continued)

Dissolve the yeast in ¼ cup lukewarm water with the sugar. Let stand for 5 minutes.

Heat the milk to lukewarm and pour it into a mixer bowl. Add the yeast with 2 cups of the flour. Beat for 5 minutes.

Add the eggs, butter, the remaining flour, and the salt. Beat well.

Turn the batter into a greased and floured Bundt pan. Cover and let rise until doubled and light.

Bake at 400°F. for 30 minutes. Turn out onto a rack and cool.

Serve this cake with preserves of good quality, as close to homemade as possible.

NOTE: You can make this into a sweet coffee cake by pinching off bits of dough, forming it into balls, and rolling it in melted butter and then cinnamon-sugar. Pile up the balls in an angel food cake pan. Let the dough rise until it is light, then bake the cake at 400°F. for 30 minutes.

SOUR CREAM PECAN COFFEE CAKE

Serves 8

½ cup butter
1 cup sugar
2 eggs
1¾ cups flour
1½ teaspoons baking powder
½ teaspoon baking soda
½ teaspoon salt
1 cup sour cream
½ teaspoon vanilla extract
2 teaspoons ground cinnamon
½ cup brown sugar
1 cup chopped pecans

Preheat oven to 350°F.

Cream the butter and sugar together until light. Beat in the eggs and blend well.

Combine the flour, baking powder, baking soda, and salt and add them to the creamed mixture alternately with the sour cream. Beat in the vanilla.

Combine the cinnamon, sugar, and pecans to make a topping and set it aside.

Turn half of the batter into a well greased and floured 9-inch tube pan. Cover the batter with half of the pecan mixture. Add the remaining batter and top it with the remaining pecan mixture.

Bake the cake for 45 to 50 minutes until it tests done. A good way to test a deep cake is to push a piece of raw spaghetti into the cake. If it comes out clean the cake is done. Let the cake rest in the pan for 10 minutes. Turn it out onto a rack.

NOTE: This coffee cake freezes well. After thawing, heat the cake before serving. For 24 people, triple the recipe, making each cake separately.

SHORTBREAD

Makes 32 pieces

1 cup butter (no substitute)
½ cup confectioners' sugar
2 cups flour
¼ teaspoon salt
¼ teaspoon baking powder

Preheat oven to 350°F.

Cream the butter in a mixer until it is very light. Beat in the sugar, blending until the butter mixture is smooth. Beat in the flour, salt, and baking powder.

Divide the mixture in half. Pat each half into an ungreased 7-inch round pan. With fork tines, prick the dough all over.

Bake for 20 to 25 minutes until the shortbread is golden brown.

While it is warm, cut each circle into 16 wedges with a sharp knife. Remove the wedges to racks.

NOTE: Shortbread will keep for several days in an airtight tin.

TUNNEL CAKE

Serves 5

2 eggs
1½ cups heavy cream
1 cup flour
1 cup sugar
1 teaspoon baking powder
¼ teaspoon salt
¼ cup pralines, crushed
Butter Cream Icing (see recipe, page 213)

Preheat oven to 350°F.

Break the eggs into an 8-ounce measuring cup and fill it with cream. Combine the flour, sugar, baking powder, and salt in a mixing bowl and add the eggs and cream. Beat the mixture quickly with a wooden spoon until it is well blended.

Turn the batter into a well greased and floured 5-cup ring mold. Bake for 40 minutes until the cake tests done when a straw inserted in the middle comes out clean.

Remove the cake from the oven and let it stand for 10 minutes. Run a knife around the outer edge and turn the cake out onto a rack to cool.

Cut off the top of the cake, about 1 inch in depth. Hollow out the inside, making a trough and leaving a ½-inch wall. Also make a trough in the top ring you have cut off.

Whip ½ cup of cream and fold in ¼ cup of crushed pralines. Fill the trough with this mixture and put the top ring back on.

Frost the whole cake with butter cream icing. Pipe rosettes of icing around the top.

Refrigerate the cake until 1 hour before serving.

NOTE: This cake will freeze. For 10 servings you will need two cakes but make each cake separately, since the recipe does not double successfully.

WEDDING CAKE

Serves 100

I am grateful to Susan Layton for providing me with the details on wedding cake procedure. She suggests that you invest in commercial baking pans for this wedding cake, since they are the required 3 to 3½ inches in depth. The cake uses 3 pan sizes, 6 inches, 9 inches, and 12 inches. Prepare the 3 pans by greasing them well and flouring them.

Ingredients and procedure for 6- and 9-inch layers:

- 1½ cups butter
- 3 cups sugar
- 6 cups cake flour, sifted
- 6 teaspoons baking powder
- 2 cups lukewarm milk
- 1 teaspoon vanilla extract
- 1 teaspoon almond extract
- 12 egg whites

Cream the butter and sugar together until they are very light.

Combine the flour and baking powder and add them alternately with the milk to the creamed mixture, beating well between each addition. Mix in the vanilla and almond extracts.

Beat the egg whites until they form soft peaks and fold them into the creamed mixture.

Turn the batter into the prepared pans, so that the pans are two-thirds full. If you have extra batter, make some cupcakes.

Ingredients for 12-inch layer:

- 2 cups butter
- 4 cups sugar
- 8 cups cake flour, sifted
- 8 teaspoons baking powder
- 2⅔ cups lukewarm milk
- 1 teaspoon vanilla extract
- 1 teaspoon almond extract
- 16 egg whites

Follow the same procedure as for the 6- and 9-inch layers.

BAKING TIMES:

Bake all the layers at 350°F. for 20 minutes. Reduce heat to 325°F. Bake the 6-inch layer for 1¼ hours, 9-inch layer for 1½ hours, 12-inch layer for 1¾ hours.

Be sure to test for doneness shortly before cakes should be done, since ovens vary.

Cool the layers on racks for 15 minutes, then turn them out and cool.

Chill or freeze the layers before icing them to prevent crumbs in the icing.

FILLING:

- 1 eight-ounce jar apricot preserves
- Kirsch or orange juice

Put the apricot preserves in a food processor and purée. Turn the puréed preserves into a saucepan and heat.

Add enough kirsch or orange juice to make a spreadable mixture and brush it over the top of each layer.

ICING:
- 2 cups butter
- 2 cups solid vegetable shortening
- 4 pounds confectioners' sugar
- 2 teaspoons vanilla extract
- ½–¾ cup milk

Beat all the ingredients together until the mixture is very smooth and shiny.

A very tiny speck of blue food coloring added to the icing on the end of a toothpick will give it an icy-white effect.

Ice the sides and top of each layer.

To put cake together, cut rounds of cardboard the size of each layer. Place each layer on a round.

Measure the height of the layers including the frosting and cut six ⅜-inch wooden dowels in the right height, 3 for each layer. Put the dowels down through the cake layers in three places making a 3-legged stool support.

Place a doily on the cake platter and balance the 9-inch layer on the dowels placed in the 12-inch layer. Rest the 6-inch layer on the dowels placed in the 9-inch layer. The top layer will not be cut for serving. The bride can take it home.

The dowel support system is necessary, especially in warm weather, or the cake will slide.

BASIC PIE PASTRY

Makes two 9-inch pie crusts

- ½ cup vegetable shortening
- ¼ cup butter
- 2½ cups flour
- ½ teaspoon salt
- 3–4 tablespoons ice water

Mix all the ingredients together with a mixer or food processor. The pastry should be firm and smooth, not sticky. Roll out the pastry on a floured board to the desired diameter and thickness.

PUFF PASTRY

Makes about 2½ pounds

- 1 pound butter
- 1 pound flour
- 1 cup ice water
- 1 teaspoon salt

(Continued)

(Continued)

Cut the butter into tablespoon-sized pieces and distribute them evenly around the bowl of a food processor. This may have to be made in 2 batches. Cover the butter with flour.

Process by pulsing the machine about 15 times. The butter now should be in small pieces, lightly coated with flour.

Add the ice water in 3 parts, pulsing the food processor with each addition. The pastry will resemble crumbs.

Turn it out onto a floured pastry cloth. Gather the pastry together into a rough rectangle with your hands.

Roll out the pastry with a floured rolling pin into a rectangle whose width is half its length. Do not allow the butter to show through the flour. To prevent this, pat more flour over the visible butter spots.

Fold the pastry in thirds, making 3 layers. Turn it so that the open end is facing you and roll it out again into a rectangle. Fold the pastry in thirds again. Wrap and chill it for 30 minutes.

Repeat this folding and turning process four more times, chilling the pastry for at least 30 minutes between each folding.

The pastry is now ready to use. After it is filled or shaped, it should be chilled. Before baking the pastry should be brushed with egg wash, being careful not to let the egg drip onto the baking sheet, which will prevent the pastry from rising.

TO MAKE FLEURONS:

Puff pastry

Egg wash: 1 egg yolk beaten with 1 tablespoon water

Cut out rounds of puff pastry with a 1½-inch fluted cutter. Brush with egg wash and bake the fleurons at 375° F. for 20 minutes.

NOTE: Puff pastry may be frozen.

BLUEBERRY CHARLOTTE

Serves 10 to 12

2 tablespoons cornstarch
1 cup sugar
½ cup water
4 cups fresh blueberries
1 teaspoon ground cinnamon
2 tablespoons gin
Grated rind of 1 lemon
4 dozen ladyfingers, split
1½ quarts vanilla ice cream, softened
½ cup heavy cream, whipped
Garnish: ½ cup blueberries

Combine the cornstarch, sugar, and water in a saucepan. Cook the mixture over medium heat until thickened. Stir in 4 cups of blueberries and the cinnamon. Cook until the berries are soft and the sauce is thick. Stir in the gin and lemon rind. Cool.

Line the bottom and sides of a 2-quart soufflé dish with split ladyfingers, fitting them together so there are no empty spaces.

Pour in one-third of the blueberry mixture. Cover with half (3 cups) of the softened ice cream. Put in another layer of ladyfingers, followed by another third of the sauce. Cover with the remaining ice cream, then another layer of ladyfingers. Pour the remaining sauce on top.

Freeze the charlotte for 24 hours. Remove it from the freezer 1 hour before serving and let it stand at room temperature.

Run a knife around the outer edge and turn it upside down onto a serving platter. Spread the top of the charlotte with whipped cream and sprinkle it with blueberries.

NOTE: This dessert may be made several days ahead and frozen until needed.

FRUIT TARTS

Three 8-inch tarts

PASTRY:

1½ cups cold butter, cut into small pieces
1½ cups flour
½ cup confectioners' sugar
2 egg yolks

Combine all the ingredients in the bowl of a food processor. Mix them briefly until the pastry is just bound together. Divide it into 3 parts.

Line the bottoms and sides of three 8-inch tart pans, pushing the pastry into place with the palms of the hands. Chill the tart pans.

FILLING:

½ cup flour
½ cup sugar
6 egg yolks
2 cups milk
1 teaspoon vanilla extract
3 cups sliced peaches, nectarines or strawberries, uncooked
Currant jelly, melted

In a bowl, whisk together the flour, sugar, and egg yolks. Scald the milk in a saucepan. Pour the milk over the yolk mixture, whisking constantly.

Return the mixture to the saucepan and cook it over medium heat, stirring, until the mixture is thick and smooth.

When the custard coats the back of the spoon so that your finger can make a path down it, the custard is ready. Chill. Stir in the vanilla.

Preheat oven to 425°F. Bake the pastry shells for 15 minutes until they are lightly browned. If desired, these now can be frozen for future use.

(Continued)

(Continued)

Assemble the tarts about an hour before serving them. Spread the custard over the pastry shell. Cover the custard with sliced fruit. Glaze the tart by brushing melted currant jelly over the fruit, custard, and pastry edges.

LEMON CHESS TART

Serves 6 to 8

- 1 nine-inch pie shell (see recipe, page 207)
- 1 egg yolk, beaten
- 2 cups sugar
- 2 tablespoons flour
- 4 eggs
- ¼ cup milk
- ¼ cup lemon juice
- Grated rind of 1 lemon
- ¼ cup melted butter

Preheat oven to 425°F.

Place the pie shell in the oven and bake for 8 minutes.

Remove the pie shell and brush it with beaten egg yolk. Return to the oven for 2 minutes. Cool.

Combine the sugar and flour.

Beat together the eggs, milk, lemon juice, and lemon rind. Stir in the butter.

Combine the flour-sugar mixture and the egg-lemon mixture and pour the filling into the pie shell.

Bake the pie at 375°F. for 35 to 40 minutes until it is golden and set. Serve the pie warm or at room temperature.

PEAR CRUNCH PIE

Serves 6 to 8

PASTRY:

- ½ cup plus 2 tablespoons unsalted butter
- 1 cup plus 2 tablespoons flour
- 5 tablespoons confectioners' sugar
- 1 hard-cooked egg yolk, mashed

Mix all the ingredients together and turn the pastry into a 9-inch tart pan. With the heel of the hand cover the bottom and push the pastry onto the sides of the pan, making sure the sides are high. Chill.

Preheat oven to 425°F.

Bake the pie shell for 10 minutes. Cool.

FILLING:
- ½ cup sugar
- 3 tablespoons apricot preserves
- 1 tablespoon rum
- 1 tablespoon grated lemon rind
- 5 pears, peeled and sliced
- ½ cup brown sugar
- ½ cup flour
- ⅓ cup butter
- ½ teaspoon ground cinnamon
- ½ teaspoon ground nutmeg
- ¼ teaspoon ground ginger
- Garnish: Whipped cream

Heat together the sugar, apricot preserves, and rum until they are blended. Stir in the lemon rind. Fold in the pears.

Turn the pear filling into the pie shell.

Combine the brown sugar, flour, butter, and spices. Crumble this mixture over the pears.

Bake at 400°F. for 35 to 40 minutes until the pears are tender. Serve the pie with whipped cream.

NOTE: Pear crunch pie can be made in advance. Cool the pie, wrap it in plastic, and freeze. To serve, bring it to room temperature, then warm in a 325°F. oven for 10 minutes.

BAKED PEAR CRUMBLE

Serves 6 to 8

- 4 large ripe pears
- Juice and grated rind of 1 lemon
- 2 tablespoons rum
- ½ cup butter
- ½ cup brown sugar
- ¼ cup unbleached flour
- ¼ cup whole wheat flour
- ½ teaspoon ground cinnamon
- Frozen vanilla yogurt

Peel the pears, core, and cut them in half. Place them in one layer in a buttered baking dish.

Sprinkle the pears with the lemon juice and rind and the rum.

In a food processor combine the remaining ingredients. Process until the mixture is crumbly. Spread the topping over the pears.

Bake the pears at 350°F. for 30 minutes. Serve the pear crumble warm with frozen vanilla yogurt.

RHUBARB CRUMBLE WITH BRANDIED WHIPPED CREAM

Serves 20

4 cups sugar
1 cup water
12 cups rhubarb, cut into 1-inch pieces
3 cups brown sugar
1½ cups butter
2¼ cups flour
2 teaspoons ground ginger
Grated rind of 2 oranges
2 cups heavy cream
½ cup confectioners' sugar
Brandy

Boil the sugar and water together until syrupy.

Put the rhubarb in a large kettle and pour in the syrup. Cover and cook over medium heat until the rhubarb is just tender.

Remove the rhubarb with a slotted spoon to two shallow 2-quart baking dishes.

Mix together until crumbly the brown sugar, butter, flour, and ginger. This may be done in the food processor. Spread the crumble over the rhubarb. Sprinkle with orange rind. Bake at 350°F. for 40 minutes until crisp and sugary.

Whip 2 cups heavy cream with ½ cup confectioners' sugar and brandy to taste. The flavor should not be too strong. Cut the warm rhubarb crumble into squares and top with the whipped cream.

NOTE: The rhubarb crumble may be baked a day in advance. The cream can be whipped in the morning and placed in a cheesecloth-lined sieve over a bowl of ice, then refrigerated.

SOUR CREAM APPLE PIE

Serves 6 to 8

PASTRY:

½ cup butter
½ cup ground walnuts
½ teaspoon salt
1 egg yolk
1½ cups flour

Combine all the ingredients quickly and work them into a ball of pastry dough. Wrap and chill the dough for 1 hour.

Line a 9-inch pie pan with the pastry. Prick the bottom.

Preheat oven to 425°F.

Bake the pie shell for 8 minutes. Cool.

FILLING:

½ cup sugar
1 teaspoon ground cinnamon
½ teaspoon ground nutmeg
½ teaspoon ground ginger

5–6 cups sliced tart apples
1 three-ounce package cream cheese, softened
2 eggs
½ cup sour cream
½ cup sugar
Grated rind of ½ lemon

Combine the sugar, cinnamon, nutmeg, and ginger and toss the apples with the mixture. Fill the pie shell with the apples.

Beat together the cream cheese, eggs, sour cream, sugar, and lemon rind and pour over the apples.

Bake at 375°F. for 35 to 45 minutes until golden. Cool the pie to room temperature before cutting.

BASIC BUTTER CREAM ICING

Enough frosting for 2 tunnel cakes

¾ cup butter
¾ cup margarine
4 egg yolks
3 cups confectioners' sugar
Flavoring (see below)

Beat the butter and margarine until they are creamy. Beat the yolks into the butter. Beat in the sugar until it is very well blended.

Flavoring: For chocolate butter cream, beat in 3 squares melted, cooled unsweetened chocolate. For coffee or mocha butter cream, flavor with 2 teaspoons instant coffee and 1 tablespoon coffee liqueur. For orange butter cream, use orange liqueur and grated orange rind.

VANILLA BUTTER CREAM ICING

Makes 2 cups

2 egg yolks
½ cup butter
½ cup margarine
3 cups confectioners' sugar
1 teaspoon vanilla extract

Combine all the ingredients in the bowl of a mixer and beat until the icing is smooth.

PRALINES

1 cup sugar
½ cup chopped nuts

Heat the sugar in a heavy skillet over medium heat until the sugar is golden and syrupy. Do not stir. Rotate the pan on the burner to incorporate the uncooked sugar with the already melted sugar.

(Continued)

(Continued)

When all the sugar is bubbling, add the chopped nuts.
Pour the mixture onto foil.
When it is hard, pulverize it in a food processor.

FROZEN PACKAGED FOODS

CHICKEN ROLLS INDIENNE

Makes 24

4 ounces cream cheese	1 tablespoon chutney, chopped
2 tablespoons mayonnaise	½ teaspoon salt
1 cup finely chopped cooked chicken	1–2 teaspoons curry powder
½ cup chopped almonds	½ cup grated fresh coconut

In a bowl combine all the ingredients, except the coconut, and blend them well. If a food processor is used, be careful not to make a mushy consistency.

Form the mixture into small balls and roll them in the grated coconut.

Freeze the chicken rolls on a baking sheet. Package.

NOTE: This recipe can be doubled or tripled.

Labeling suggestion: CHICKEN ROLLS INDIENNE. A spicy bite to serve with drinks. Serve at room temperature.

ARTICHOKE PUFFS

Makes 36 squares

2 (six ounces each) jars marinated artichoke hearts	½ teaspoon dried oregano
1 small onion, chopped fine	2–3 drops Tabasco sauce
4 eggs	½ pound sharp Cheddar cheese, grated
¼ cup wheat germ	1 clove garlic
Salt and freshly ground black pepper to taste	2 tablespoons chopped parsley

Preheat oven to 325°F.

Drain the artichoke hearts, reserving 2 tablespoons of the marinade. In a skillet, cook the onion in the reserved marinade until it is soft. Finely chop the artichokes.

FROZEN PACKAGED FOODS / 215

In a large bowl beat the eggs, adding the wheat germ, salt, pepper, oregano, Tabasco, and grated cheese to them.

Put the garlic clove through a garlic press. Mix the artichokes, onion, parsley, and garlic into the eggs.

Turn the mixture into two 6- × 8-inch foil pans and bake for 25 minutes. Cool. Cut the artichoke puffs into small squares and freeze them. Package in plastic bags or foil pans with clear covers.

Labeling suggestion: ARTICHOKE PUFFS. That something different to thaw and serve with drinks or soup.

CHILLED CUCUMBER AND MINT SOUP

Serves 8

- 3 medium cucumbers
- 1 medium onion, thinly sliced
- 6 cups chicken bouillon
- 3 tablespoons flour
- 1 cup heavy cream
- 2 tablespoons chopped fresh mint
- Salt to taste
- Dash of Tabasco sauce

Peel, seed, and dice the cucumbers.

Combine the cucumbers, onion slices, and chicken bouillon in a saucepan. Bring the liquid to a boil, then reduce the heat. Cover the pan and simmer until the vegetables are tender, about 30 minutes.

Turn the vegetables and liquid into a blender or food processor. Add the flour, cream, and chopped mint. Blend until the soup is smooth. This will have to be done in two stages. Season to taste with salt and Tabasco sauce.

Cool the soup rapidly by placing its container in a pan of ice cubes.

When the soup is cold, pour it into 2 quart or 4 pint containers. Freeze.

Labeling suggestion: Keep Your Cool with Chilly CUCUMBER AND MINT SOUP. Serve garnished with a dab of whipped cream.

PUMPKIN SOUP

Makes 10 cups

- 6 tablespoons butter
- 4 leeks chopped, white part only
- 1 onion, minced
- 2 stalks celery, chopped
- 2 medium potatoes, peeled and diced
- 2 cups cooked pumpkin, puréed
- 6 cups chicken bouillon

(Continued)

(Continued)

  1 cup heavy cream
  Salt and freshly ground
    black pepper to taste
  ½ teaspoon freshly ground
    nutmeg

Melt the butter in a large heavy saucepan. Add the leeks, onion, and celery. Sauté the vegetables until they are soft. Stir in the potatoes. Cover and simmer the vegetables for 10 minutes.

Add the puréed pumpkin and chicken bouillon. Cook for 20 minutes longer.

Purée the vegetables and liquid in a blender or food processor. Add the cream, salt, pepper, and nutmeg, and blend well.

Cool the soup rapidly by placing its container in a pan of ice cubes.

When the soup is cold, fill 5 pint containers or 2 quart and 1 pint containers to within ½ inch of the top. Cover and freeze.

Labeling suggestion: Celebrate Autumn with PUMPKIN SOUP. Heat slowly and serve with grilled sausages, sautéed apples, and pecan pie.

SPICY TEX-MEX CHILI

Serves 6

  2 pounds lean beef (chuck or round), trimmed and diced
  1 pound smoked sausage (kielbasa or bratwurst)
  3 tablespoons vegetable oil
  2 medium onions, chopped fine
  1 clove garlic, minced
  1 tablespoon ground cumin
  1–2 tablespoons chili powder
  1 teaspoon salt
  Tabasco sauce to taste
  2 cups crushed or chopped tomatoes
  2 cups hot water
  2 cups canned red kidney beans, drained
  1 cup grated Cheddar cheese

Trim the beef and dice it very small. Chop the sausage into small pieces.

Heat the oil in a heavy skillet and brown the beef quickly. Reduce the heat to medium and cook the meat until all the moisture evaporates. Remove the beef and set it aside.

Add the sausage to the skillet and brown it. Add the onions and garlic and cook them until they are soft. Add more oil if necessary. Stir in the spices and Tabasco sauce to taste.

Add the chopped tomatoes and 2 cups of hot water to the skillet and bring them to a boil. Reduce the heat. Stir in the beef.

Cover and simmer the meat and vegetables over the lowest heat for 1 hour. Add the beans and continue cooking for another ½ hour to an hour until the meat is tender.

Turn the chili into four 4- × 5- × 2-inch foil pans. Sprinkle the grated cheese over each container and broil until the cheese is melted.

Cool the containers quickly and cover them with fitted plastic tops. Freeze.

Labeling suggestion: SPICY TEX-MEX CHILI. Heat and serve with corn bread and avocado salad.

HAM AND VEAL LOAF EN CROÛTE

Serves 6

PASTRY:
- 1 cup butter
- 2 cups flour
- 6 tablespoons sour cream
- ½ teaspoon salt
- 1 egg white

Combine all the ingredients and work them together until a smooth dough is formed. Shape the dough into a flat cake and wrap it in plastic. Chill.

HAM AND VEAL LOAF:
- 1 pound ground ham
- 1 pound ground veal
- ½ cup Madeira
- 1 clove garlic
- 2 shallots
- 1 medium onion
- 1 tart apple
- 1 cup fresh bread crumbs
- 1 egg
- 2 tablespoons chopped parsley
- Salt and freshly ground black pepper to taste
- 1 pinch powdered sage
- 2 tablespoons butter
- 6 chicken livers, washed and trimmed of fat
- 10–12 pistachio nuts
- 1 egg white
- Egg wash: 1 egg yolk beaten with 1 tablespoon water

Preheat oven to 375°F.

Place the ground meats in a bowl, pour in the Madeira, and set aside.

Mince the garlic, shallots, and onion. Peel and dice the apple. Add them and the bread crumbs to the meats. Add the egg, parsley, and seasonings into the meat mixture and mix well.

Melt butter and sauté the chicken livers for 5 minutes, browning them on all sides.

Roll out half the pastry into a rectangle. Shape half of the meat mixture into a rectangle on the pastry, leaving a ½-inch edge of pastry all around.

Place the chicken livers down the center of the meat. Sprinkle the pistachio nuts around the livers. Cover with a layer of the remaining meat. The resulting loaf should be 2½ to 3 inches in height.

(Continued)

(Continued)

Brush the pastry rim with the egg white and press it up onto the loaf.

Roll out the remaining pastry into a rectangle and place it over the loaf. Shape it to fit the loaf, press it against the rim of the bottom pastry. Trim away the extra pastry. Cut decorations out of the pastry scraps and glue them on top of the loaf with egg white. With fork tines prick around the bottom edge where the two pieces of pastry meet.

Chill the loaf for 1 hour.

Brush the loaf with the egg wash and bake on a baking sheet for 40 minutes until it is golden.

Cool, and freeze it on the baking pan. Then place the loaf in a plastic bag and tie tightly.

Labeling suggestion: HAM AND VEAL LOAF EN CROÛTE. Do not thaw. Heat in a 350°F. oven, loosely covered with foil, for 1½ hours.

CHICKEN CORDON BLEU

Serves 6

- 3 whole chicken breasts, skinned and boned
- 6 thin slices prosciutto ham
- 6 thin slices Swiss or Gruyère cheese
- Juice of 1 lemon
- 2 tablespoons butter
- ½ teaspoon salt
- Sauce Suprême (recipe follows)

Preheat oven to 425°F.

Split the chicken breasts and pound the halves between sheets of waxed paper until they they are thin and spread out. Place 1 slice of ham and 1 slice of cheese on each half-breast. Roll up the chicken, tucking in the sides. Place the rolls in a greased baking dish. Sprinkle lemon juice and salt over the rolls and dot them with butter. Cover the dish tightly with foil and bake for 15 minutes. The chicken should be opaque, not pink. Drain off the liquid into a measuring cup and reserve. Place two rolled chicken breasts in a 3½- × 6- × 3-inch foil container. Cover it with sauce suprême.

SAUCE SUPRÊME:

- 4 tablespoons butter
- 4 tablespoons flour
- 4 tablespoons reserved poaching liquid plus heavy cream and white wine to equal 2 cups
- 1 teaspoon brandy
- Salt and freshly ground black pepper to taste
- 1 teaspoon Dijon mustard, optional

Melt the butter in a saucepan and add the flour, stirring constantly until they are bubbly and well blended.

Add the 2 cups of poaching liquid combined with cream and wine and cook, stirring, until the sauce is thick and smooth. Stir in the brandy and season with salt and pepper. If desired, add the Dijon mustard.

Divide the sauce evenly among the 3 containers and garnish with parsley. Freeze.

Labeling suggestion: CHICKEN CORDON BLEU. Thaw and heat in a 325°F. oven until warm through. Serve with rice and a green salad.

SPICY CHICKEN WITH GINGER

Serves 6

3 whole chicken breasts, skinned and boned
Juice of ½ lemon
½ teaspoon salt

3 cups cooked rice
Ginger Sauce (recipe follows)

Preheat oven to 425°F.

Split the chicken breasts and place them in a single layer in a baking pan. Sprinkle the chicken with lemon juice and salt. Cover the pan tightly with foil.

Bake for 12 to 15 minutes, until the breasts are no longer pink. They should be opaque and firm to the touch. Cool.

Place each breast in a 3½- × 6- × 3-inch foil container over ½ cup of cooked rice, cover with ginger sauce, and freeze.

GINGER SAUCE:
½ cup orange juice
½ cup Port wine
⅓ cup ginger marmalade

Grated rind of 1 orange
⅓ cup heavy cream

Combine the orange juice, Port wine, marmalade, and orange rind in a saucepan. Heat the ingredients, stirring, until the marmalade is melted. Cook until the sauce is thickened and reduced.

Add the cream and boil for 2 to 3 minutes.

When the sauce is well blended, pour it over the chicken breasts in each container.

Labeling suggestion: SPICY CHICKEN WITH GINGER. Dinner for one can be fun! Thaw and heat until the sauce is bubbling.

ZESTY ZITI

Serves 6

1 pound ziti	2 tablespoons vegetable oil
Salted water	1 cup grated Parmesan cheese
2 (ten ounces each) packages frozen artichoke hearts	4 cups well-seasoned tomato sauce
7 tablespoons butter	½ pound provolone cheese
1 pound mushrooms, sliced	

Preheat oven to 350°F.

Cook the ziti for about 10 minutes in boiling salted water until it is "al dente." Drain and rinse the pasta.

Cook the frozen artichoke hearts in salted water for 5 to 7 minutes. Slice them into quarters.

Melt 6 tablespoons of butter and sauté the mushrooms over high heat for about 5 minutes.

Heat 1 tablespoon of butter and the oil together and toss with the ziti, coating it well.

Divide the ziti evenly among four 8- × 2-inch round foil pans. Sprinkle each portion with 3 tablespoons of Parmesan cheese. Divide the artichoke hearts evenly and arrange them over the ziti. Arrange a layer of the sautéed mushrooms over the artichokes. Season each layer with salt and pepper.

Pour 1 cup of tomato sauce into each container. Slice the provolone very thinly and arrange slices over the sauce. Sprinkle each container with the remaining Parmesan cheese.

Bake the ziti casseroles for 30 minutes. Cool them quickly and seal the containers with plastic covers. Freeze.

Labeling suggestion: ZESTY ZITI—A HEARTY CASSEROLE. Serve with garlic bread and salad.

INDIVIDUAL CHEESE SOUFFLÉS

Makes 4 soufflés

3 tablespoons butter	½ teaspoon prepared mustard, preferably Dijon
3 tablespoons flour	
1 cup milk	2–3 drops Tabasco sauce
6 eggs, separated	1⅓ cups grated cheese, Swiss and Parmesan mixed
Salt and freshly ground black pepper to taste	
	¼ teaspoon cream of tartar

Melt the butter in a saucepan and add the flour, stirring constantly over medium-high heat until they are well blended and bubbly. Add the milk and cook, stirring, until the mixture is smooth and thickened.

Remove the pan from the heat and beat in the egg yolks, one at a time. Season with salt, pepper, mustard, and Tabasco. Stir in the grated cheese.

Beat the egg whites until they are foamy. Add the cream of tartar and beat until the whites are stiff. Fold one-third of the whites rapidly into the soufflé mixture, stirring well. Gently fold in the remainder of the whites.

Turn the mixture into 4 buttered 1½-cup round foil containers.

When cool, freeze the soufflés. Package them in clear plastic bags.

Labeling suggestion: SINGLES' SOUFFLÉ. Place in a preheated 325°F. oven. Bake for 45 to 50 minutes until puffed and firm. Eat immediately.

ORANGE KUMQUAT BREAD

Makes 3 loaves

6 kumquats	½ cup orange juice
Grated rind of 1 orange	1 cup milk
½ cup sugar	3½ cups flour
¼ cup melted butter	4 teaspoons baking powder
1 egg	1 teaspoon salt

Preheat oven to 350°F.

Grease and flour three 5½- × 3- × 2-inch loaf pans.

Halve the kumquats and remove the seeds and white membrane. Place the kumquats in the container of a food processor fitted with a metal blade.

Add the orange rind and sugar. Grind them for 10 seconds. Add the melted butter, egg, orange juice, and milk. Process until the mixture is smooth, and turn it into a bowl.

Combine the flour with the baking powder and salt. Mix the flour into the kumquat mixture.

Turn the batter into the pans and bake for 50 minutes until the bread tests done.

Remove the loaves from the pans and cool them on racks. Freeze, then place the loaves in plastic bags and tie tightly.

Labeling suggestion: ORANGE KUMQUAT BREAD. Thaw at room temperature. Serve sliced thin with cream cheese or toasted with butter.

STOVEPIPE BREAD

Makes 2 loaves

1 package yeast
½ cup lukewarm water
3 tablespoons sugar
1 thirteen-ounce can evaporated milk
2 teaspoons salt
4 tablespoons melted butter
4–5 cups flour

Dissolve the yeast in ½ cup of lukewarm water in a large bowl with 1 tablespoon of sugar. Let it stand until it is bubbly.

Stir in the remaining sugar, the milk, salt, and melted butter.

Beat in the flour 1 cup at a time. The dough should be very heavy and too sticky to knead.

Turn the dough into 2 well-greased 1-pound coffee cans. Cover them with well-greased plastic lids. Let the cans stand in a warm place until the dough rises and pops off the lids, about 1 hour and 15 minutes.

Discard the lids and bake at 350°F. for 45 minutes. The tops of the bread will be very brown.

Remove the cans from the oven and let them stand for 10 minutes. Carefully run a sharp knife around the top edges and slide the breads out of the cans.

Allow the bread to cool standing upright. Freeze. Package.

Labeling suggestion: STOVEPIPE BREAD. Slices in the round. Good, toasted, with soup. Wrap in foil and defrost in 350°F. oven for 30 minutes.

BRANDIED ORANGE CRÊPES

Serves 6

4 tablespoons unsalted butter
¼ cup sugar
½ cup orange juice
2 tablespoons orange liqueur
1 tablespoon brandy
Grated rind of 1 orange
½ cup apricot preserves
18 crêpes (see recipe, page 176)
¼ cup slivered almonds

Heat the butter, sugar, and orange juice in a skillet. Simmer until they are blended. Add the orange liqueur, brandy, and orange rind.

Spread each crêpe with a thin layer of apricot preserves. Fold the crêpes into envelopes.

Place the folded crêpes in the skillet and simmer in the sauce, basting, until they are well soaked.

Arrange the crêpes in 6- × 4-inch foil pans, overlapping them in two rows, six to a pan. Pour the remaining sauce over the crêpes and sprinkle them with almonds. Freeze. Package.

Labeling suggestion: BRANDIED ORANGE CRÊPES. For a gala dessert, heat crêpes in sauce in chafing dish. Flame with brandy.

FROSTED ORANGE-ALMOND MERINGUE

Serves 8

MERINGUE SHELL:

- 3 egg whites at room temperature
- Pinch of salt
- 1 cup confectioners' sugar
- ½ cup finely chopped almonds
- 1 tablespoon cornstarch

Preheat oven to 225°F.
Lightly grease a 9-inch pie pan.
Beat the egg whites with a pinch of salt until they are foamy. Add the sugar one tablespoon at a time until you have used ¾ cup.
Mix the remaining sugar with the almonds and cornstarch. Fold them into the meringue.
Spread the meringue onto the prepared pan. Bake in the oven for 2 hours until the meringue is no longer sticky to the touch.

FILLING:

- 1 can sweetened condensed milk
- ¾ cup orange juice
- ¼ cup orange liqueur
- 1 cup heavy cream, whipped
- 2 tablespoons grated unsweetened chocolate
- 2 tablespoons grated orange rind

Combine the condensed milk, orange juice, orange liqueur, and the whipped cream. Turn the filling into the baked meringue shell. Freeze the pie overnight.
Sprinkle the pie with the grated chocolate and orange rind.
Package and store in the freezer.
Labeling suggestion: FROSTED ORANGE-ALMOND MERINGUE. Cool and refreshing. A mid-winter treat. Thaw for 20 minutes before serving.

FROZEN WALNUT SOUFFLÉ

Makes 2 soufflés; each serves 6

- ¾ cup granulated sugar
- ½ cup walnuts
- 4 eggs
- ¼ cup strong coffee

(Continued)

(Continued)

Hot water
1 cup heavy cream
⅔ cup confectioners' sugar
1 cup sour cream
2 tablespoons dark or amber rum

Heat the sugar in a heavy skillet until it turns liquid and dark brown. Shake the skillet frequently; do not stir.

When the sugar is smoking and syrupy, add the walnuts. Turn the caramel out onto foil. Cool it completely, then break it up and pulverize it in a food processor.

Combine the eggs and coffee in a bowl over a pan of hot water, as in a double boiler. Place the pan over medium heat. Beat the egg mixture until it is thickened. Remove the bowl from the pan of hot water and beat the mixture until it is cool.

Whip the cream into stiff peaks, adding confectioners' sugar gradually.

Combine the whipped cream with the sour cream. Stir in the rum and caramel-walnut mixture.

Turn the mixture into two 7- × 1½-inch round foil containers and freeze.

When the soufflés are solid, pipe whipped cream on the top of each soufflé. Freeze again.

Cover the foil containers with clear plastic tops.

Labeling suggestion: FROZEN WALNUT SOUFFLÉ. A little goes a long way. Let stand at room temperature for 15 minutes before serving.

BISCUIT TORTONI

Serves 8

½ (eight-ounce) package almond toast or almond cookies
2 cups heavy cream
4 egg yolks
½ cup sugar
¼ cup dry sherry

Break up the almond toast and grind it into fine crumbs in the blender or food processor.

Beat the cream into stiff peaks. Beat the egg yolks with the sugar until they are light in color.

Combine the whipped cream with the beaten eggs. Stir in the sherry.

Turn half the mixture into an 8- × 5-inch loaf pan. Sprinkle it with 4 to 6 tablespoons of the crumbs. Cover with a layer of the remaining cream mixture.

Freeze. When the loaf is solid, turn it out onto the counter. Cover the top and sides with the remaining crumbs.

Refreeze the loaf on foil-covered cardboard. Then, seal it in a plastic bag.

Labeling suggestion: A LOAF OF BISCUIT TORTONI. Just slice and serve right from the freezer.

ALMOND-GRAND MARNIER TEA CAKE

Serves 6 to 8

- 3 eggs, separated
- ¾ cup sugar
- ⅓ cup Grand Marnier or other orange liqueur
- ¼ teaspoon almond extract
- ¾ cup flour
- ¾ cup finely ground almonds
- ½ cup unsalted butter, melted
- ¼ teaspoon salt
- Butter for greasing
- Whole blanched almonds

Preheat oven to 350°F.

Beat the egg yolks until they are light in color. Gradually beat in ½ cup of sugar plus 2 tablespoons.

Add the orange liqueur and almond extract. Beat in the flour. Stir in the almonds, then the melted butter.

Beat the egg whites with ¼ teaspoon of salt until they are foamy. Beat in the remaining 2 tablespoons of sugar gradually and continue beating until the egg whites are stiff. Fold the whites into the cake batter.

Turn the batter into a well-greased and floured 1½-quart mold or a small Bundt cake pan. Bake for 30 minutes until the cake tests done.

Cool the cake in the pan for 10 minutes. Turn it out onto a rack and allow it to cool.

Decorate the cake with whole blanched almonds. Freeze the cake. Place the cake on a cardboard tray and package it in a plastic bag.

Labeling suggestion: SPIRITED TEA CAKE. Serve this almond-orange-flavored cake at your next luncheon or tea.

MOCHA APPLESAUCE CAKE

Serves 8

- ½ cup butter
- 1 cup sugar
- 1 tablespoon instant coffee
- 1¼ cups applesauce
- 1 egg
- 1¾ cups flour
- 1 teaspoon baking soda
- ½ teaspoon salt
- 1 teaspoon ground cinnamon
- ½ teaspoon ground nutmeg

(Continued)

(Continued)

½ teaspoon ground ginger
1 cup chopped walnuts

Mocha Butter Cream Icing
(see recipe, page 202)

Preheat oven to 350°F.
Grease and flour a 9-inch round foil pan.
Cream the butter and sugar until they are light.
Dissolve the instant coffee in the applesauce.
Beat the egg into the butter mixture.
Combine the flour, baking soda, salt, and spices, and add them alternately with the applesauce to the creamed mixture. Stir in the walnuts.
Turn the batter into pan and bake for 35 to 40 minutes until the cake tests done.
Cool the cake, then frost it with mocha butter cream icing.
Freeze and package the cake in a plastic bag, tightly tied.

Labeling suggestion: MOIST MOCHA APPLESAUCE CAKE with creamy Mocha Butter Cream Icing. Bring to room temperature for best flavor.

APRICOT CAKE

Serves 10

½ cup butter
8 ounces cream cheese
1¼ cups sugar
2 eggs
1 teaspoon vanilla extract
½ teaspoon almond extract
2 cups flour
1 teaspoon baking soda
1 teaspoon baking powder
¼ teaspoon salt

¼ cup milk
1 twelve-ounce jar apricot preserves
1 tablespoon brandy
Vanilla Butter Cream Icing (see recipe, page 213), flavored with almond extract
½ cup toasted slivered almonds

Preheat oven to 350°F.
Grease and flour two 8-inch cake pans.
Cream the butter and cream cheese until they are light, beating in the sugar. Beat in the eggs, vanilla, and almond extract.
Combine the flour, baking soda, baking powder, and salt, and add them alternately with milk to the cream cheese mixture. Turn the batter into the prepared cake pans.
Heat the apricot preserves with 1 tablespoon of brandy, until it becomes liquid. Spread half the melted preserves over each pan of batter.
Bake for 30 to 40 minutes until the layers test done. Remove them to racks.

Let the layers stand for 10 minutes, then remove them from the pans. When they are cool, spread vanilla butter cream icing flavored with almond extract between the two layers and on the top and sides of the cake.

Sprinkle the top with almonds and decorate it with icing piped through a pastry tube.

Place the cake on a cardboard round and freeze it. Package the cake in a plastic bag and tie it tightly.

Labeling suggestion: SPECIAL ALMOND-APRICOT PARTY CAKE. Thaw to room temperature before serving.

BLUEBERRY SQUARES

Makes 9 squares

¼ cup butter
1 cup brown sugar
2 eggs
1 cup flour
1 teaspoon baking powder
½ teaspoon ground cinnamon

⅛ teaspoon salt
1 tablespoon lemon rind
1 teaspoon vanilla extract
1 cup blueberries
½ cup chopped walnuts

Preheat oven to 350°F.
Grease and flour an 8-inch square pan.
Cream the butter and sugar until it is light in color. Beat in the eggs.

Combine the flour, baking powder, cinnamon, salt, and lemon rind and stir them in. Add the vanilla. Stir in the blueberries and walnuts.

Turn the batter into a pan and bake for 40 to 45 minutes, or until done.

Cool the cake on a rack. Cut it into squares and remove them from the pan.

Place them on a baking sheet and freeze. Then place them in plastic bags or foil pans and store in the freezer.

Labeling suggestion: SUMMER FRESH BLUEBERRY SQUARES. Great for parties or picnics, especially with lemon sherbet.

BOURBON-PECAN CAKE

Makes 1 loaf

½ cup butter
½ cup brown sugar
2 eggs
2 cups flour
2½ teaspoons baking powder

½ teaspoon salt
½ cup maple syrup
½ cup bourbon whiskey
1½ cups chopped pecans
Confectioners' sugar

(Continued)

(Continued)

Preheat oven to 350°F.

Grease and flour a small tube pan, 8- × 5-inch loaf pan, or small Bundt pan.

Cream the butter and brown sugar until they are light in color. Beat in the eggs one at a time.

Combine the flour, baking powder, and salt. Beat the dry ingredients into the creamed mixture alternately with the maple syrup and bourbon. Mix the batter well. Stir in the pecans.

Turn the batter into the prepared pan and bake for 45 to 50 minutes until the cake tests done. Let it stand in the pan for 10 minutes.

Turn out the cake onto a rack and allow it to cool. Sprinkle the cake with confectioners' sugar.

Package in plastic bags and freeze the cake.

Labeling suggestion: BOURBON-PECAN CAKE. Southern comfort in a dessert! Serve with fresh fruit.

BUCHE DE NOËL

Makes 1 log; serves 10

CAKE:
4 eggs, separated	1 teaspoon baking powder
¾ cup sugar	¾ cup flour
Pinch of salt	1 teaspoon vanilla extract

Preheat oven to 375°F.

Prepare a 10- × 15-inch jelly roll pan. Grease the pan and line it with greased waxed paper extending 1 inch over either end.

Beat the egg yolks until they are light in color, adding the sugar gradually.

Beat the egg whites with a pinch of salt until they are stiff.

Combine the baking powder and flour.

Quickly mix one-third of the egg whites into the yolk mixture. Fold the remaining whites and the flour mixture gently but rapidly into the egg yolks, sifting the flour mixture over the top as you fold. Add the vanilla.

Spread the batter in the prepared pan. Bake for 12 minutes.

Turn the cake out onto a clean towel. Allow the cake to stand for 5 minutes, then strip off the paper. Roll the cake up. Unroll it and cool.

CHOCOLATE ICING:
6 tablespoons margarine	3 cups confectioners' sugar
6 tablepoons butter	3 squares unsweetened
4 egg yolks	chocolate, melted

Beat together the margarine and butter. Beat in the egg yolks. Add the sugar and beat well. Add the chocolate and beat again.

Chill until the icing is of a spreadable consistency.

MERINGUE MUSHROOMS:
  3 egg whites
  ⅛ teaspoon salt
  ¾ cup superfine sugar

Beat egg whites with salt until foamy. Add the sugar by tablespoonfuls. Beat until the whites are stiff and shiny.

Fill a pastry bag fitted with a ½-inch tip with the meringue. Holding the pastry bag directly over a lightly greased baking sheet, form the mushroom caps, by piping 1-inch "blobs" of meringue. Hold pastry bag almost horizontal with baking sheet and pipe 1 to 1½-inch separate stems. With a wet fingertip, smooth out "tails," or drippings.

Bake at 225°F. for 1 to 2 hours until meringues are completely dry. Remove them from the pan and freeze the mushrooms in plastic bags.

To assemble the log, spread the cake roll with chocolate icing. Roll it up and cover the outside with more icing.

With a serrated knife, cut off each end of the roll at an angle to resemble a log. Cut a piece off one of the ends and stick it into the log to make a twig. The icing should look somewhat bumpy to resemble bark.

With the sharp point of a knife, make a hole in the top of each mushroom. Fill the hole with icing and stick in a stem. Glue the mushrooms to the sides of the log with icing. Use three mushrooms on one side, two on the other.

Combine the cocoa and confectioners' sugar in a small strainer and sprinkle them over mushrooms to resemble snow and dirt.

Make a piece of holly for the top of the log using long strips of citron and small bits of red candied cherries for berries.

Refrigerate the log before packaging it, so the frosting won't stick to the plastic bag.

NOTE: This is a good item to have on order for the holidays. The meringue mushrooms and icing can be made ahead and frozen. The whole cake can be assembled and frozen, although it is better when freshly made. Have ready long pieces of cardboard to place the log on and extra long plastic bags for wrapping.

Labeling suggestion: BUCHE DE NOËL. The traditional holiday log. Transfer to a platter before thawing at room temperature.

CHOCOLATE CAKE

Serves 8

2 squares unsweetened
   chocolate
¼ cup butter
1 cup sugar
½ cup boiling water
¾ teaspoon baking soda
¼ cup sour cream
1 egg
1 teaspoon vanilla extract
1 cup flour
Pinch of salt
Vanilla Butter Cream Icing
   (see recipe, page 213)

Preheat oven to 375°F.
Grease and flour a 7-inch round cake pan.

Heat the chocolate and butter in a saucepan until they are melted and well blended. While the pan is still over the flame, stir in the sugar and ½ cup of boiling water. Stir until the sugar dissolves, then remove the pan from the heat.

Dissolve the baking soda in the sour cream. Add the sour cream, egg, and vanilla to the chocolate mixture in the saucepan and mix well. Beat in the flour and salt. Turn the batter into the prepared pan.

Bake for 40 to 45 minutes until the cake tests done. Remove the pan to a rack. Let it stand for 10 minutes.

Run a knife around the edge of the pan and turn out the cake onto the rack. Cool. With a serrated knife, cut the cake into two layers.

Frost it with vanilla butter cream icing. With a pastry tube decorate the top.

Refrigerate before packaging the cake in a plastic bag and freezing it.

Labeling suggestion: MOIST CHOCOLATE CAKE. A small, family-sized cake with a big chocolate flavor.

DOUBLE CHOCOLATE CAKE

Serves 8 to 10

2 (three ounces each)
   packages cream cheese
¾ cup butter
1 teaspoon vanilla extract
6 cups confectioners' sugar
¼ cup hot coffee
4 squares unsweetened
   chocolate, melted
2¼ cups flour
1½ teaspoons baking soda
1 teaspoon salt
3 eggs
¾ cup buttermilk
Pecan or walnut halves

Preheat oven to 350°F.
Grease and flour two 9-inch cake pans.

Cream until smooth the cream cheese and 4 tablespoons of butter mixed with the vanilla. Beat 3 cups of confectioners' sugar into the cream cheese mixture. Beat in the remaining sugar and the coffee. Blend in the melted chocolate. Remove and set aside half the mixture to use as frosting.

Combine the flour, baking soda, and salt.

Beat the remaining ¼ cup of butter into the remaining chocolate-cream cheese mixture. Beat in the eggs, one at a time. Then beat buttermilk alternately with dry ingredients into the chocolate batter.

Turn it into the prepared pans and bake for 30 to 40 minutes until the cake tests done. Cool the layers in the pans for 10 minutes. Turn them out onto racks.

When they are cold, stack them with a layer of frosting between and cover the top and sides with frosting. Decorate the top of the cake with nut halves.

Freeze the cake uncovered. Place the cake on a cardboard tray and package in a plastic bag, tightly tied.

Labeling suggestion: DOUBLE CHOCOLATE CAKE. For chocolate lovers only!

DOBOS TORTE

Serves 8 to 10

1 sixteen-ounce frozen pound cake
2 recipes Chocolate Butter Cream Icing (see recipe, page 213)
Caramel pieces (recipe follows)

Make the caramel and break it up into small pieces.

With a serrated knife, cut the partially thawed cake into 5 slices. Spread the slices with the chocolate butter cream icing and stack up the layers.

Put the remaining icing into a pastry tube with a star tip. Make a wall-like border around the outer edge of the top of the cake by piping two rows of icing. Fill the space between the two rows with the broken caramel. Pipe rosettes of icing at each corner of the cake.

Refrigerate the cake until the icing is hard, then place it in a plastic bag and freeze it.

CARAMEL:
1 cup sugar

Pour the sugar into a heavy skillet over medium heat. When the sugar starts to darken and become syrupy, rotate the pan occasionally to incorporate the uncooked sugar. Do not stir.

(Continued)

(Continued)

When the sugar is completely melted, dark, and syrupy and is bubbling, pour it onto a piece of foil. Break it into small pieces after it has hardened.

Labeling suggestion: DOBOS TORTE. Pure party food. Transfer while frozen to a serving platter.

LEMON TEA CAKE

2 loaves

Grated rind of 2 lemons
1 cup vegetable oil
1½ cups sugar
6 eggs
1⅓ cups flour
¼ teaspoon salt
⅓ cup wheat germ
½ teaspoon ground mace
2 teaspoons baking powder
½ cup finely chopped almonds

Preheat oven to 300°F.

Beat together the lemon rind, oil, and sugar. Beat in the eggs, one at a time.

Combine the flour, salt, wheat germ, mace, and baking powder and stir them into the egg mixture. Add the chopped almonds. Turn the batter into 2 greased and floured 8- × 5-inch loaf pans.

Bake for 1 hour and 10 minutes or until the cakes test done. Let them stand for 10 minutes.

Run a knife around the edges and turn the cakes out onto racks to cool. Freeze. Package.

Labeling suggestions: LIGHT AND LEMONY TEA CAKE with a hint of almonds. Good plain or heated and spread with apricot jam.

MELON CAKE

Serves 8

1 cup sugar
1 cup flour
1 teaspoon baking powder
⅛ teaspoon salt
2 large eggs
Heavy cream (⅔ cups, plus ½ cup, whipped)
Pralines (see recipe, page 213)
Mocha Butter Cream Icing (see recipe, page 202)

Preheat oven to 350°F.

Combine the sugar, flour, baking powder, and salt in a bowl.

Break the eggs into a measuring cup and fill the cup with heavy cream to make one liquid cup. Stir the eggs and cream into the dry ingredients, beating until they are smooth.

Turn the batter into a well-buttered and floured 6-cup melon mold. Bake in the oven for 50 to 60 minutes, until the cake tests done in the center. Let it stand for 10 minutes.

Carefully turn the cake out onto a rack. Cool it completely.

With a serrated knife, cut a 1½-inch slice off the bottom—flat side. Hollow out the rounded top of the cake and fill it with the ½ cup of cream that has been whipped and mixed with the pralines. Put the two pieces back together again and frost the cake with Mocha Butter Cream.

Decorate it with a pastry tube to give a melon-like appearance. Freeze the cake, then wrap it.

Labeling suggestion: MOCHA MELON CAKE. A light, non-butter cake filled with whipped cream and pralines, and iced with rich buttercream. A very special dessert.

FRENCH ORANGE CAKE

Serves 10 to 12

- 1 cup boiling water
- 1 pound pitted dates, chopped
- ½ cup butter
- 1 cup sugar
- 2 eggs, separated
- 2 cups flour
- 1 teaspoon baking soda
- 2 teaspoons baking powder
- Grated rind of 3 oranges
- 2 cups chopped toasted almonds
- ⅛ teaspoon salt

Preheat oven to 300°F.

Lightly grease and flour one angel food cake pan.

Pour 1 cup of boiling water over the dates. Cream the butter and sugar until they are very light. Beat in the egg yolks. Combine the flour, baking soda, and baking powder. Add them alternately with the date mixture to the creamed mixture. Stir in the orange rind and chopped almonds. Beat the egg whites with ⅛ teaspoon of salt until they are stiff. Fold the egg whites into the batter. Turn it into the prepared pan and bake for 1 hour or until the cake tests done. Pour the following topping over the cake before removing it from the pan.

TOPPING:

- ½ cup orange juice
- ¼ cup orange liqueur
- 1 cup sugar
- Grated rind of 1 orange

Combine all the ingredients in a saucepan and heat until the sugar is dissolved. Pour it over the warm cake.

(Continued)

(Continued)

When the cake is cool, remove it from the pan. Place it on a cardboard round and freeze it. Put it in a plastic bag and tie the end tightly.

Labeling suggestion: FRENCH ORANGE CAKE with triple orange flavor. Thaw to room temperature before serving.

Index for A Cookbook for Caterers

Almond(s)
 barbecued, 116
 brown rice with, 159
 –Grand Marnier tea cake, 225
 -orange meringue, frosted, 223
 tarts, tiny, 196
Amber glazed onions, 162–63
Appetizers
 almonds, barbecued, 116
 brandade de morue, 118
 caponata with black bread, 113
 caviar mold, 118
 cheese
  Edam, stuffed, 127
  strudels, tiny, 126–27
 chicken
  balls, crispy, 123
  canapés, curried, 123
  liver pâté, 122
 coquilles seviche, 119
 crab- and shrimp-filled éclairs, 119–20
 croissants, stuffed, 125
 crudités
  with guacamole, 113
  tapenade with, 117
 cucumber-shrimp rounds, 116
 curried lamb meatballs, 124
 fish timbales with sauce Aurore, 121–22
 garlic popcorn, 116
 gougère ring filled with ham, 127–28
 mushroom(s)
  herbed marinated, 114
  stuffed, 115
  turnovers, 114–15
 sardine deviled eggs, 117
 sausage en brioche, 124–25
 shrimp
  -filled éclairs, 119–20
  toast, 120–21
 veal and spinach pâté, 125–26
Apple(s)
 -blueberry soup, 129
 pie, sour cream, 212–13
 roast veal with, in orange sauce, 139–40
 slices, glazed, 185–86
Applesauce cake, mocha, 225–26
Apricot cake, 226–27
Artichoke(s)
 puffs, 214–15
 tarragon chicken with, 151–52
Asparagus soup, 129–30
Aspic, salmon or striped bass in, 136–37
Avocado(s), guacamole, crudités with, 113

Barbecued almonds, 116

INDEX FOR A COOKBOOK FOR CATERERS / 235

Beef, dried, and horseradish sandwiches, 174
Biscuit tortoni, 224–25
Biscuits, buttermilk, 181–82
Blueberry
 -apple soup, 129
 charlotte, 208–9
 muffins, 181
 squares, 227
Bourbon
 balls, 196
 -pecan cake, 227–28
Brandade de morue, 118
Bread
 black, caponata with, 113
 French, 184
 herb, 185
 orange kumquat, 221
 pudding with brandied fruits, 193–94
 refrigerator rolls, 182
 stovepipe, 222
Brie en croûte, 198
Brioche, 180–81
 sausage en, 124–25
Broccoli
 purée, corn timbales on, 166
 puréed, and winter squash, 161
Brownies, 196–97
Buche de Noël, 228–29
Butter cream icing
 basic, 213
 vanilla, 213
Butterflied leg of lamb, 142
Buttermilk biscuits, 181–82

Cabbage, stuffed, 139
Cake(s), 225–33
 apricot, 226–27
 bourbon-pecan, 227–28
 buche de Noël, 228–29
 carrot, 199–200
 cheese-, baby, 199
 chocolate, 230
  double, 230–31
 coffee, sour cream pecan, 204
 Danish cream, 200
 melon, 232–33
 mocha applesauce, 225–26
 orange, French, 233–34
 pound, lemon yogurt, 201–2

rum raisin, holiday, 203
Sally Lunn, 203–4
tea
 almond-Grand Marnier, 225
 lemon, 232
 tunnel, 205
 wedding, 206–7
Canapés, curried chicken, 123
Cannelloni, crêpes, 176–77
Caponata with black bread, 113
Caramel sauce, floating islands with, 190–91
Carrot(s)
 cake, 199–200
 parslied, 162
 potage Parmentier with, 130
 rapées, 168
 veal and, roulade, 141–42
Casserole, pork and sausage, 143–44
Caviar mold, 118
Celery root remoulade, 168
Cheese(s)
 bread sticks, 183
 Edam, stuffed, 127
 gougère ring filled with ham, 127–28
 macaroni with three, 157
 mushrooms stuffed with, 115
 soufflés, individual, 220–21
 strudels, tiny, 126–27
Cheesecakes, baby, 199
Cherry tomatoes with cucumbers, sautéed, 163
Chestnuts, puréed spinach with, 161–62
Chicken
 balls, crispy, 123
 breasts, duxelles, 147–48
 canapés, curried, 123
 cordon bleu, 218–19
 and corn chowder, 131
 country captain, 145
 drumsticks, stuffed, 154
 Florentine, 150–51
 with ginger, spicy, 219
 hash à la Ritz, 152–53
 Kiev, 146–47
 liver pâté, 122
  croissants stuffed with, 125
  mushrooms stuffed with, 115
 Marengo, 146
 Marsala, 151
 and oyster pie, 153

poulet vert, 149–50
rolls Indienne, 214
salad
  in curry ring, 172–73
  romaine leaves filled with, 173
tarragon, with artichokes, 151–52
turban of, with watercress sauce, 148–49
Chili, spicy Tex-Mex, 216–17
Chocolate
  cake, 230
    double, 230–31
  cream, 192–93
Chowder, corn and chicken, 131
Cod, brandade de morue, 118
Coffee
  macaroon cream, 193
  mousse, frozen, 188–89
  soufflé, Irish, 194
Coffee cake, sour cream pecan, 204
Compote, hot fruit, 187–88
Cookies, oatmeal, 197
Coquilles seviche, 119
Corn
  popcorn, garlic, 116
  soufflé, 166
  timbales on broccoli purée, 166
Country captain, 145
Crab(meat)
  -filled éclairs, 119–20
  finnan haddie roulade with, 133–34
  pasties, 135–36
  soufflé, 133
Crêpes
  cannelloni, 176–77
  Florentine, 179–80
  onion, filled with smoked salmon, 178
  orange, brandied, 222–23
  seafood, 178–79
Croissants, stuffed, 125
Crudités
  with guacamole, 113
  tapenade with, 117
Cucumber(s)
  cherry tomatoes with, sautéed, 163
  and green pepper salad, 169
  and mint soup, chilled, 215
  mousse, 169
  ring, seafood vinaigrette in, 132–33
  -shrimp rounds, 116

and tomatoes, marinated, 163
Curried chicken canapés, 123
Curried lamb meatballs, 124
Curry ring, chicken salad in, 172–73

Dacquoise, 189–90
Danish cream cake, 200
Desserts, 185–214
  almond tarts, tiny, 196
  apple slices, glazed, 185–86
  apricot cake, 226–27
  biscuit tortoni, 224–25
  blueberry charlotte, 208–9
  blueberry squares, 227
  bourbon balls, 196
  bourbon-pecan cake, 227–28
  bread pudding with brandied fruits, 193–94
  brie en croûte, 198
  brownies, 196–97
  buche de Noël, 228–29
  butter cream icing, 213
  carrot cake, 199–200
  cheesecakes, baby, 199
  chocolate cake, 230
    double, 230–31
  chocolate cream, 192–93
  coffee macaroon cream, 193
  coffee mousse, frozen, 188–89
  dacquoise, 189–90
  Danish cream cake, 200
  Dobos torte, 231–32
  floating islands with caramel sauce, 190–91
  fruit compote, hot, 187–88
  fruit tarts, 209–10
  gingered fruit, 186
  Irish coffee soufflé, 194
  lemon chess tart, 210
  lemon curd, 192
  lemon sponge roll, 201
  lemon tea cake, 232
  lemon yogurt pound cake, 201–2
  mango mousse with rum sauce, 189
  melon cake, 232–33
  melon crescents in wine, 188
  meringue cups with lemon curd, 191
  mocha applesauce cake, 225–26
  mocha soufflé, cold, 195
  mocha torte, five-layer, 202–3

INDEX FOR A COOKBOOK FOR CATERERS / 237

oatmeal cookies, 197
orange-almond meringue, frosted, 223
orange cake, French, 233–34
orange crêpes, brandied, 222–23
peaches, poached, with raspberry sauce, 187
peaches, sliced, in honey and brandy, 186
pear crumble, baked, 211
pear crunch pie, 210–11
pralines, 213–14
puff pastry, 207–8
rhubarb crumble with brandied whipped cream, 212
rum raisin cake, holiday, 203
Sally Lunn, 203–4
shortbread, 205
sour cream apple pie, 212–13
sour cream pecan coffee cake, 204
strawberry soufflé, cold, 195
walnut oatmeal roll with whipped cream, 197–98
walnut soufflé, frozen, 223–24
Deviled eggs, sardine, 117
Dobos torte, 231–32

Eclairs, crab- and shrimp-filled, 119–20
Edam cheese, stuffed, 127
Egg(s)
  mollet Florentine, 155
  sardine deviled, 117
Eggplant, caponata with black bread, 113
Endive and watercress, julienne of, 170

Finnan haddie roulade with crabmeat, 133–34
Fish
  brandade de morue, 118
  finnan haddie roulade with crabmeat, 133–34
  kedgeree, 134–35
  salmon or striped bass in aspic, 136–37
  seviche, 119
  timbales with sauce Aurore, 121–22
  See also Seafood
Floating islands with caramel sauce, 190–91
French bread, 184
French orange cake, 233–34
Frozen packaged foods, 214–34

Fruit
  brandied, bread pudding with, 193–94
  compote, hot, 187–88
  gingered, 186
  sauce, pork olives with yams and, 144–45
  tarts, 209–10
  See also specific fruits

Game hens with ginger sauce, 154–55
Garlic popcorn, 116
Gazpacho, 128
Ginger
  chicken with, spicy, 219
  sauce, game hens with, 154–55
Gingered fruit, 186
Gnocchi, 160
Gougère ring filled with ham, 127–28
Grapefruit ring with watercress, 171
Green bean salad, 170
Green noodles, baked, 156
Green pepper salad, cucumber and, 169
Green sauce, noodles in, 156–57
Guacamole, crudités with, 113

Ham
  gougère ring filled with, 127–28
  and veal loaf en croûte, 217–18
Hens, game, with ginger sauce, 154–55
Herb bread, 185
Herbed marinated mushrooms, 114
Holiday rum raisin cake, 203
Hors d'oeuvres, *see* Appetizers

Icing, butter cream
  basic, 213
  vanilla, 213
Irish coffee soufflé, 194

Julienne of endive and watercress, 170

Kasha, with mushrooms, 159–60
Kedgeree, 134–35
Kidney pie, steak and, 137–38

Lady Curzon soup, 131–32

Lamb
butterflied leg of, 142
meatballs, curried, 124

Lasagne, verde Bolognese, 138

Lemon
chess tart, 210
curd, 192
   meringue cups with, 191
sponge roll, 201
tea cake, 232
yogurt pound cake, 201–2

Macaroni, with three cheeses, 157
Macaroon cream, coffee, 193
Mango mousse with rum sauce, 189
Mayonnaise tomatoes, broiled, 164
Meatballs: lamb, curried, 124
Melba toast, 183

Melon
cake, 232–33
crescents in wine, 188

Menu suggestions, 107–12
Meringue, orange-almond, frosted, 223
Meringue cups with lemon curd, 191

Mocha
-applesauce cake, 225–26
soufflé, cold, 195
torte, five-layer, 202–3

Mousse
coffee, frozen, 188–89
cucumber, 169
mango, with rum sauce, 189

Muffins, blueberry, 181

Mushroom(s)
herbed marinated, 114
kasha with, 159–60
pie, 167
stuffed, 115
turnovers, 114–15

Noodles
green, baked, 156
in green sauce, 156–57

Oatmeal
cookies, 197
walnut oatmeal roll with whipped cream, 197–98

Onion(s)
amber glazed, 162–63
crêpes filled with smoked salmon, 178

Orange
-almond meringue, frosted, 223
cake, French, 233–34
crêpes, brandied, 222–23
kumquat bread, 221
sauce, roast veal with apples in, 139–40

Oyster and chicken pie, 153

Pan bagna, 175
Parslied carrots, 162

Pâté
chicken liver, 122
   croissants stuffed with, 125
   mushrooms stuffed with, 115
veal and spinach, 125–26

Pea soup, fresh, 130–31

Peaches
poached, with raspberry sauce, 187
sliced, in honey and brandy, 186

Pear
crumble, baked, 211
crunch pie, 210–11

Pecan
cake, bourbon-, 227–28
coffee cake, sour cream, 204

Picnics, menu suggestions for, 112

Pie
apple, sour cream, 212–13
chicken and oyster, 153
mushroom, 167
pastry, basic, 207
pear crunch, 210–11
steak and kidney, 137–38

Pizza rustica, 175
Popcorn, garlic, 116

Pork
olives with yams and fruit sauce, 144–45
sausage, see Sausage
and sausage casserole, 143–44

Potage Parmentier (with carrots), 130
Poulet vert, 149–50
Pound cake, lemon yogurt, 201–2
Pralines, 213–14
Pudding, bread, with brandied fruits, 193–94

INDEX FOR A COOKBOOK FOR CATERERS / 239

Puff pastry, 207–8
Pumpkin soup, 215–16

Raspberry sauce, poached peaches with, 187
Refrigerator rolls, 182
Rhubarb crumble with brandied whipped cream, 212
Rice
  baked, with vegetables, 158
  brown, with almonds, 159
  pilaf, 157–58
  with raisins and pine nuts, 158–59
  salad, cold, 171–72
Rolls, refrigerator, 182
Romaine leaves filled with chicken salad, 173
Rum
  raisin cake, holiday, 203
  sauce, mango mousse with, 189

Salad(s), 168–74
  carrotes rapées, 168
  celery root remoulade, 168
  chicken
    in curry ring, 172–73
    romaine leaves filled with, 173
  cucumber and green pepper, 169
  cucumber mousse, 169
  grapefruit ring with watercress, 171
  green bean, 170
  julienne of endive and watercress, 170
  rice, cold, 171–72
  salad bar, 170–71
  tabbouli, 172
  vinaigrette dressing for, 173–74
Sally Lunn, 203–4
Salmon
  in aspic, 136–37
  smoked, onion crêpes filled with, 178
  smoked, pâté sandwiches, 174
Sandwiches, 174–75
Sardine deviled eggs, 117
Sauce(s)
  Aurore, fish timbales with, 121–22
  caramel, floating islands with, 190–91
  fruit, pork olives with yams and, 144–45

green, noodles in, 156–57
orange, roast veal with apples in, 139–40
raspberry, poached peaches with, 187
rum, mango mousse with, 189
watercress, turban of chicken with, 148–49
Sausage(s)
  en brioche, 124–25
  mushrooms stuffed with, 115
  and pork casserole, 143–44
  in white wine, 143
Scallops seviche, 119
Seafood
  crêpes, 178–79
  soufflé, 133
  vinaigrette in cucumber ring, 132–33
  See also Fish; *and specific types of fish and shellfish*
Shortbread, 205
Shrimp
  -cucumber rounds, 116
  -filled éclairs, 119–20
  soufflé, 133
  toast, 120–21
Side dishes, 156–60
Soufflé(s)
  cheese, individual, 220–21
  corn, 166
  Irish coffee, 194
  mocha, cold, 195
  seafood, 133
  strawberry, cold, 195
  walnut, frozen, 223–24
Soup
  apple-blueberry, 129
  asparagus, 129–30
  corn and chicken chowder, 131
  cucumber and mint, chilled, 215
  gazpacho, 128
  Lady Curzon, 131–32
  pea, fresh, 130–31
  potage Parmentier (with carrots), 130
  pumpkin, 215–16
  zucchini, cold, 128–29
Sour cream
  apple pie, 212–13
  pecan coffee cake, 204

Spinach
chicken Florentine with, 150–51
crêpes Florentine with, 179–80
eggs mollet Florentine with, 155
puréed, with chestnuts, 161-62
tart, 167–68
and veal pâté, 125–26

Squash
winter, puréed broccoli and, 161
zucchini soup, cold, 128–29

Steak and kidney pie, 137–38
Stovepipe bread, 222
Strawberry soufflé, cold, 195
Striped bass in aspic, 136–37
Strudels, cheese, tiny, 126–27
Summer potpourri, 165

Tabbouli, 172
Tapenade with crudités, 117
Tarragon chicken with artichokes, 151–52
Tex-Mex chili, spicy, 216–17

Tomato(es)
broiled
  mayonnaise, 164
  parmesan, 164
cherry, sautéed, with cucumbers, 163
cucumbers and, marinated, 163

Tortoni, biscuit, 224–25
Tunnel cake, 205
Turban of chicken with watercress sauce, 148–49
Turnovers, mushroom, 114–15

Vanilla butter cream icing, 213

Veal
and carrot roulade, 141–42
and ham loaf en croûte, 217–18
ragoût, 140–41
roast, with apples in orange sauce, 139–40
and spinach pâté, 125–26

Vegetable(s), 161–68
à la Grecque, 164–65
rice with, baked, 158
summer potpourri, 165
See also Crudités; and specific vegetables

Vinaigrette
dressing, 173–74
seafood, in cucumber ring, 132–33

Walnut
oatmeal roll with whipped cream, 197–98
soufflé, frozen, 223–24

Watercress
grapefruit ring with, 171
julienne of endive and, 170
sauce, turban of chicken with, 148–49

Wedding cake, 206–7

Wine
melon crescents in, 188
white, sausages in, 143

Winter squash, puréed broccoli and, 161

Yams, pork olives with, and fruit sauce, 144–45
Yogurt pound cake, lemon, 201–2

Ziti, zesty, 220
Zucchini soup, cold, 128–29

General Index

Advertising, 21–22
Agreement, letter of, 41–43
American Women's Economic Development Corporation (AWED), 90–91
Appearance of your business, 23–24
Appetizers, garnishing, 58

Baked goods, freezing, 79–80
Baking dishes, 96–97
Baskets
   as containers for take-home foods, 76
   as table decoration, 60, 61
Bids for a job, 44–45
Bookkeeping, 88–90
Breads, decorative uses of, 60, 61
Brunch, table decoration for, 60
Bûche de Noël (Yule Log), 60
   packaging, 75
Buffet, table decoration for, 61
Business expenses, keeping records of, 88–89

Cake logs, packaging, 75
Cakes, 75
   freezing, 79–80
   See also Baked goods
Cancellations, 43
Carlton, Nancy, 77, 78
Catering (catering business)
   advantages of, 6–8
   basic requirements for succeeding in, 11–12
   drawbacks of, 8–9
   market for, 12–13, 20–21
   new wave, *see* New wave catering
   starting out in, 15–26
   story of the development of a caterer, 68–72
Centerpieces, edible, 59–61
Children, 9
Christmas dessert party, centerpiece for, 61
Christmas Eve supper, table decoration for, 60
Cleaning up, 66
Cleanliness, 87
Clients, 44–50, 67
   cheating by, 49
   confidentiality of relationship with, 46
   first contact with, 44–45
   kitchen equipment of, 48–49
   visiting, 45–48
Colors of foods, 33
Competing for a job, 44–45
Containers
   disposable, 76
   for picnics, 76–77
   with see-through tops, 77
   See also Packaging
Contracts, 41–43
Convection ovens, 94
Cookbooks, 34, 98
Cooking classes, giving, 24–25
Cooking schools, 16
Cooking utensils, 97–98

GENERAL INDEX

Costs
  pricing and, 36–40
  See also Pricing
Crises (emergencies), 50, 56
Crudités as decoration, 61
Curries, packaging, 76
Customers, *see* Clients

Decorating, 57–59
Delivery, 65
Delivery charges, 40
Deposits, 41–43
Desserts, garnishing, 59
Dinner with a French theme, table decorations for, 60
Disease prevention, 87
Dowling, Roberta, 14, 22, 46, 52, 86
Dry ice, 77
Duval, Sally, 6

Eggplant, garnishing, 58
Emergencies (crises), 50, 56
Entrées, garnishing, 58
Equipment, *see* Kitchen equipment
Exchanges, 19
Expenses, keeping records of, 88–89

Family, 9–10
Financial aspects of planning, 5–6
  pricing, 21, 36–40
  record-keeping, 88–90
Flowers, 63
Food processor, 92–93
Food service inspection, 87
Freezers, 95
Freezing, 79–80
French theme dinner, table decoration for, 60
Frozen packaged foods
  freezing, 79–80
  packaging, 75–77
Fruits, seasonal, 31–32

Garnishing, 57–59
Gushee, Kitty, 7, 14, 17, 50, 86

Health code, 85
Health inspection, 87
Hilliard, Karen, 14, 17, 34–35
Hobart Kitchen Aid mixer, 93
Hors d'oeuvres, 29–30
  garnishing, 58
  skewers for, 75

Ice, dry, 77
Ice cream, storing, 79
Icemaker, automatic, 94–95
Inspection, 87
Insurance, 88

Kedgeree, garnishing, 57
Kettles, 95–96
Kitchen Aid mixer, 93
Kitchen equipment, 24, 92–101
  availability in client's kitchen, 48–49
  cooking utensils, 97–98
  food processor, 92–93
  mixer, 93
  ovens, 94
  pots and pans, 95–97
  refrigerators and freezers, 94–95
  rentals of, 62–63

Labeling, 80–82
Labor costs, 66
Lawyers, 91
Legal aspects of catering, 84–88
Letter of agreement, 41–43
License to cater, 21
Luncheon, table decoration for, 60

Marcus, Gail, 14, 40, 46
Market for a catering business, 12–13
Marketing, 51–52
Matchett, Ada, 14, 17, 44, 52
Meeting with clients, 44–49
Menus (menu planning), 29–33, 66
  colors and textures of foods and, 33
  price ranges for, 30
  pricing considerations and, 37–40
  replacements and substitutes in, 30, 32

GENERAL INDEX / 243

revising, 34
seasonal, 31–33
Microwave ovens, 94
Mixer, 93
Molds, 96
Mousses, packaging, 74–75

New wave catering, 15, 17
take-home catering business, *see* Take-home catering business

Ovens, 94
Ovenware, 96–97
disposable, 76
Overhead, 41

Packaging, 74–77
cake logs and other long shapes, 75
frozen foods, 75–77
for picnics, 76–77
Party planning, 62–66
Peppermills, 97
Picnics, containers for, 76–77
Planning, 52–56
party, 62–66
Portions, 35
of take-home foods, 74–75
Pots and pans, 95–97
Poultry, freezing, 79
Pricing (prices), 21, 36–40, 71
auxiliary services, 66
confirming, 51
take-home foods, 77–78
talking to client about, 47–48
See also Costs
Publicity, 21–25

Recipes, 98
creating or adding new, 34–36, 67
increasing, 35
testing new, 34–35
Record-keeping, 24, 88–90
Regional cookbooks, 34
Regional differences, 17–18
Rentals of equipment, 62–63

Restaurant, professional experience gained from working in, 15–16
Rolling pins, 97

Salads, garnishing, 58–59
Salsman, Bob, 46, 62
Schedules, 53–56
Seafood, 37
Seasonal menus, 31–33
Service, 63–66
charging for, 66
Serving dishes, 49, 59, 96
Serving food, 40
Shopping, 51–52
Skewers, 75
Small Business Administration, 90
Soufflés, cold, containers for, 76
Soups, garnishing, 58
Specialties, 34–35
choosing your, 17, 18, 29–30
Stewart, Martha, 34
Stoves, 94
Supermarkets, specials at, 53
Supper, table decorations for, 60

Table decorations, 59–61
Take-home catering business (new wave catering), 63, 73–82
market for, 74
Take-home foods, 73–82
baskets as containers for, 76
labeling, 80–82
non-frozen items, 80
outlet for, 73–74
portions of, 74–75
pricing, 77–78
See also Frozen packaged foods
Taxes, 88–89
Temperature requirements, 87–88
Textures of foods, 33
Thermometers, 97
Thermoses, 77

Vegetables
decorative uses of, 61

garnishing, 58–59
  seasonal, 31–32
Vitello tonnato, garnishing, 57–58

Waitresses and waiters, 63–64, 66
Wedding cakes, 29, 72
Whisks, 97
White, Donald Bruce, 34
Wholesalers, 52
Williams, Ken, 12, 14, 86

Wolfe, Elsie de, 45
Women's Exchange, 19
Work schedules, 53–56
Working hours, keeping a record of, 90

Youngblood, Pug, 14, 17, 50, 92
Yule Log (bûche de Noël), 60
  packaging, 75

Zoning regulations, 16, 85–86

WOMEN'S
BUSINESS BOOKS

____ 16806	THE LANDAU STRATEGY Suzanne Landau & Geoffrey Bailey	$2.50
____ 16816	MONEY MANAGEMENT FOR WOMEN Rosalie Minkow	$2.50
____ 16909	RE-ENTERING Eleanor Berman	$2.25
____ 16899	SUCCESSFUL NEGOTIATING SKILLS FOR WOMEN John Ilich & Barbara S. Jones	$2.25
____ 16835	WHAT EVERY WOMAN NEEDS TO KNOW ABOUT THE LAW Martha Pomroy	$3.95

1081-1

PBJ BOOKS, INC.
Book Mailing Service
P.O. Box 690 Rockville Centre, New York 11571

NAME_____

ADDRESS_____

CITY_____STATE_____ZIP_____

Please enclose 50¢ for postage and handling if one book is ordered; 25¢ for each additional book. $1.50 maximum postage and handling charge. No cash, CODs or stamps. Send check or money order.

Total amount enclosed: $_____